# Crack Pipe as Pimp

# Crack Pipe as Pimp

*An Ethnographic Investigation
of Sex-for-Crack Exchanges*

*Edited by*

Mitchell S. Ratner

Lexington Books
*An Imprint of Macmillan, Inc.*
New York

Maxwell Macmillan Canada
Toronto

Maxwell Macmillan International
New York   Oxford   Singapore   Sydney

Library of Congress Cataloging-in-Publication Data

Crack pipe as pimp : an ethnographic investigation of sex-for-crack exchanges / edited by
   Mitchell S. Ratner.
      p.   cm.
   Includes bibliographical references and index.
   ISBN 0-02-925725-5
   1. Crack (Drug)—United States.   2. Prostitution—United States.
   3. Drug abuse and crime—United States.   4. United States—Social conditions.
   I. Ratner, Mitchell S.
   HV5825.C695 1993       76537
   362.29′8—dc20                                                    92-29042
                                                                       CIP

Lexington Books
An Imprint of Macmillan, Inc.
866 Third Avenue, New York, N.Y. 10022

Maxwell Macmillan Canada, Inc.
1200 Eglinton Avenue East
Suite 200
Don Mills, Ontario M3C 3N1

Macmillan, Inc. is part of the Maxwell Communication Group of Companies.

Printed in the United States of America

printing number
1   2   3   4   5   6   7   8   9   10

# Contents

# Preface

At the heart of this study are seven site reports from the streets of urban America. They are finely grained, often graphic descriptions and analyses of what we call the sex-for-crack phenomenon: the exchange of sexual services for crack cocaine or for money to buy crack cocaine. Collectively, the reports paint a disturbing picture of a life-style that frequently combines compulsive drug use, promiscuous sex, despair, degradation, and the possibility of HIV (human immunodeficiency virus) infection.

As ethnographers, we have sought to document and explain the values and actions of individuals engaging in sex-for-crack exchanges. We have tried to present not just the facts but also the world as our subjects understand it to be. Our presentations include large sections of verbatim text from interviews and the explication of indigenous terms. Inevitably, many of the words we use and the subjects we broach are "impolite" in the context of mainstream American values. Our goal is not to shock or to titillate but to develop a fuller understanding of the sex-for-crack phenomenon and the social forces that influence it.

The first chapter discusses the origin and methodology of the study and provides a general conceptual framework for understanding the interaction of forces that influence the sex-for-crack phenomenon. It also makes some general recommendations regarding future research and government policy. The other seven chapters discuss aspects of the sex-for-crack phenomenon as it was observed in one or more neighborhoods or user communities. Six chapters focus on the metropolitan areas of Chicago, Denver, Los Angeles, Miami, New York, and San Francisco. A seventh report integrates research conducted in Philadelphia and Newark.

Because each chapter is an independently developed site report, a number of topics, such as the symbiotic relationship between compulsive crack use and prostitution, are discussed at several points in the text. To some extent, this repetition bolsters the validity of the findings in that it suggests a cross-site structuring of the phenomenon that is greater than any one individual's subjective interpretation of it.

Minor disagreements and contradictions among the chapters can also be found. These may be attributed to differences in the populations studied but may also reflect differences in methodological approaches and in the theoretical and personal perspectives of the authors.

Many colleagues who reviewed the manuscript commented that it was admirably thick, providing material capable of capturing the complexities involved, and powerful, in the sense of eliciting a strong emotional response. A few went on to say that the report was so thick and so powerful it was possible that readers might arrive at conclusions different from any the authors intended. Two erroneous conclusions are particularly worth discussing.

The first erroneous conclusion is, "Exchanging sex for crack is typical of crack smokers." This study went looking for a particular phenomenon—regular crack users who exchange sex for crack—found it, and comprehensively described and analyzed its many variations. Given its public health consequences, the sex-for-crack phenomenon warrants detailed consideration. But the prominence of such exchanges among our respondents should not be equated with the prevalence of such exchanges among crack smokers in general. While looking for individuals who exchanged sex for crack, study researchers also encountered many individuals whose crack use was not compulsive and/or whose sexual behavior was extremely circumscribed. A study very different from this one would be needed to estimate reliably the number of crack smokers who smoke regularly or who engage in sex-for-crack exchanges.

The other erroneous conclusion is, "The sex-for-crack phenomenon arises from the moral failing, poor judgment, inadequate socialization, or depravity of the participants." This is the classic blaming-the-victim argument that locates the cause of a social problem in the defects imputed to those who are injured, while systematically ignoring the social forces that may contribute to the problem.* The perspective developed throughout this book is more subtle; it shifts back and forth between the analysis of individual lives and the identification of social forces that shape the behavior of groups.

In contrast, among the conclusions of the authors are that the sex-for-crack phenomenon comprises multiple complex patterns of human behavior, that ethnographic methods provide insight into the nature and causes of the phenomenon, and that ameliorative action is both possible and needed.

**Mitchell S. Ratner**
Sex-for-Crack Study Director
Silver Spring, Maryland

---

*Ryan, William. 1971. *Blaming the Victim*. New York: Vintage Books.

# 1

# Sex, Drugs, and Public Policy: Studying and Understanding the Sex-for-Crack Phenomenon

*Mitchell S. Ratner*

> Life as we find it is too hard for us: it entails too much pain, too many disappointments, impossible tasks. We cannot do without palliative remedies. There are perhaps three of these means: powerful diversions of interest . . . ,substitute gratifications which lessen it, and intoxicating substances which make us insensitive to it.
> —Sigmund Freud, *Civilization and Its Discontents*

## Origin and Scope of the Study

Prior to the passage of the Harrison Act in 1914, the first national attempt to regulate the use of habit-forming substances, cocaine was widely used in the United States. It was imbibed as a wine (Vin Mariani), it was (until 1906) part of Coca-Cola's secret formula, and it was the active ingredient in innumerable patent medicines, often unbeknown to the users.

Cocaine was also injected and snorted and in this form raised considerable public concern, often directed at nonmainstream segments of society. For example, the American Public Health Association's Committee on the Acquirement of the Drug Habit noted in 1902 that "the use of cocaine by unfortunate women generally, and by Negroes in certain parts of the country, is simply appalling. No idea of this can be had unless personally investigated. The police officers of these . . . districts tell us that the habitués are made madly wild by cocaine, which they have no difficulty at all in buying, sometimes being peddled around from door to door, but always adulterated." (cited by Musto 1987:17).

After passage of the Harrison Act, which essentially banned the importation, distribution, and use of the drug, the price of cocaine increased dramatically, and its presence in America decreased proportionately, though for the next half-century it continued to be popular among some musicians, artists, and drug connoisseurs. In the 1960s and 1970s, cocaine again became a major drug of abuse, its popularity fueled by the drug explorations of the jet set and counterculture and by a sophisticated new generation of illicit drug importers (see Adler 1985). Increased supplies led to reductions in street prices; cocaine once again became accessible to drug users on limited budgets. According to the National Institute on Drug Abuse's (NIDA) National Household Survey, the number of people who tried cocaine at least once increased from 5.4 million in 1974 to 25 million in 1985 (cited by Kleber 1988:4).

In the late 1980s, the widespread sale and use of crack cocaine became a major public issue; few other health-related topics received such widespread media attention. Although overall national trends in illicit use had been decreasing, as demonstrated by national student and household epidemiological studies, crack cocaine use, especially in poor and minority communities, appeared to be epidemic. Arrestees in major cities presented the clearest indicators of skyrocketing cocaine use. For example, during the first three months of 1989, 76 percent of male arrestees in New York City, 74 percent in Philadelphia, and 42 percent in San Diego tested positive for cocaine. Rates for female arrestees during this period were almost as high: 72 percent, 74 percent, and 41 percent, respectively (Wish and O'Neil 1989:4).

National concern about crack use began to center not only on the devastation experienced by users but by their families as well. Public attention seemed riveted for a time on the effects of crack on prenatal development and the surging number of what came to be called crack babies. Soon broader socioeconomic and public health consequences emerged. The criminal activities users engaged in to support drug use, the increasing violence associated with the lucrative and changing drug trade, and the impact that huge drug profits might have on legitimate institutions and aspirations loomed as serious threats to the general economy and social well-being.

In terms of the AIDS (acquired immunodeficiency syndrome) epidemic, crack cocaine at first seemed benign in comparison to opiates or even cocaine powder. Because crack cocaine is always smoked—never injected—its use would not contribute to the spread of HIV, or so it seemed. This sanguine view was soon challenged, however, by early reports that promiscuous sex might be endemic to the crack-using subculture in American cities. The underlying apprehension, concretized in 1988 by Willard Cates, Jr., the director of the Center for Disease Control's Sexually Transmitted Diseases Division, was that "the crack house of today has become what the gay bathhouse was yesterday with regard to all sexually transmitted diseases" (Goldsmith 1988:2009).

For its part, the NIDA, already deeply involved with AIDS research, was particularly sensitive to crack's potential for spreading the human immunodeficiency virus (HIV) to new populations. Staff within NIDA's Division of Clinical Research noted that while crack cocaine use, and particuarly sex-for-crack exchanges, had been described in media accounts and discussed in personal communications, the phenomenon was poorly described in the scientific literature. To spur research in this area, NIDA contracted with Birch & Davis Associates to coordinate an ethnographic study of the sex-for-crack phenomenon. The Statement of Work authorizing the project noted that NIDA expected the research to provide descriptive data on individuals engaging in sex-for-crack exchanges and to describe more fully the potential for HIV transmission in this population.

## Methodology

### Ethnographic Studies of Drug Use

The tradition of studying drug-abuse issues through qualitative research methods goes back at least fifty years. One of the most influential of the early qualitative researchers was Alfred Lindesmith, who in the 1940s conducted lengthy qualitative interviews with heroin users and former users in order to understand the nature of addiction (Lindesmith 1947). Another seminal study was Howard Becker's exploration of socialization to marijuana use among musicians (Becker 1953).

Qualitative studies of drug use bloomed in the 1960s and 1970s, especially the subspecialty known as street ethnography, which investigated crime and drug use in natural settings (see Weppner 1977). One of the earliest and best known articles in this genre was Edward Preble and J. J. Casey's 1969 analysis of the active and focused life-style of many inner-city black heroin users; this analysis caused a generation of drug-abuse researchers to reevaluate their narrow stereotypes of heroin users as social and psychological failures.

Since the late 1960s, qualitative studies of drug use have usually focused on particular user communities or particular drugs.[1] A publication of particular relevance for this book is *Angel Dust*, the report of a four-city ethnographic study funded by NIDA (and coordinated by Birch & Davis Associates) that explored through ethnographic methods patterns of PCP use as the drug was first entering the U.S. illicit drug pharmacopeia (Feldman, Agar, and Beschner 1979).

This book continues this ethnographic tradition. The primary research tools employed were naturalistic observations and lengthy qualitative interviews exploring the behavior, knowledge, and attitudes of participants in sex-for-crack exchanges.

Although NIDA is best known for its periodic statistical surveys of drug use, it has also recognized the importance of qualitative studies. They are, from NIDA's perspective, particularly useful for studying emergent and little-understood phenomena and for learning more about hidden populations: "the homeless and transient, chronically mentally ill, high school dropouts, criminal offenders, prostitutes, juvenile delinquents, gang members, run-aways, and other 'street people' " (Lambert and Wiebel 1990:1). These hidden populations are often omitted from nationally representative surveys because they have no fixed address, live in areas where interviewers prefer not to go, are not at home during typical interviewing hours, or directly or indirectly choose not to participate.

Ethnography is also valued by NIDA research staff as a complement to medically oriented research. Sander Genser, a psychiatrist (and the study's project officer), recently noted that although most physicians are taught a bio-psycho-social-environmental approach to behavior disorders such as drug dependence, in practice physicians and treatment agencies "focus most on the biological factors and show decreasing focus on psychological, social and environmental variables." They are subtly biased "toward discovering only those problem areas that are considered treatable and that are compatible with the interventions available to the physician or the treatment program." The ethnographic approach, however, usually begins at the other end. It concentrates "on environmental and social elements and to a lesser extent on individual psychological elements and least on biological intra-individual elements. Because ethnographic researchers are usually not committed to an established treatment approach, they are often able to suggest innovative intervention approaches."[2]

Ethnographers themselves, when they reflect on the contribution of their approach to drug-abuse research, most often stress its interpretive power.[3] Drug-abuse ethnographies are part of a social science tradition established by Wilhelm Dilthey and Max Weber that insists that the scientific study of human behavior must include the meaning of events and actions for the participants. Drug-abuse ethnographies are notable for their rich descriptions; through them, readers develop an appreciation for both the complexities of individual lives and the subtle patterning of social and cultural relationships. Often drug-abuse ethnographers explore social patterns through counterpoising street (or folk) schema with "professional" schema, such as those of police, treatment providers, and policymakers (Agar 1985).

Because their interest is in developing rich descriptions informed by the users' perspective, ethnographers usually spend more time with their subjects and develop better rapport with them than is customary or possible in survey studies. As ethnographic data collection unfolds (whether based on a two-hour interview or a two-year field study), there is time to sift and evaluate responses. Additionally, in most studies, interviewing is joined with field observations. As additional information is gathered, old answers take on new meaning, and more meaningful questions can be asked. Consequently, ethnographers are able to move beyond the stereotyped and manipulative responses drug users often develop for professional ears and engage them in dialogues more meaningful to both parties.

## Study Sites and Staff

In choosing study sites and study staff, the goal was to provide geographic and social diversity while capitalizing on the expertise and resources of senior drug-abuse researchers working in communities they know well.

According to the project research design, each city was essentially an independent field study headed by a senior site ethnographer who would conduct the research over an eighteen-month period with the help of one or more interviewers and a transcriber. Senior staff were able to restructure the allotment of hours and responsibilities within their teams as long as the site budget of roughly $25,000 (including respondent fees and other expenses) was not exceeded. Over time, a number of different field team structures developed.

In Chicago the team leader was Wayne Wiebel, a sociologist and professor at the Universityof Illinois-Chicago, School of Public Health, and the director of the school's AIDS Outreach Intervention Project. Interviewing and analysis in Chicago was done primarily by ethnographers who direct the three field stations for the AIDS project: Lawrence Ouellet, Antonio Jiminez, and Wendell Johnson.

The Denver site was headed by Steven Koester, an anthropologist and research director of Project Safe, an AIDS IV drug user outreach project sponsored by the University of Colorado Health Sciences Center. Koester worked closely with Judith Schwartz, a public health specialist, who interviewed subjects and collaborated on the analysis.

The Los Angeles site was headed by Douglas Anglin, a research psychologist who directs the UCLA Drug Abuse Research Group. Anglin assumed a relatively minor supervisory role and delegated the research and analysis to Kathleen Boyle, a Ph.D. candidate in psychology who had worked on several other projects with the UCLA Drug Abuse Research Group.

James A. Inciardi, a professor of criminal justice and the director of the Center for Drug and Alcohol Studies at the University of Delaware, headed the research team in Miami, where he has been conducting street studies for two decades. Inciardi worked closely with several street outreach projects being conducted by the Comprehensive Drug Research Center at the University of Miami School of Medicine, with which he is also affiliated, and with Spectrum Programs, one of Miami's major drug treatment structures. Much of the more systematic interviewing was done by researchers Rose Anderson and Mary Comerford; Inciardi conducted all of the crack house observations and interviews.

John French, sociologist and director, data analysis and epidemiology, Division of Alcoholism, Drug Abuse, and Addiction Services, New Jersey State Department of Health, conducted research in Newark and Philadelphia. He collaborated closely with Atiba Akili-Obika, a colleague from the state office.

The New York component of the study was headed by Philippe Bourgois, a social anthropologist and assistant professor at San Francisco State University who when the study began was in the third year of a study of crack use in Spanish Harlem. The study extension from Spanish Harlem into Black Harlem was facilitated through a close working relationship with Eloise Dunlap, a sociologist able to develop extraordinary rapport with black street users.

Finally, the San Francisco efforts were headed by Harvey Feldman, a social worker and sociologist who was research director of YES, a San Francisco–based AIDS outreach to IV drug users project. Interviewing in San Francisco was conducted mainly by Frank Espada, a writer and photojournalist, and by two outreach workers: Sharon Penn and Sharon Byrd.

Overall supervision, coordination, and support of the research effort was provided by staff from Birch & Davis Associates. The project director established research priorities, developed instruments, maintained contact with field staff, and made site visits to each of the research locations. The director also submitted the research plan to B&D's Institutional Review Board to ensure that subjects' rights were protected and applied for and obtained a NIDA grant of confidentiality that would allow researchers to protect the names of subjects from police or judicial subpoena. Research coordination was facilitated on the three occasions when ethnographers from each of the sites came together with B&D staff: at an initial start-up meeting, at a mid-term project conference, and at an end-of-study conference presentation and review of the draft final report.

## Field Procedures

Although senior site ethnographers were experienced in street studies of drug users, with the exception of two (Bourgois and Inciardi), this was their first research focused on crack users. In the initial stages of the research, most field teams conducted general ethnographic fieldwork to identify and document the basic framework of attitudes and behavior that constitute the lifestyle of heavy crack users. A number of the researchers used existing subject networks, composed of IV drug users, as a base from which to look for crack users. Others had streetwise outreach workers and friends introduce them to crack users and to locales where crack was sold or consumed. The ethnographers talked to people using and selling crack, and they observed street scenes, homeless shelters, and other places where crack users congregate.

In addition to the general ethnographic work on crack users, each field site was given the goal of conducting forty taped interviews with individuals who exchanged sex for crack or were knowledgeable about sex-for-crack exchanges. Rules for inclusion in this ethnographic sample varied somewhat by site. Some site leaders adhered to an exchange requirement, including only regular crack users who within the prior thirty days had provided sexual services in direct exchange for crack, provided sexual services for money to purchase crack, or received sexual services in exchange for crack. Other site leaders felt that their research goals would benefit by including some individuals who had exchanged in the past but not in the last thirty days, as well as a few individuals who had never exchanged sex for crack but could provide specific information because of their role in the crack subculture.

Various strategies were used to identify subjects for the taped interviews. Boyle, in Los Angeles, identified most of her subjects in jails just after their arrest and through homeless shelters. Inciardi, in Miami, worked closely with a treatment facility. Many of the sites employed outreach workers and street contacts as finders.

Once identified (and possibly qualified through a few screening questions), prospective respondents were informed about the study and its confidentiality procedures and asked to participate. In most cases, they were also told that they would be paid for their participation if they completed the full interview, usually lasting one to two hours.

Researchers associated with storefront outreach projects often conducted interviews there, but the interviews took place almost anywhere. Many were conducted on the street or in cars, parks, restaurants, and other public facilities. In several cities, researchers interviewed subjects in rooms rented by the hour in crack houses or apartments.

As part of each interview, the interviewer or site ethnographer completed a face sheet, documenting basic demographic information (age, race, residence, education, and employment), drug use (historical and current), sexual behavior (historical and current), and AIDS knowledge and behavior. After completing the face sheet, the interviewers asked a series of qualitative questions on such topics as drug use, sexual behavior, and AIDS knowledge. The qualitative questions differed with the respondents' knowledge and cooperativeness and with the researchers' immediate substantive interests.

After the tapes were transcribed, they were periodically reviewed, along with the face sheets, to assess progress and identify new areas to be approached during interviews.

## Characterizing the Ethnographic Sample

The significant demographic and social characteristics of the individuals who completed taped interviews are noted in table 1–1. Of the 340 respondents, roughly two-thirds are female, and one-third are male. Women predominate because most sites chose to concentrate on the providers of sexual services, who were mainly women. Part of the rationale for this choice was that sexual providers are the central feature of the sex-for-crack phenomenon. They often serve thirty or more customers per day. In contrast, few of the purchasers of these sexual services, who are almost all men, engage in three or more exchanges per week.

## Table 1–1
### Demographic Characteristics of Ethnographic Sample

| Characteristic | Number | Percentage |
|---|---|---|
| Total | 340 | 100 |
| **Sex** | | |
| Female | 233 | 69 |
| Male | 107 | 31 |
| **Race** | | |
| African-American | 244 | 72 |
| White | 51 | 15 |
| Hispanic | 37 | 11 |
| Asian | 1 | * |
| Native American | 1 | * |
| Missing | 6 | 2 |
| **Age** | | |
| 15–17 | 6 | 2 |
| 18–25 | 94 | 28 |
| 26–35 | 170 | 50 |
| 36+ | 67 | 20 |
| Missing | 3 | * |
| **Years of education completed** | | |
| 4–6 | 3 | * |
| 7–9 | 53 | 16 |
| 10–11 | 129 | 38 |
| 12 | 95 | 28 |
| 13+ | 37 | 11 |
| Missing | 23 | 7 |
| **Primary street hustles** | | |
| Prostitution | 161 | 47 |
| Drug dealing | 36 | 11 |
| Street hustler | 13 | 4 |
| Shoplifting | 13 | 4 |
| Crack house worker | 5 | 1 |
| Begging | 4 | 1 |
| Robbery | 1 | * |
| No reported hustle | 102 | 30 |
| Missing | 5 | 1 |
| **Income from government assistance (e.g., welfare, food stamps)** | | |
| Yes | 108 | 32 |
| No | 227 | 67 |
| Missing | 5 | 1 |

*Less than 1 percent.

In the cities studied, street-level sales of crack and sex-for-crack exchanges occur mainly in inner-city African-American neighborhoods. It is not surprising, then, that the ethnographic sample is largely African-American (73 percent). Whites and Hispanics involved in the inner-city crack scene usually participated as peripheral members of the African-American dominated networks. There were numerous exceptions, however—notably gay hustles and white street prostitutes.

Contrary to our expectations (and mass media reports), most respondents were between 26 and 35 years of age. Except in Miami, site ethnographers reported being unable to find many (or any) young people under 18 years of age willing to be interviewed about their involvement in sex-for-crack exchanges. Nor could they elicit many stories about such individuals.

Most respondents (58 percent) had less than a high school education, and many engaged in street hustles to support themselves or to buy drugs; most common was prostitution, followed by drug dealing, and shoplifting. Only about one-third of the sample received government financial assistance in the form of family assistance, food stamps, or general disability payments.

Table 1–2 highlights the sample's drug-using patterns. Not surprisingly, the most commonly used drug was crack (at least 86 percent of the sample). But the population was a polydrug-using group. Next to crack, the drugs most used were alcohol (65 percent) and marijuana (46 percent). About a quarter of the sample, of both males and females, were IV drug users; they had injected at least once during the previous thirty days. Roughly an additional quarter, again of both males and females, had injected drugs at some point in their history.

For those who used crack, the common pattern was to use it extensively: 58 percent indicated they used it twenty days or more per month. Attempts to clarify how much crack was used in a day were generally unsuccessful because drug dose and purity is uncertain, because vials of crack are often shared, and because the most common reply to the question of how much per day was, "As much as I can, as often as I can."

Table 1–3 provides an overview of involvement in sex-for-crack exchanges. Of the 340 subjects, 191 were women who provided sexual services for crack or for money to buy crack. In the thirty days prior to the interview, relatively few (14) of these women provided sex only for dugs. More commonly, if trading sex for drugs, they were, to a greater or lesser extent, also trading sex for money. A significant number (71) were crack-using prostitutes; although almost all their income might go to crack, they reported that in the previous thirty days, they had not exchanged sex directly for crack (though they might have received it as a bonus in addition to a cash payment). Of the 107 men in the ethnographic sample, 29 were providing sex for drugs or money—almost always to other males—and 40 were obtaining sex with drugs or money—almost always from females.

Ten subjects (4 females and 6 males) indicated that in the last thirty days they had both provided and received sexual services in exchange for money or drugs.

The 36 females and 32 males in the "other" category include individuals who had not engaged in sexual trading in the last thirty days (although they may have actively traded during an earlier period) and individuals who had

**Table 1–2**
**Drug Use Characteristics of Ethnographic Sample**

| Characteristic | Number | Percentage |
|---|---|---|
| Total | 340 | 100 |
| Drugs used during last thirty days* | | |
| Crack | 291 | 86 |
| Alcohol | 221 | 65 |
| Marijuana | 155 | 46 |
| Cocaine (powder, non-IV) | 59 | 17 |
| IV cocaine | 51 | 15 |
| IV heroin | 43 | 13 |
| Heroin (snort or smoke) | 30 | 9 |
| Downers (barbiturates, etc.) | 28 | 8 |
| Inhalants (amyl nitrate, etc.) | 16 | 5 |
| Hallucinogens (LSD, PCP, etc.) | 12 | 4 |
| Uppers (amphetamines, etc.) | 10 | 3 |
| IV speed (methamphetamine) | 8 | 3 |
| IV speedball (heroin and cocaine) | 6 | 2 |
| Number of days per month using crack | | |
| 0 | 11 | 3 |
| 1–9 | 51 | 15 |
| 10–19 | 43 | 13 |
| 20+ | 197 | 58 |
| Missing | 38 | 11 |
| Intravenous drug use within last thirty days | | |
| Females ($N$ = 233) | | |
| Yes | 52 | 22 |
| No | 181 | 78 |
| Males ($N$ = 107) | | |
| Yes | 33 | 31 |
| No | 74 | 69 |
| History of intravenous drug use | | |
| Females ($N$ = 233) | | |
| Yes | 105 | 45 |
| No | 128 | 55 |
| Males ($N$ = 107) | | |
| Yes | 50 | 47 |
| No | 57 | 53 |

Note: Because of missing data on some forms, the number and percentage using each of the drugs is probably somewhat higher than indicated.

engaged in exchanges but could not be further categorized for lack of data. (Because "missing information on sex-for-crack exchanges" was not always clearly distinguished from "does not engage in sex-for-crack exchanges," we are not able to subdivide this group meaningfully.)

Finally, a useful way of explaining some differences in the reports that follow is to look at sexual behavior by site (Table 1–4). More than at other sites, study staff in Chicago and Denver talked with individuals who, though

Table 1–3
Current Sexual Behavior of Ethnographic Sample

| Current Sexual Behavior (Last 30 Days) | Number of Females | Number of Males |
|---|---|---|
| Total | 233 | 107 |
| Providing sex | | |
| Sex for money | 71 | 13 |
| Sex for drugs | 14 | 3 |
| Sex for money or drugs | 106 | 13 |
| Receiving sex | | |
| Drugs or money for sex | 2 | 40 |
| Both providing and receiving sex | 4 | 6 |
| Not providing or receiving sex in the time noted or inadequate information to classify | 36 | 32 |

associated with the crack scene, had not exchanged sex for drugs or money in the month preceding the interview. More than at the other sites, study staff in Newark and Philadelphia interviewed men receiving sex. The New York team focused more on prostitutes who trade sex for money to buy crack. Compared to other sites, study staff in Miami, Philadelphia, and San Francisco interviewed more individuals trading sex directly for crack.

## Types of Sex-for-Crack Exchanges

Sex-for-crack exchanges were defined as transactions in which a crack user trades sex for crack or money to buy crack. Although the site reports that follow richly elaborate a number of different patterns, three basic, qualitatively different types emerge: casual exchanges, sex-for-money-for-crack exchanges, and sex-for-crack-or-money exchanges.

*Casual exchanges* are distinguished by their infrequency, usually occurring no more than two or three times a week and often less than that. The exchanges are often opportunistic: a slightly known acquaintance at a party may make it known that he has a supply of crack and is looking for a woman to share it with. But they may also be quite premeditated: a crack user temporarily without funds may occasionally go to bars looking for someone to supply drugs in exchange for sex. Often these casual exchanges occur repeatedly between the same individuals. A number of the women talked about having their drug money come from one or two regular customers with whom they traded sex for money. Others talked about having "sugar daddies": older men who regularly provided them with drugs and money in exchange for sex and companionship.

**Table 1–4**
**Ethnographic Sample by Current Sexual Behavior and Site**

| Site | Total | Providing Sex | | | Receiving Sex | Both Providing and Receiving Sex | Other (including unable to classify) |
|---|---|---|---|---|---|---|---|
| | | For Money Only | For Drugs Only | For Money and for Drugs | | | |
| **Chicago** | | | | | | | |
| Female | 24 | 5 | 1 | 9 | | | 9 |
| Male | 16 | 1 | | | 2 | | 13 |
| **Denver** | | | | | | | |
| Female | 27 | 5 | | 8 | | | 14 |
| Male | 6 | | 2 | | 1 | | 3 |
| **Los Angeles** | | | | | | | |
| Female | 30 | 12 | 4 | 12 | | | 2 |
| Male | 21 | 4 | | 2 | 5 | 1 | 9 |
| **Miami** | | | | | | | |
| Female | 35 | 10 | 2 | 22 | | 1 | |
| Male | 17 | 7 | | 3 | 2 | 4 | 1 |
| **Newark** | | | | | | | |
| Female | 22 | 3 | 4 | 6 | 1 | 1 | 7 |
| Male | 24 | | | 4 | 14 | 1 | 5 |
| **New York** | | | | | | | |
| Female | 34 | 24 | | 8 | | 1 | 1 |
| Male | 6 | 1 | 1 | 1 | 2 | | 1 |
| **Philadelphia** | | | | | | | |
| Female | 26 | 3 | 2 | 18 | 1 | 1 | 1 |
| Male | 12 | | | 1 | 11 | | |
| **San Francisco** | | | | | | | |
| Female | 35 | 8 | 2 | 22 | | | 3 |
| Male | 5 | | | 2 | 3 | | |

Some respondents reported that engaging in casual exchanges was a transitional state—the beginning of a slide into more frequent sex-for-crack exchanges or a career as a prostitute. In other cases, individuals engaged in casual exchanges for years and planned to continue to do so.

*Sex-for-money-for-crack exchanges* occur in the context of prostitution. The provision of sexual services is considered to be an income-generating activity. It is conceptually separate from smoking crack, which is a consumption activity. The crack-using prostitute usually insists that all her exchanges are for money, though she may accept crack for use during the exchange or as a bonus. A number of skills are needed to work successfully as a street prostitute or gay hustler; most important is the ability to control and manage the sexual encounters.

What distinguishes sex-for-money-for-crack exchanges from prostitution in general is the compulsiveness of the drug use. For many in our study, each day is a constant repetition of finding customers, exchanging sex, and smoking crack alone or with friends. Usually prostitution is the sole source of income, and all the money earned in a day is spent that day on crack, even to the disregard of essentials such as rent and food.

*Sex-for-crack-or-money exchanges* are typified by desperation. They are entered into by women and men whose whole being is dominated by their craving for crack. They are willing to provide sexual services, typically oral sex, in exchange for a small amount of crack or for almost any sum of money. In their extreme neediness, they are minimally able to negotiate the terms of the encounter and are readily exploited and degraded. They are almost universally disdained by those who exploit them and by others such as dealers and street prostitutes. As the site reports relate, a colorful array of derogatory street terms, such as "skeezer," "chickenhead," and "rock prostitute," have been coined to refer to the women (and men) who engage in these exchanges.

Such exchanges often occur in sexually oriented crack houses. They may involve young women or men who regularly come in on their own with a little bit of money or crack and then extend their visit (and crack use) by providing sexual services to the "houseman" (the proprietor or manager of the crack house) or to other men present. Some of the women in our sample worked essentially as employees of the crack house: they were supplied with crack, food, and shelter in exchange for providing whatever sexual services customers desired.

Sex-for-crack-or-money exchanges occur outside crack houses as well. Crack-using men may pick up a woman on the street to provide sexual services or perform sex shows while they smoke crack in an apartment or home. Quick and furtive exchanges occur in automobiles, alleys, and darkened stairways.

In certain respects, there is nothing dramatically new about all three types of exchanges. Throughout this century, sex has been traded casually, for money, and in desperation for heroin, cocaine, and other drugs. In his history of American drug control, David Musto (1987:17,19) mentions that cocaine use was reputed to be widespread among prostitutes in the South during the first decade of the century and was one of the drug fears that led to the passage of the Harrison Act of 1914. In a study of prostitution and drugs conducted in the 1970s, Paul Goldstein (1979:54) noted that thirteen of the thirty-three female heroin addicts in his sample had at some time in their lives been "bag brides" who exchanged sex for heroin. And in a 1979–1981 study of cocaine use in Miami, well before the appearance of crack as a common street drug, Morningstar and Chitwood (1987:138) described the behavior of "coke whores," women who "knowingly and consciously take a man's cocaine and then go to bed with him or simply go out with a man because he has cocaine."

What does seem different, though, is the magnitude of the sex-for-crack phenomenon today, in all its manifestations. Ethnographically, perhaps the clearest indicator of the size of the phenomenon are the reflections of street prostitutes with ten years or more of experience. Many complained that the sex-for-crack phenomenon has lowered the street value of their sexual services: too many crack-using women are offering sex for the price of the smallest unit of crack sold, often as little as three to five dollars. "Old-timers," both prostitutes and their customers, also noted that the relationship between drug use and prostitution seems to have changed. When heroin was the most popular drug among street prostitutes, it was often viewed as helping prostitutes to cope with the hassles of their trade. But in this current era of crack prostitution, the trading of sex for money is viewed as a means to enable the prostitute to stay high.

Although the sex-for-crack phenomenon is too complex to be explained by an all-encompassing single factor theory, it is useful to look systematically at a number of factors, discussed in more detail in the site reports, that appear to have influenced its growth.

# Drug, Set, and Setting

In his book *Drug, Set, and Setting*, Norman Zinberg (1984:5) contends that to understand a drug-related phenomenon, one needs to understand the interaction of the pharmacologic action of the substance itself (the drug); the attitude of the person at the time of use, including his or her personality structure (the set); and the influence of the physical and social setting within which the use occurs (the setting). This drug-set-setting framework provides a useful structure through which to explore influential factors (schematically summarized in figure 1–1).

## *The Drug: The Pharmacologic Action of the Substance Itself*

As several of the site reports point out, the technology for transforming cocaine into crack cocaine was not invented in the mid-1980s; rather, it was rediscovered by a new generation of drug entrepreneurs. All forms of cocaine are derived from an active alkaloid in the leaf of the coca plant. Until recently, cocaine was almost always sold as a powder in the form of a hydrochloride salt. Usually ingested by snorting, it could also be sprinkled on tobacco or marijuana and smoked, or dissolved in water and injected.

Cocaine powder, which is often adulterated, can also be transformed into highly purified "freebase" cocaine by removing the hydrochloric acid with a liquid base such as ammonia or baking soda and then dissolving the product in a solvent such as ether. "Freebasers," who desire the increased

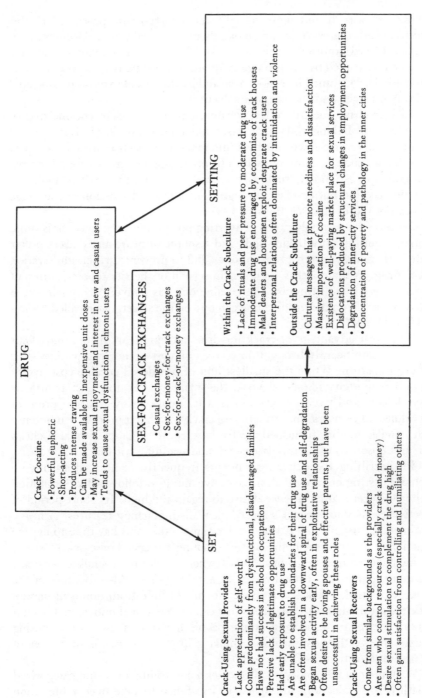

**DRUG**

**Crack Cocaine**
- Powerful euphoric
- Short-acting
- Produces intense craving
- Can be made available in inexpensive unit doses
- May increase sexual enjoyment and interest in new and casual users
- Tends to cause sexual dysfunction in chronic users

**SEX-FOR-CRACK EXCHANGES**
- Casual exchanges
- Sex-for-money-for-crack exchanges
- Sex-for-crack-or-money exchanges

**SETTING**

**Within the Crack Subculture**
- Lack of rituals and peer pressure to moderate drug use
- Immoderate drug use encouraged by economics of crack houses
- Male dealers and housemen exploit desperate crack users
- Interpersonal relations often dominated by intimidation and violence

**Outside the Crack Subculture**
- Cultural messages that promote neediness and dissatisfaction
- Massive importation of cocaine
- Existence of well-paying market place for sexual services
- Dislocations produced by structural changes in employment opportunities
- Degradation of inner-city services
- Concentration of poverty and pathology in the inner cities

**SET**

**Crack-Using Sexual Providers**
- Lack appreciation of self-worth
- Come predominantly from dysfunctional, disadvantaged families
- Have not had success in school or occupation
- Perceive lack of legitimate opportunities
- Had early exposure to drug use
- Are unable to establish boundaries for their drug use
- Are often involved in a downward spiral of drug use and self-degradation
- Began sexual activity early, often in exploitative relationships
- Often desire to be loving spouses and effective parents, but have been unsuccessful in achieving these roles

**Crack-Using Sexual Receivers**
- Come from similar backgrounds as the providers
- Are men who control resources (especially crack and money)
- Desire sexual stimulation to complement the drug high
- Often gain satisfaction from controlling and humiliating others

**Figure 1–1.** Sex-for-Crack Phenomenon as Interaction of Drug, Set, and Setting

intensity of a rush and high brought about by cocaine processed in this manner, crush the crystals and smoke them in special pipes. Although freebasers achieved notoriety in the 1960s and 1970s, their number was always somewhat restricted by the prodigious quantities of expensive powder cocaine that could be consumed in a short time and by the risk of explosion associated with open flames and the use of a solvent.

Like freebase cocaine, crack cocaine is processed from cocaine hydrochloride (with baking soda as a base) and then crystallized. But the end product is different: fewer of the adulterants have been removed, and part of the baking soda remains as a salt. The processing also allows for additional adulterants to be added, such as lidocaine or benzocaine, which look and taste like cocaine but produce no high. (For a fuller discussion of the range of coca-derived drugs, see Inciardi 1987.)

Because the technology for converting powder cocaine to crack is quite simple, requiring only baking soda and a source of heat, many users prefer to do it themselves, both to save money and to prevent further adulteration of the drug. In many areas, as noted in several of the site reports, different terms are used to distinguish the cocaine one has converted oneself, often called "rock," from the product one can buy on the street, often called "ready rock" or "crack."

The great advantage of crack for drug entrepreneurs of the mid-1980s was that it significantly brought down the unit cost of the drug while raising the profit margin. While the smallest unit of powdered cocaine cost five or ten dollars in a city like New York, the smallest crack dose cost as little as three dollars, and twenty dollars of powder might easily return a profit of sixty dollars. For users, the attraction of crack was that it produced an intense high, similar to that furnished by freebase cocaine. Crack was also cheap (per unit dose), conveniently packaged, and readily available.

In describing the drug, respondents frequently mentioned an intense euphoria, lasting no more than three or five minutes, followed by diminution of the euphoria and an intense desire to regain the high. Its short period of effectiveness is one of crack's most salient distinguishing features. A heavy heroin addict usually fixes three to five times a day and has time to engage in activities away from home or the shooting gallery. For crack smokers, staying high requires being near a place where crack can be smoked—a crack house, an apartment, a hotel room, or a quiet corner. Also, because of the smoke and smell, crack use is more difficult to hide from nonusing family and close acquaintances than drugs that can be consumed undetected behind a door. For many, especially young people living at home with nonusing parents, one of the advantages of smoking in crack houses is to be free of the fear of detection.

A number of respondents called crack a controlling drug and categorized it with heroin, alcohol, and speed in its ability to take over a life. John French, in his Newark-Philadelphia report, observes that unlike heroin distributors, crack distributors rarely employ known users of the sales product as street dealers. Nevertheless, the "addictiveness" of crack may also be somewhat overemphasized in the site reports because our sample selection procedures focused attention on that segment of the user community engaged in chronic and uncontrolled use. There is some evidence, from both our interviews and other sources (Murphy, Reinarman, and Waldorf 1989; Treaster 1991), that some individuals may be able to moderate their cocaine and crack use, especially now that the dangers of unmoderated use are better understood in the user community.

Cocaine has long had a reputation as an aid to sexual interest or performance (Grinspoon and Bakalar 1976; Gay et al. 1982). Many subjects reported increased sexual pleasure when they first used crack, but this may be as much due to the disinhibiting quality of the drug as to its action as a direct sexual stimulant. Whatever the initial effect, however, long-term chronic use tends to decrease sexual interest and function. Most of the women in the study reported that once they became steady crack users, they had little interest in the pleasures of sex, especially when using the drug. For men, there is a slightly different pattern. Although many of the crack-using men in our sample continued to engage in sexual activities and often desired to combine it with crack use, most respondents confirmed the common street knowledge that prolonged cocaine use inhibits the ability to achieve erection or ejaculation. A very few long-time users, however, reported that crack increased their sexual desire or at least did not decrease it. (These patterns are similar to those found by MacDonald et al. 1988.)

## The Set: The Attitudes and Personality Structures of the Participants

A core theme that pervades the relationships of participants in sex-for-crack exchanges is the low value they place on human life. The women and men providing the sex do not value themselves, and the men obtaining the sex do not attribute intrinsic worth to others. As one woman in Denver characterized men who come to crack houses for crack and for sex: "For them a woman is a commodity."

This lack of appreciation for self and others is understandable, given the backgrounds and circumstances of many of our subjects. Although the ethnographic sample contained a few children of stable middle- and working-class families, the subjects came overwhelmingly from dysfunctional families, hard-pressed by poverty. Many respondents reported growing up with alcoholic and drug-using parents who were unable to nurture them; others reported early abandonment or spending time in an orphanage and moving through childhood without ever having a satisfactory living arrangement. For most, the family was just the first of many social institutions that did not involve or nurture them. Few succeeded in school. Though many had worked, few had found psychologically or economically rewarding jobs. Most perceived a lack of legitimate opportunities open to them.

Commonly they began their drug-using careers as young teenagers. Some began even sooner. A few began their drug use with the concurrence of their parents. Ethnographers in several cities have documented intergenerational drug use: families in which adult or near-adult children used crack with one of their parents.

A common characteristic of the men and women offering sex in these exchanges was their inability to set limits on drug use. When craving crack, they devalue everything else in their life. Many respondents detailed the possessions, relationships, and self-esteem they had lost in chasing a crack-induced euphoria. Many felt that crack controlled their life, as a pimp, demon, or devil might.

A downward spiral of drug use and degradation was frequently reported. Drug use began for many as self-medication—a way of allaying feelings of ill ease and lack of self-esteem. Then the respondents were faced with having to do something they would rather not do in order to obtain more of the drug: stealing from a friend or family member, spending the rent money, or engaging in a degrading sexual act. After the deed was done and the short-lived drug euphoria wore off, a new cycle began, with the addition of self-disgust for having done the deed. This led to more ill ease, more lack of self-esteem, and a greater need for the drug-induced euphoria.

For most, sexual experience as well as drug use began early. For many of the females, it began through rape—commonly by a relative or friend of the family. Many of the sexual providers were strongly ambivalent about their sexual activities. While in one breath they might describe the activities as mechanical manipulation devoid of any meaning for them, at other times they expressed considerable guilt and shame about their actions.

Many female respondents were also deeply ambivalent about traditional female gender roles. While they valued their social freedoms and enjoyed aspects of their fast-paced lives, at times they felt alone and without satisfying relationships. Many held out hope of a futuure when they would be loving wives and mothers, though they felt powerless to take actual steps toward that future.

The men in the crack subculture who purchased sexual services came from backgrounds similar to those of the women offering the services. Although the men might not control significant resources by middle-class standards, twenty dollars was usually more than enough to purchase crack and sexual services in a crack house. For dealers, even those on the bottom of the pyramid, the amount of crack given over to satisfy a sexual desire or fantasy was an insignificant part of the day's trade.

Men desire sexual services for their own sake and to complement the drug high. But the desire to humiliate and degrade the provider—male or female—was also implicit in many of the actions and openly mentioned by many respondents. Many men appeared to desire a sense of mastery and control denied them in other arenas. They might obtain this feeling by dominating every aspect of the sexual encounter or by totally controlling another's actions in front of peers—as several respondents phrased it, "making them perform like circus dogs." In the extreme, the desire for mastery and control turned to violence, with reports of women being beaten and raped not uncommon. In some instances, the tendency toward humiliation and violence may also be fueled by male frustration associated with crack-induced sexual dysfunction.

## The Setting: Influence of the Physical and Social Environment

In *Drug, Set, and Setting*, Norman Zinberg was primarily interested in individual variation: why some individuals were able to control their heroin use and others were not. The concept of setting he employed was fairly restricted: the immediate physical and social setting in which use occurs. For the purposes of this book (which addresses not only the question of individual variation but also asks why the sex-for-crack phenomenon exists to the extent it does), the notion of setting has been expanded to include outside forces directly and indirectly impinging on the immediate setting.

**The Immediate Setting.** One of the most important findings from this study is the degree to which sex-for-crack exchanges take place in a defined subcultural space. In each of the studied cities, there exists one or more identifiable crack subcultures in which groups of users (and suppliers) interact frequently and share a set of values, attitudes, behaviors, and linguistic conventions. Many participants in sex-for-crack exchanges live almost entirely in the crack subculture in the sense that it is the context for their activities during most of their waking hours. Their experiences differ dramatically from those of the physician addicted to pharmaceutical opiates, whose drug use is almost totally separate from the social world he or she usually inhabits.

Zinberg argues that controlled drug use is supported by rituals, sanctions, and peer pressures encouraging moderation (e.g., limiting drug use to certain times or places). As described in our site reports, one of the most striking aspects of the drug-use patterns of men and women who regularly trade sex for crack is a lack of rituals and peer pressure that might limit the destructive potential of crack use. Rather than moderating drug use, friends often encourage friends to use as much as they can for as long as they can. Binges are common and accepted. Once crack use begins, it often continues until resources are depleted or physical exhaustion sets in after days of nonstop use. Most of the respondents were not just using drugs; their lives were totally organized around their drug use.

Although lack of moderation was common among respondents who regularly traded sex for crack, others in the crack scenes were less fully involved in the crack subculture. They were more like binge drinkers who join their drinking buddies several times a week but otherwise maintain relationships in contexts that do not include alcohol.

The crack house or smoke house, amply described in many variations in the following chapters, contributes to the lack of moderation. Most commonly, a crack house is an arrangement whereby some crack users support their drug use by setting up an environment—apartment, house, abandoned building—where other crack users can smoke crack, socialize, and possibly engage in sex. The people running the crack house extract a payment, in crack or money, for a range of services, including entry, remaining in the crack house, use of equipment such as pipes or matches, providing crack (or arranging to buy crack outside if the drug is not sold within the house), use of a room for sex, and in some cases, providing a person to supply sexual services. Because the house's "take" depends on how long people stay and how much they smoke, it is in the house's interest to encourage excess. Some of the cons run in crack houses are reminiscent of those used in bars for fleecing sailors home on leave. The crack house's objective is to ensure that no one leaves while still in possession of crack or money.

Males employed in the crack distribution system are a critical element of the setting. Often, especially at the distributor and dealer levels, their crack use is moderate or nonexistent. Their work, however, puts them into contact with individuals whose crack use is not moderated. Many of the sex-for-crack exchanges begin with a woman's telling a dealer (or anyone with enough crack to spare) that she will do anything for a rock. The dealer can then set the terms of the exchange—most commonly, to have the woman perform oral sex on him and possibly his friends or customers.

Much of the violence and degradation accompanying sex-for-crack exchanges can be best understood as part of the generalized use of intimidation and violence in the inner cities (a phenomenon Bourgois and Dunlap call the "culture of terror"). The tendency toward violence is especially prominent in the crack subculture, where, in the absence of any legitimate authority, violence is used to settle disputes and enforce discipline and boundaries.

**Outside Forces.** In a review of public health approaches, Mosher and Yanagisako (1991:281) caution that "problems associated with drug use are likely to be explained primarily as failures of the individual user, because of moral weakness, disease, or other shortcomings, while systemic factors that place individuals at risk are likely to be ignored." Although we cannot comprehensively delineate all the forces outside of the crack subculture that have contributed to the growth of the sex-for-crack phenomenon, it is worthwhile to highlight a few.

A critical element underlying the sex-for-crack phenomenon, and all other forms of drug abuse as well, is the ubiquitous message in American society that one needs something from outside oneself to feel good. The most aggressive purveyor of this message is the television, which for seven hours a day in the average American home stimulates artificial needs: for soft drinks, alcohol, snack foods, candy, new cars, fashion, music, and cosmetics (Ashbach and Scott 1989:26). Television is also a mind-altering substance (product) that stimulates its own need: "With the touch of a button, it takes you out of the 'real' world in which you reside and can place you at a basketball game, the back alleys of Miami, the streets of Bucharest, or the cartoony living rooms of Sitcom Land" (Hamil 1990:109). Inner-city minority youth, whose sense of self-worth is already often tenuous because of the insults from their immediate environment, are most susceptible to media-manipulated images that leave them feeling chronically dissatisfied.

An equally critical factor contributing to the sex-for-crack phenomenon, though on a different level, is the multibillion-dollar-a-year industry that imports cocaine into the United States. The low unit price of crack was made possible not only by the introduction of a different processing method but also by an increased supply, and hence lowering of the street price, of powdered cocaine from $65,000 per kilo in 1981 to $14,000 in 1989 (Inciardi 1992:90).

Another force critical to sex-for-money-for-crack exchanges is the existence of men outside the crack culture who desire to pay money for sex. Some of these men are part of inner-city communities in which crack and sex are openly sold; others drive in from the suburbs. Some prefer women; others prefer men. But without the demand they create, there could not be as many suppliers of sexual services.

More generalized societal forces, less immediate to the exchanges themselves, also appear to underlie the growth of the sex-for-crack phenomenon. William J. Wilson, in his book *The Truly Disadvantaged*, asks why inner-city black neighborhoods are so much bleaker, meaner, and characterized by more social pathology than they were forty or fifty years ago. His answer is summed up by the terms "concentration effect" and "social buffer":

> The former refers to the constraints and opportunities associated with living in neighborhoods in which the population is overwhelmingly socially disadvantaged—constraints and opportunities that include the kinds of ecological niches that the residents of these communities occupy in terms of access to jobs, availability of marriageable partners, and exposure to conventional role models. The latter refers to the presence of sufficient working- and middle-class professional families to absorb and cushion the effect of uneven growth and periodic recessions on inner-city neighborhoods. The basic thesis is not that ghetto culture went unchecked following the removal of higher-income families in the inner city, but that the removal of these families made it more difficult to sustain the basic institutions in the inner

city (including churches, stores, schools, recreational facilities, etc.) in the face of prolonged joblessness. (Wilson 1987:144)

While Wilson emphasizes joblessness caused by structural changes in the labor force and cyclical economic cycles, Rodrick Wallace, in a detailed analysis of "urban desertification" in the Bronx, argues that the driving force behind worsening conditions in inner-city minority communities is the withdrawal of adequate municipal services, especially fire services. The lack of municipal services leads to low-income housing loss, depopulation, and disruption of social networks and structures, all of which, according to Wallace, "is closely and causally associated with a broad spectrum of pathological outcomes, including raised death rates from homicide and substance abuse, and the distribution of the AIDS epidemic in both geographic and social space" (1990:801).

Finally, there is the issue of increasing poverty. In his book *The Politics of Rich and Poor: Wealth and the American Electorate in the Reagan Aftermath* (1990), Kevin Phillips, a Republican political analyst, argues that national economic and tax policies since the mid-1970s have resulted in a major redistribution of wealth that has benefited the rich while undercutting the poor. According to census data, while the percentage of income received by the lowest quintile decreased steadily from 5.6 percent in 1969 to 4.6 percent in 1988, the percentage received by the highest quintile increased from 40.6 percent to 44 percent (p. 13). Not only did the poor have relatively less money, they also received fewer services: the percentage of federal outlays for human resources (such as housing, urban, and social services) decreased between 1980 and 1987 from 28 to 23 percent (p. 87). The effects are particularly acute for black Americans: "In 1987 the income of the typical black family—at $18,098—equaled just 56.1 percent of the typical white family's income, the lowest comparative percentage since the 1960s" (p. 207). The last twenty years were also difficult for children: the percentage living in poverty had bottomed at 14 percent in 1968, climbed to 16 percent in the 1970s, and went over 20 percent in the 1980s (p. 204).

## Sex-for-Crack Exchanges and the Transmission of AIDS

Since the inception of this study, a key concern has been that sex-for-crack exchanges might be a mechanism through which HIV could spread to low-incidence populations. The ethnographic work detailed in the following chapters confirms that this concern is justified by the high-risk behavior of many respondents. Many women and men providing sexual services for crack or for money to buy crack often have sexual relations with numerous partners, sometimes numbering more than several hundred per month. Much of the sex is unprotected, especially for individuals who are not experienced prostitutes able to negotiate condom use and other conditions of the encounters. Although anal intercourse is not commonly practiced, and is considered "deviant" and "unacceptable" by many respondents, it does occur, especially in exchanges in which humiliation and degradation play a large role. As a number of the chapters highlight, it is precisely those individuals most dependent on crack who are most likely to be involved in degrading sexual encounters and least able to insist on safer sex pratices.

In addition to the generalized risk of infection due to unprotected sex with hundreds (or thousands) of partners, individuals engaging in sex-for-crack exchanges appear to be at increased risk for HIV transmission through blood or semen because of open sores on the tongue and lips from crack pipe burns, because of ulcers caused by other sexually transmitted diseases, and, as Inciardi identifies, because of penile abrasion associated with the difficulty many crack-using men have in achieving orgasm.

The principal factor that might lessen the risk of HIV transmission is that, overwhelmingly, the sexual service most requested is fellatio. Many AIDS researchers and educators (as well as many of our subjects) have characterized this activity as "less risky." But how much less risky than anal or vaginal sex is still a contested matter. Recently, Lifson and his colleagues (1990) provided extensive documentation on the sero-conversion of two homosexual men who reported no anal intercourse during the preceding five years and no IV drug use or receipt of blood products, but both had engaged in multiple acts of receptive oral intercourse with ejaculation. Because many gay men previously engaged in a wide repertoire of sexual acts including anal sex, the dangers of "less risky" sexual acts have been difficult to detect in large multifactorial studies. Lifson and his colleagues predict that for the homosexual community, "as the frequency of anal intercourse declines, transmission through receptive oral intercourse may become more apparent" (1990:1510).

In terms of our study sample, there is an important difference between saying that the population might be at risk for HIV infection because of their sexual practices and documenting that the transmission has occurred and is likely to continue. As initial findings were analyzed, it became evident that information regarding the current HIV status of ethnographic sample subjects was not being collected in a reliable manner. Although subjects were routinely asked about their HIV status, many had never been tested and did not know. Also, many of those who said they knew were basing their answers on tests conducted one or more years earlier.

To provide a better indication of HIV infection than was available from the ethnographic sample, serological testing was conducted at five sites (Denver, Los Angeles, Miami, New York, and San Francisco), and confirmed HIV status results were obtained for 195 individuals. Criteria for inclusion in the "serostatus" sample were stricter than for inclusion in the ethnographic sample in that persons not directly involved in sex-for-crack exchanges could not be included. All of the 195 individuals in the sample were crack users who, within the prior thirty days, had provided sexual services in direct exchange for crack, provided sexual services for money to purchase crack, or received sexual services in exchange for crack. Although it would have been preferable to have the same individuals in both the ethnographic and sero-status samples, there is relatively little overlap between the two samples because funding for HIV testing was received only after ethnographic interviewing was nearly complete at most sites.

Although field procedures differed somewhat at each of the five sites, usually HIV testing began with informed consent procedures followed by a short interview. Subjects also received pretest counseling, from the study interviewer or, more commonly, from the staff of the hospital or agency cooperating with the testing. Blood samples were tested for the presence of the HIV virus and also, at three of the sites, for the presence of syphilis antibodies.[4] Once the results were known, subjects were notified of their status, provided with counseling, and, when appropriate, provided with medical or psychological referrals.

The sero-status sample demographics (table 1–5) are similar to the ethnographic sample in regard to sex, race, age, years of education completed, and income from street hustles. The most important finding from the HIV testing was that significant rates of HIV infection were found among both women and men engaging in sex-for-crack exchanges, whether or not the individuals had a history of intravenous drug use and whether or not they now engaged in homosexual or bisexual practices (table 1–6). Extreme caution should be taken in interpreting table 1–6 beyond the basic assertion that HIV was found within each category. Not only was the site sample small and nonrandom, but the rates of infection within each category differed greatly by site.

The general conclusion, however, seems clear: sex-for-crack exchanges appear to be implicated in the spread of the AIDS virus. In every city, we found individuals who through their sex-for-crack exchanges were having unprotected sex with large numbers of partners. We found a significant number of individuals in our target population who were already infected with the virus.

## Research and Policy Implications

One of the most important lessons of the study was not only that it could be done but it could be done well. Chronic crack smokers, drug dealers, crack house operators, and other members of the crack subculture became (at least much of the time) cooperative and insightful subjects for a research study on sex-for-crack exchanges. Many did it simply for the money. Others,

## Table 1–5
## Demographic Characteristics of Serostatus Sample

| Characteristics | Number | Percentage |
|---|---|---|
| Total | 195 | 100 |
| Sex | | |
| Female | 139 | 71 |
| Male | 56 | 29 |
| Race | | |
| African-American | 138 | 71 |
| White | 26 | 13 |
| Hispanic | 31 | 16 |
| Age | | |
| 18–25 | 50 | 26 |
| 26–35 | 95 | 49 |
| 36+ | 50 | 26 |
| Years of education completed | | |
| 4–6 | 7 | 4 |
| 7–9 | 19 | 10 |
| 10–11 | 64 | 33 |
| 12 | 70 | 36 |
| 13+ | 27 | 14 |
| Missing | 8 | 4 |
| Primary street hustles | | |
| Prostitution | 107 | 55 |
| Drug dealing | 29 | 15 |
| Street hustler | 1 | * |
| Shoplifting | 6 | 3 |
| Crack house worker | 1 | * |
| Begging | 6 | 3 |
| No reported hustle | 28 | 14 |
| Missing | 17 | 9 |
| Income from government assistance (e.g., food stamps or welfare) | | |
| Yes | 54 | 27 |
| No | 158 | 81 |
| Missing | 3 | 2 |

*Less than 1 percent.

however, gave more than they got. They appreciated that someone else wanted to hear about their experiences and they wanted to make sure the researcher got the story right. Among conditions that made the study possible, perhaps most important was having patient, determined, street-smart, and nonjudgmental interviewers and a flexible approach to the research process.

A great strength of the site reports is that they collectively provide as

**Table 1–6**
**HIV Serostatus by Gender, Sexual Activity, and Drug Use History**

| Gender and Current Sexual Activity (Last Thirty Days) | Drug Use History | HIV Positive Proportion (%) |
|---|---|---|
| Women providing sex in heterosexual sex-for-crack exchanges | No IV | 8/75 (11%) |
|  | IV | 5/65 (8%) |
| Men receiving sex in heterosexual sex-for-crack exchanges | No IV | 3/24 (12%) |
|  | IV | 5/19 (26%) |
| Men providing or receiving sex in same-sex sex-for-crack exchanges | No IV | 2/6 (33%) |
|  | IV | 4/6 (67%) |
| Total |  | 27/168 (14%) |

perceptive an analysis of sex-for-crack exchanges (and, indirectly, of the inner-city crack subculture) as now exists. But in documenting the variety of patterns and complexity of issues involved, they are more preface than summation. Clearly more research is needed.

This book as a whole emphasizes what appears to be the core of the sex-for-crack phenomenon: women exchanging sexual services for crack in crack houses and women, as street prostitutes, exchanging sexual services for money to buy crack. But, as noted in each chapter, the sex-for-crack phenomenon is much larger than these two patterns. Several of the reports were able to explore other patterns more fully, especially the Los Angeles study, which spotlights homelessness and the exchange of sex for crack, and the Denver study, which analyzes the interplay of drugs and sex in youth gang networks.

Many other aspects of the sex-for-crack phenomenon touched on in the site reports need to be more fully developed. Perhaps most needed is an ethnographic study describing and analyzing the sex-for-crack phenomenon in relation to gay and bisexual men.[5] Other aspects of the phenomenon that could be profitably addressed through ethnographic study include:

• Sex-for-crack exchanges among youth 18 and under.
• Sex-for-crack exchanges in non-inner-city crack subcultures.
• The participation of non-crack-using men in sex-for-crack exchanges.
• Behavioral changes among participants in sex-for-crack exchanges associated with increased knowledge of HIV transmission routes.

Other kinds of studies are also needed. Although it would face many methodological challenges, an epidemiological study that could credibly estimate the prevalence and incidence of crack use, chronic crack use, and sex-for-crack exchanges would complement this study and contribute to a fuller understanding of the sex-for-crack phenomenon. Another study sorely needed is a large-scale longitudinal sero-conversion study that could document the life-styles of HIV-infected participants in sex-for-crack exchanges before and after their infection.

## What Is to Be Done: Sick Individuals and Sick Populations

During their eighteen months of fieldwork, the study ethnographers and interviewers were frequently shocked and dismayed—not so much by the drug use but by the violence associated with drug dealing, the degradation and brutality associated with many of the sex-for-crack exchanges, and the adverse health and mental health consequences. Certainly the sex-for-crack phenomenon is not a pleasant subject to investigate. Site teams encountered many individuals in physical and psychological pain and foresaw tragedies still to come. Ameliorative action seems both possible and needed—but what is to be done?

The epidemiologist Geoffrey Rose provides a conceptual distinction helpful to developing programmatic recommendations based on the findings of this study. In "Sick Individuals and Sick Populations" (1985), Rose writes that there are fundamentally two different approaches to public health—the "high-risk" strategy and the population strategy. The two strategies, in turn, are related to two very different etiological questions:

> The first seeks the causes of cases, and the second seeks the causes of incidence. "Why do some individuals have hypertension?" is a quite different question from "Why do some populations have much hypertension, whilst in others it is rare?" The questions require different kinds of study, and they have different answers. (p. 33)

The high-risk public health strategy emphasizes identifying and treating sick individuals or individuals likely to be sick in the near future. Among its advantages, it provides intervention appropriate to the immediate circumstances of the individuals: salt restriction for the hypertensive, dietary change for those with high serum cholesterol. Among its disadvantages are that it is essentially palliative and temporary: "It does not seek to alter the underlying causes of the disease but to identify individuals who are particularly susceptible to those causes" (p. 36). In contrast, the population strategy emphasizes removing the underlying causes that make an illness common in a population. Put another way, it seeks to reduce the mean level of the relevant risk factors in a population. If intervention is effective, through changing environmental factors or social norms, then the rates of illness are permanently reduced.

This is its great advantage. Here we look at specific high-risk and population strategy recommendations relating to the sex-for-crack phenomenon.

## Programs for Affected Individuals

**Harm Reduction Approaches.** There is an immediate need to establish culturally sensitive programs to reduce health risks associated with the sex-for-crack phenomenon, especially the spread of the AIDS virus and other sexually transmitted diseases.

AIDS outreach programs for intravenous drug users and their sexual partners have demonstrated the feasibility and effectiveness of public health programs addressed to drug-using populations. Such programs typically employ indigenous outreach workers, many of them previously heavy drug users. The programs offer street-based AIDS education, prevention supplies such as condoms and bleach for disinfecting needles, risk-reduction counseling, and referrals to health and drug-treatment agencies. A key element in their success has been their acceptance by user communities. Outreach staff were abstinent and often served as role models for ending illicit drug use, but health and prevention services were provided to drug users whether or not they abstained from drug use.

Several site reports describe outreach programs in which the chapter authors played instrumental roles. These programs employed ethnographically oriented social scientists in the development, implementation, evaluation, and redirection of the intervention. Their involvement ensured that the materials, messages, programs, and procedures were appropriate for the targeted community.

The ethnographic evidence from this study supports extension of such outreach efforts to populations not now benefiting from special attention, especially female and male sexual providers who frequently engage in unprotected sex-for-crack exchanges. One model of proactive outreach, developed by the Philadelphia Department of Public Health, is to send caseworkers into sexually oriented crack houses specifically to conduct serological testing and make medical referrals (Mellinger et al. 1991). Creative solutions must especially be found to provide social and health services to individuals in this population who are already infected with the AIDS virus.

The receivers of the sexual services are also in need of AIDS outreach information. Although they are probably at less risk than providers of sexual services, they dominate most of the high-risk exchanges. The non-crack-using customers are especially likely to be more risk conscious once the AIDS implications of their actions are made clear.

Outreach programs for participants in sex-for-crack exchanges might tailor their messages to specific misconceptions, such as the common one noted in several of the site reports that HIV-positive persons have a distinct look or smell. A special effort should also be made to explain, in terms the population can completely understand, the conditions and precautions that can raise or lower the risks associated with oral sex. For many in our sample, oral sex is not considered to be "real sex" and is discounted as an AIDS-transmission mechanism.

Another way of conceptualizing outreach programs and other harm-reduction health programs directed to drug users is to think of them as treatment recruitment programs. One of the key findings of this study concerns the social isolation of chronic crack users. Their meaningful interactions are often only with other chronic crack users. Health programs are an effective way to provide bridges back to mainstream institutions, such as schools, social service agencies, and drug-abuse treatment programs.

**Drug Treatment Approaches.** There appears to be considerable need for a variety of drug-abuse treatment modalities targeted specifically to crack users and women participating in sex-for-crack exchanges. Repeatedly in our study we talked with women and men who told us they wanted to quit using crack. They had hit bottom or burned out; their drug use was not fun anymore. However, they did not know how to quit. Similar in many ways to cigarette smokers who want to quit, they are defeated day after day, time after time.

To a great extent, the drug-treatment community has not adapted to the changing characteristics of those seeking treatment. Although heroin and crack users share many common characteristics, crack users tend to be younger and have special needs that traditional treatment approaches often fail to address. For example, given the pervasiveness of crack in the families and home neighborhoods of many recovering crack users, specific after-treatment relapse prevention techniques may need to be taught to counter the intense crack cravings induced by environmental cues.

Many more treatment programs could direct their efforts to the special needs and aspirations of crack-using women, who comprise such a large percentage of all crack abusers. Several reports note that the strongest internal force for positive change in many of these women is their desire to be more responsible and effective as mothers. Treatment programs that involve children and incorporate family therapy techniques might be particularly successful with these women.

## Programs for Affected Populations

Most respondents in our study began life with deficits in terms of the competencies of their families, schools, and communities to engage them and sustain them. It comes as little surprise that many of them have failed academically, occupationally, and in developing supportive personal relationships.

In many respects, the crack subculture offers an appealing alternative to individuals who do not have respected roles in mainstream institutions or sustaining relationships. To dealers, it offers material rewards and positions of power and respect. To users, it offers the pleasure of the drug, a generally accepting community of fellow users, and an answer to the question, "What should I do today?" (In the long run, of course, the crack subculture also offers the risks of incarceration, violent injury, infection, addiction, and depletion of resources.)

The real and long-term solution to reducing the incidence of chronic drug use and accompanying pathologies is not simply to set up programs to stop young people from using drugs but rather to support, from an early age, their active participation in institutions that will engage them in healthier pursuits. There are myriad means through which the health of families, schools, and communities might be nurtured—some aimed at directly supporting these institutions, others at affecting them indirectly. For example, William J. Wilson (1987:151) would have us initiate a "macroeconomic policy designed to promote both economic growth and a tight labor market" as well as job training and apprenticeship programs for those without job skills. Rodrick Wallace (1990) suggests that urban decay could be reversed by improving municipal services; encouraging the reknitting of "frayed" personal, domestic, and community networks; and increasing government investment in low-income housing. Kevin Phillips (1990:220) calls for new economic policies at the national level that would counter the "excessive individualism, greed, and insufficient concern for America as a community" that characterized the 1980s. For his part, Rose (1985:38) observes that the greatest impediment to population approaches in public health is "the enormous difficulty for medical personnel to see health as a population issue and not merely as a problem for individuals." The most difficult part of a strategy to reduce the incidence of crack abuse and accompanying pathologies may not be devising the requisite programs but rather developing the consensus that these programs are necessary.

## Notes

1. To date, the largest number of ethnographic drug use studies address heroin use. Among the most often cited are Agar (1973a, 1978); Biernacki (1979, 1986); Feldman (1968, 1973); Hanson et al. (1985); Rosenbaum (1981); Stephens and McBride (1976); Sutter (1966, 1969, 1972); Weppner (1973), and Waldorf (1973). Stephens (1991) has recently reviewed the sociocultural literature on heroin users and developed a theoretical model of the "street addict role."

    Other drugs that have been the focus of significant qualitative studies include marijuana (Fields 1984, 1986); cocaine (Adler 1985; Cleckner 1967a); crack (Bourgois 1989; Hamid 1990; Williams 1989); speed (Carey and Mandel 1968); methadone (Agar 1977a; Agar and Stephens 1975; Preble and Miller 1977; Soloway

1974); and multidrug abuse (Caven 1972; Cleckner 1976b, 1977; Feldman 1977; Moore et al. 1978).

2. Genser's remarks were made during a session on Sex and Crack in Urban America at the Society for Applied Anthropology's Annual Meeting in Charleston, South Carolina, in March 1991. He was one of three designated discussants who commented on findings from this study.

3. The field of illicit drug ethnography is well enough established that a number of practitioners have reflected on its (and their own) contributions to the field of drug-abuse research. These include Adler (1990); Agar (1973b, 1976, 1977b, 1985); Bennett (1990); Feldman (1974); Feldman and Aldrich (1990); Plant and Reeves (1976); Power (1989); Waldorf (1979); and Weppner (1977).

4. Serological testing was done with the cooperation of the San Francisco Department of Health; Foundation for Research on Sexually Transmitted Diseases (New York City); Denver AIDS Prevention, Department of Public Health, City and County of Denver; and the University of Miami School of Medicine. At all sites, serum was initially determined to be positive with an ELISA and confirmed with a Western Blot.

5. Morse and his coauthors (1991) recently outlined, in their study of New Orleans male street prostitutes, how bisexual male prostitutes providing sexual services to gay men and bisexual customers receiving sexual services from gay prostitutes may be important bridges through which HIV may spread to currently low-incidence heterosexual populations.

# References

Adler, Patricia, 1985. *Wheeling and Dealing: An Ethnography of an Upper-Level Drug Dealing and Smuggling Community*. New York: Columbia University Press.

———. 1990. "Ethnographic Research on Hidden Populations: Penetrating the Drug World." In *The Collection and Interpretation of Data from Hidden Populations*, pp. 96–112. NIDA Research Monograph 98. Rockville, Md.: National Institute on Drug Abuse.

Agar, Michael H. 1973a. *Ripping and Running: A Formal Ethnography of Urban Heroin Addiction*. New York: Seminar Press.

———. 1973b. "Ethnography and the Addict." In *Cultural Illness and Health*. Edited by L. Nader and T. Maretzki. Washington, D.C.: American Anthropological Association.

———. 1976. "One Up, One Down, Even Up: Some Features of an Ethnographic Approach." *Addictive Disease: An International Journal* 4:619–626.

———. 1977a. "Going Through the Changes: Methadone in New York City." *Human Organization* 36:291–295.

———. 1977b. "Ethnography in the Streets and in the Joint." In *Street Ethnography: Selected Studies of Crime and Drug Use in Natural Settings*. Edited by Robert Weppner. Beverly Hills: Sage Publications.

———. 1978. "When the Junk Disappeared: Historical Case of a Heroin Shortage." *Journal of Psychedelic Drugs* 10:225–261.

————. 1985. "Folks and Professionals: Different Models for the Interpretation of Drug Use." *International Journal of the Addictions* 20:173–182.

Agar, Michael, and Richard C. Stephens. 1975. "The Methadone Street Scene." *Psychiatry* 38:381–387.

Ashbach, Charles, and David Scott. 1989. *"Drugs: Demand, Depenency and Denial."* Unpublished manuscript.

Becker, Howard S. 1953. "Becoming a Marijuana User." *American Journal of Sociology* 59:235–242.

Bennett, Linda A. 1990. "Drug Studies: Anthrpology's Distinctive Imprint." In *Medical Anthropology: A Handbook of Theory and Method*. Edited by Thomas Johnson and Carolyn Sargent. Westport, Conn.: Greenwood Press.

Biernacki, Patrick. 1979. "Junkie Work, Hustles, and Social Status among Heroin Addicts." *Journal of Drug Issues* (Fall):535–551.

————. 1986. *Pathways from Heroin Addiction: Recovery Without Treatment*. Philadelphia: Temple University.

Bourgois, Philippe. 1989. "In Search of Horatio Alger: Culture and Ideology in the Crack Economy." *Contemporary Drug Problems* 16:619–651.

Carey, J. T., and J. Mandel. 1968. "A San Francisco Bay Area Speed Scene." *Journal of Health and Social Behavior* 9:164–174.

Caven, Sherri. 1972. *Hippies of the Haight*. St. Louis: New Critics Press.

Cleckner, Patricia J. 1976a. "Blowing Some Lines: Intracultural Variations Among Miami Cocaine Users." *Journal of Psychedelic Drugs* 8:37–42.

————. 1976b. "Dope Is to Get High: A Preliminary Analysis of Intracultural Variation in Drug Categories Among Heavy Users and Dealers." *Addictive Diseases* 2:537–552.

————. 1977. "Cognitive and Ritual Aspects of Drug Use Among Young Black Urban Males." In *Drugs, Rituals and Altered States of Consciousness*. Edited by B. M. DuToit. Rotterdam: A. A. Balkema.

Feldman, Harvey W. 1968. "Ideological Supports to Becoming and Remaining a Heroin Addict." *Journal of Health and Social Behavior* 9(2):131–139.

————. 1973. "Street Status and Drug Users." *Transaction/Society* 10(4):32–38.

————. 1974. *Street Status and the Drug Researcher: Issues in Participant Observation*. Washington, D.C.: Drug Abuse Council.

————. 1977. "A Neighborhood History of Drug Switching." In *Street Ethnography: Selected Studies of Crime and Drug Use in Natural Settings*, pp. 21–54. Edited by Robert Weppner. Beverly Hills: Sage Publications.

Feldman, Harvey W., Michael H. Agar, and George M. Beschner. 1979. *Angel Dust: An Ethnographic Study of PCP Users*. Lexington, Ma.: Lexington Books.

Feldman, Harvey W., and Michael Aldrich. 1990. "The Role of Ethnography in Substance Abuse Research and Public Policy: Historial Precedent and Future Prospects." In *The Collection and Interpretation of Data from Hidden Populations*. NIDA Research Monograph 98. Rockville, Md.: National Institute on Drug Abuse.

Fields, Allen B. 1984. "Slinging Weed: The Social Organization of Street-Corner Marijuana Sales." *Urban Life* 13(2–3):274–280.

————. 1986. "Young Black Marijuana Dealers." In *Teen Drug Use*, pp. 85–104. Edited by G. Beschner and A. S. Friedman. New York: Lexington Books.

Gay, George R., John A. Newmeyer, Michael Perry, Gregory Johnson, and Mark

Kurland. 1982. "Love and Haight: The Sensuous Hippie Revisited. Drug/Sex Practices in San Francisco, 1980–91." *Journal of Psychoactive Drugs* 14(1–2):111–123.

Goldsmith, Marsha F. 1988. "Sex Tied to Drugs = STD Spread." *Journal of the American Medical Association* 260:2009.

Goldstein, Paul. 1979. *Prostitution and Drugs.* New York: Lexington Books.

Grinspoon, Lester, and James B. Bakalar. 1976. *Cocaine: A Drug and Its Social Evolution.* New York: Basic Books.

Hamid, Ansley. 1990. "The Political Economy of Crack-Related Violence." *Contemporary Drug Problems* 17:31–78.

Hamill, Pete. 1990. "Crack and the Box." *New Age Journal* 7(6):52–53, 109–110.

Hanson, Bill, George Beschner, James W. Walters, and Elliott Bovelle. 1985. *Life with Heroin: Voices from the Inner City.* New York: Lexington Books.

Inciardi, James A. 1987. "Beyond Cocaine: Basuco, Crack, and Other Coca Products." *Contemporary Drug Problems* 14:461–492.

———. 1992. *The War on Drugs II: The Continuing Epic of Heroin, Cocaine, Crack, Crime, AIDS, and Public Policy.* Mountain View, Calif.: Mayfield Publishing.

Kleber, Herbert D. 1988. "Introduction: Cocaine Abuse: Historical, Epidemiological, and Psychological Perspectives." *Journal of Clinical Psychiatry* 49:2 (Supplement) (February).

Lambert, Elizabeth, and W. Wayne Wiebel. 1990. Introduction to *The Collection and Interpretation of Data from Hidden Populations.* NIDA Research Monograph 98. Rockville, Md.: National Institute on Drug Abuse.

Lifson, Alan R., Paul M. O'Malley, Nancy A. Hessol, Susan P. Buchbinder, Lyn Cannon, and George W. Rutherford. 1990. "HIV Seroconversion in Two Homosexual Men After Receptive Oral Intercourse with Ejaculation: Implications for Counseling Concerning Safe Sexual Practices." *American Journal of Public Health* 80:1509–1511.

Lindesmith, Alfred R. 1947. *Opiate Addiction.* Bloomington, Ind.: Principia Press.

MacDonald, Patrick T., Dan Waldorf, Craig Reinarman, and Sheigla Murphy. 1988. "Heavy Cocaine Use and Sexual Behavior." *Journal of Drug Issues* 18:437–455.

Mellinger, M. D., M. Goldberg, A. Wade, et al. 1991. "Alternative Case-Finding Methods in a Crack-Related Syphilis Epidemic in Philadelphia." *Morbidity and Mortality Weekly Report* 40(5):77–80.

Moore, J., L. Cerea, C. Garcia, R. Garcia, and F. Valencia. 1978. *Homeboys: Gangs, Drugs, and Prison in the Barrios of Los Angeles.* Philadelphia: Temple University Press.

Morningstar, Patricia J., and Dale D. Chitwood. 1987. "How Women and Men Get Cocaine: Sex-Role Stereotypes and Acquisition Patterns." *Journal of Psychoactive Drugs* 19:(2):135–142.

Morse, Edward V., Patricia M. Simon, Howard J. Osofsky, Paul M. Balson, and H. Richard Gaumer. 1991. "The Male Street Prostitute: A Vector for Transmission of HIV Infection in the Heterosexual World." *Social Science and Medicine* 32:535–539.

Mosher, James F., and Karen Yanagisako. 1991. "Public Health Not Social Warfare: A Public Health Approach to Illegal Drug Policy." *Journal of Public Health Policy* 12(3):279–324.

Murphy, Sheigla, Craig Reinarman, and Dan Waldorf. 1989. "An 11-Year Follow-up of a Network of Cocaine Users." *British Journal of Addictions* 84:427–436.

Musto, David F. 1987. *The American Disease: Origins of Narcotic Control*. New Haven: Yale University Press.

Phillips, Kevin. 1990. *The Politics of Rich and Poor: Wealth and the American Electorate in the Reagan Aftermath*. New York: Random House.

Plant, M. A., and C. E Reeves, 1976. "Participant Observation as a Method of Collecting Information About Drug Taking: Conclusions from Two English Studies." *British Journal of Addictions* 71:155–159.

Power, Robert. 1989. "Participant Observation and Its Place in the Study of Illicit Drug Abuse." *British Journal of Addiction* 84(1):43–52.

Preble, Edward, and John J. Casey. 1969. "Taking Care of Business: The Heroin User's Life on the Street." *International Journal of the Addictions* 4 (March):1–24.

Preble, Edward, and Thomas Miller. 1977. "Methadone, Wine and Welfare." In *Street Ethnography*. Edited by R. S. Weppner. Beverly Hills: Sage.

Rose, Geoffrey. 1985. "Sick Individuals and Sick Population." *International Journal of Epidemiology* 14:32–38.

Rosenbaum, Marsha. 1981. *Women on Heroin*. New Brunswick, N.J.: Rutgers University Press.

Soloway, Irving H. 1974. "Methadone and the Culture of Addiction." *Journal of Psychedelic Drugs* 6:1–99.

Stephens, Richard C. 1991. *The Street Addict Role: A Theory of Heroin Addiction*. Albany: State University of New York Press.

Stephens, Richard C., and Duane L. McBride. 1976. "Becoming a Street Addict." *Human Organization* 35(1):85–93.

Sutter, Alan G. 1966. "The World of the Righteous Dope Fiend." *Issues in Criminology* 2(2):177–222.

———. 1969. "Worlds of Drug Use on the Street Scene." In *Delinquency, Crime and Social Process*. Edited by D. Cressey and D. A. Ward. New York: Harper & Row.

———. 1972. "Playing a Cold Game: Phases of a Ghetto Career." *Urban Life and Culture* 1(1):77–91.

Treaster, Joseph. 1991. "In a Crack House: Dinner and Drugs on the Stove." *New York Times*, April 6.

Waldorf, Dan. 1973. *Careers in Dope*. Englewood Cliffs, N.J.: Prentice-Hall.

———. 1979. "A Brief History of Illicit-Drug Ethnographies." In *Ethnography: A Research Tool for Policymakers in the Drug and Alcohol Fields*, pp. 21–35. Edited by Carl Akins and George Beschner. Rockville, Md.: NIDA.

Wallace, Rodrick. 1990. "Urban Desertification, Public Health and Public Order: 'Planned Shrinkage,' Violent Death, Substance Abuse and AIDS in the Bronx." *Social Science and Medicine* 31:801–813.

Weppner, Robert S. 1973. "An Anthropological View of the Street Addict's World." *Human Organization* 32(2):111–121.

———. 1977. "Street Ethnography: Problems and Prospects." In *Street Ethnography: Selected Studies of Crime and Drug Use in Natural Settings*, pp. 21–54. Edited by Robert Weppner. Beverly Hills: Sage.

Williams, Terry. 1989. *The Cocaine Kids*. Reading, Mass.: Addison-Wesley.

Wilson, William J. 1987. *The Truly Disadvantaged: The Inner City, the Underclass, and Public Policy*. Chicago: University of Chicago Press.

Wish, Eric D., and Joyce O'Neil. 1989. *DUF: Drug Use Forecasting. January to March, 1989*. Washington, D.C.: National Institute of Justice.

Zinberg, Norman E. 1984. *Drug, Set, and Setting: The Basis for Controlled Intoxicant Use*. New Haven: Yale University Press.

# 2

# Kingrats, Chicken Heads, Slow Necks, Freaks, and Blood Suckers: A Glimpse at the Miami Sex-for-Crack Market

*James A. Inciardi*

Crack was my pimp.
—A 28-year-old Miami chicken head[1]

How many of us can remember the more newsworthy events of 1986? There were many, with some standing out more prominently than others. Most notably, although the number of Americans smoking, snorting, swallowing, sniffing, shooting, or otherwise ingesting one drug or another had not changed dramatically that year, late in the spring of 1986 the majority of the national media finally discovered crack cocaine. For *Newsweek*, crack became the biggest story since Vietnam and the fall of the Nixon presidency;[2] other media giants compared the spread of crack with the plagues of medieval Europe.[3] By the end of 1986 the major dailies and weekly news magazines had served the nation more than one thousand stories in which crack figured prominently. Not to be outdone, network television offered hundreds of reports on drug abuse, capped by CBS's "48 Hours on Crack Street," a prime-time presentation that reached some 15 million viewers and became one of the highest-rated documentaries in the history of television.

For the majority of those who had spent the better part of their careers doing street research, crack was not a particularly new drug. They had been hearing about it for years. In fact, a number remembered its initial appearance on the street almost two decades ago. And well before the media started taking credit for the discovery of crack as the new drug, systematic studies of the crack phenomenon had already been initiated.

37

## Crack-Cocaine in Miami

Miami is the crack-cocaine capital of Florida, of America, of the world, of the whole damn mother uni-fucking-verse!
—Miami crack dealer

The history of crack in Miami dates back to the early 1970s, when cocaine was still known as "charlie," "corrine," "bernice," "schoolboy," and the "rich man's drug." It was available for only a short period of time before it was discarded by freebase cocaine disciples as an inferior product. In this regard, a 42-year-old Miami cocaine user commented in 1986:

Of course crack is nothing new. The only thing that's new is the name. Years ago it was called *rock*, *base*, or *freebase*, although it really isn't true "freebase." It was just an easier way to get something that gave a more potent rush, done the same way as now with baking soda. It never got too popular among the 1970s cokeheads because it was just not as pure a product as conventional freebase.[4]

The reemergence of crack occurred in Miami early in the 1980s. As a result of the Colombian government's attempts to reduce the amount of illicit cocaine production within its borders, it apparently, at least for a time, successfully restricted the amount of ether available for transforming coca paste into cocaine hydrochloride. (Coca paste, also known in South America as *basuco*, *susuko*, and *pasta basica de cocaina*, is an intermediate product in the processing of the coca leaf into street cocaine.) The result was the diversion of coca paste from Colombia, through Central America and the Caribbean, into south Florida for conversion into cocaine. Spillage from shipments through the Caribbean corridor acquainted local island populations with coca paste smoking; these populations developed the forerunner of crack cocaine in 1980.[5] Known as "baking-soda base," "base-rock," "gravel," and "rox-anne," the prototype was a smokable product composed of coca paste, baking soda, water, and rum. Migrants from Jamaica, Haiti, Trinidad, and locations along the Leeward and Windward Islands chain introduced the crack pro-totype to Caribbean inner-city populations in Miami's immigrant under-grounds, where it was ultimately produced from powder-cocaine rather than paste.

Crack was already a part of the street scene in Miami by 1982, and according to several informants, the drug could be purchased at several inner-city "get-off houses" (shooting galleries) as early as mid-1981. The use of crack and the existence of crack houses proliferated in Miami and elsewhere throughout the 1980s, with media coverage of the phenomenon focusing extensively on the addiction potential and abuse liability of the drug.[7] Sub-sequent commentaries targeted the involvement of youths in crack distribution, the violence associated with struggles to control the crack marketplace in inner-city neighborhoods, and the child abuse, child neglect, and child abandonment by crack-addicted mothers.[8] And in Miami, although the violence associated with crack distribution never reached the proportions apparent in other urban centers,[9] crack use was nevertheless a major drug problem,[10] particularly in the criminal justice sector. Early in 1987 a Miami prosecutor emphasized in this behalf: "All we ever seem to hear about any more is crack—crack dealers, crack wholesalers, crack manufacturers, crack users, crack houses, crack cases. The police are all jammed up, spending all of their time chasing the dealers; they've clogged the courts, and they've got the jails and prisons overloaded."

By 1989, the Drug Enforcement Administration estimated that there were no fewer than seven hundred operating crack houses in the greater Miami area.[11] As in other urban locales, the exchange of sex for drugs became a prominent feature of the Miami crack scene,[12] raising concerns about the increased potential for the conveyance of the human immunodeficiency virus (HIV) in a metropolitan center already experiencing high rates of AIDS.[13]

## Miami Crack Houses

> The crack house is a carnival of vice. It is one hell of a nasty place where the kingrats and pay masters rule, where the gut buckets give slow necks for a penny, and where the freaks, rock monsters, and blood suckers will do anything for a hit on the stem.[14]
> —Miami kingrat

At the outset of this study, I was already well acquainted with the Miami crack scene, having studied it intensively since 1986. My first direct exposure to the sex-for-crack market came in 1988, during an initial visit to a North Miami crack house.[15] I had gained entry through a local drug dealer, who had been a key informant of mine for almost a decade. He introduced me to the crack house door man as someone "straight but OK." After the door man checked us for weapons, my guide proceeded to show me around.

Upon entering a room in the rear of the crack house (what I later learned was called a freak room), I observed what appeared to be the gang-rape of an unconscious child. Emaciated, seemingly comatose, and likely no older than 14 years of age, she was lying spread-eagled on a filthy mattress while four men in succession had vaginal intercourse with her. After they had finished and left the room, however, it became readily clear that it had not been forcible rape at all. She opened her eyes and looked about to see if anyone was waiting. When she realized that our purpose there was not for sex, she wiped her groin with a ragged beach towel, covered herself with half of a tattered sheet affecting a somewhat peculiar sense of modesty, and rolled over in an attempt to sleep. Almost immediately, however, she was disturbed by the door man, who brought a customer to her for oral sex. He just walked up to her with an erect penis in his hand, said nothing to her, and she proceeded to oblige him.

Upon leaving the crack house a few minutes later, the dealer/informant explained that she was a house girl, a person in the employ of the crack house owner. He gave her food, a place to sleep, and all the crack she wanted in return for her providing sex—any type and amount of sex—to his crack house customers.

In subsequent visits to this and six other Miami crack houses through September 1990, I made twenty-two observations. Based on these, combined with data obtained from more than seventy informants, it became evident that the term "crack house" can mean many different things—a place to use, a place to sell or do both, a place to manufacture and package crack—and the location may be a house, an apartment, a small shack at the back of an empty lot, an abandoned building, or even the rusting hulk of a discarded automobile. There are no fewer than seven different types of crack houses in the Miami area. In addition to what might be called "organized crack houses," there are numerous others, locally known as castles, base houses, brothels, residence houses, resorts, and graveyards.

## Castles

Reportedly few in number, castles are fortified structures where large quantities of crack are manufactured from powder cocaine, packaged in plastic bags or glass vials, and sold both wholesale and retail. Crack users are not permitted inside the walls of castles. Typical fortifications include barred windows, reinforced door and window frames, steel doors with heavy slide bolts, and walls reinforced from the inside with steel mesh and/or a layer of concrete blocks. Such heavy fortifications are for the purpose of making police raids difficult. An 18-year-old former lookout for a crack house reported in 1990:

> The whole idea [of the fortification] is to keep the cops off yer backs long enough to dump the stuff [crack] before they get in. This one rock castle I was in had all the doors and walls braced with steel bars drilled into the floor and ceiling. It had TV cameras lookin' up and down the street. Nothin' could go down without them knowin' about it. The only time the DEA [Drug Enforcement Administration] got in was when they came with a tow truck to pull down the door and a battering ram to get past a concrete barrier. It took them fifteen minutes to get in, and by then we had the place clean [free of drugs].

In addition to fortifications, most castles are well armed, with workers typically carrying semiautomatic weapons at all times. Crack sales are accomplished with little or no interaction. In some houses of this type, exchanges are made through a slot or hole in the fortified door, with the money passed in and the crack passed out. In others, the transaction is accomplished by means of a basket or pail lowered from a second floor or attic window.

## Base Houses

The base house seems to be an "all-purpose drug joint," as one informant put it. Base houses are used by many kinds of drug users, especially intravenous users. A variety of drugs are available, including crack. However, smoking crack is not the primary activity. Intravenous drug use (typically cocaine) is more commonly seen and accepted here than in other types of crack houses, but sex-for-drugs exchanges rarely occur. In this regard, a 35-year-old crack-using prostitute commented in February 1990:

> You can go there and shoot drugs and she [the owner] shoot, but she didn't smoke crack. She'll let you smoke there as long as you . . . give her two dollars. If you was a smoker, a rock smoker, you can give her two dollars to smoke. If you was a cocaine shooter you give her cocaine to shoot or buy her some wine or something. The only thing she didn't let us do there is bring customers.

Another crack user offered a somewhat different description:

> OK, you go in there, and some people they have a syringe in their arm and a pipe in their mouth at the same time. You go in there and you buy crack and they rent a room or they go in the bathroom. You gotta pay fifteen dollars for this 'cause that's two different types of drugs that you get into your system. You can buy a syringe there too, but most times people bring their own syringes. And they go in there, and they shoots up first and they leave the needle in their arm and then they put the crack on top of the pipe and they tell somebody to hit them, you know, to keep the fire on the stem while they inhale it.

## Resorts

The resort is one of the more customary types of crack house in Miami. The physical layout is that of a small apartment adapted for crack use. The kitchen is used for cooking rock, at least one bedroom is set aside for sex, and the living space is used for selling and smoking. As one crack user described the resort:

> It was just an apartment house where a lot of people that smoke crack come inside and just do drugs and smoke. One of them was his main room and

the other two he would rent out, one for sexuals and one for just smoking. And sometimes there wouldn't be nobody smoking and they just come to have sex in both of them. Inside, candles burning, pillows on the floor, it wouldn't be very good for a person in his right mind.

The owners of these crack houses seem to be concerned about two things: money and crack. Many of them are addicted to crack and operate the houses to support their drug habits. Almost anything can happen in these crack houses. They were observed to be filthy, chaotic, and crowded. The crack smokers got into fights, attempted to steal each other's drugs, and exhibited extreme paranoia.

A characteristic of the resort is easy access to crack, although each house has slightly different sales procedures. Some charge an entrance fee, and customers are free to smoke and have sex. Crack is usually on a table and purchases are informal. In other houses, the crack may not be on display, and customers pay a worker to bring them a rock. For example:

> They just have it there on the table, whatever you want, give them the money for it and go in the back and then if you want another you go right to the front and buy a nickel [five-dollar rock] and then you smoke that. You have to buy your stuff from them.
> There was one where you could bring your stuff, but you would have to pay, pay them to use their equipment.

In resorts, the bartering of sex and crack occurs between the head hunter/ prostitute and her or his customer, or john. The owner of the crack house receives a fee (crack or money) from the john for the use of the freak room. As such, the customer pays both the owner of the house and the prostitute. (The sexual activities that occur in resorts are described in greater length elsewhere in this chapter.)

And finally, the crack houses known locally as resorts are termed as such because of the variety of activities that occur there. A cocaine dealer reported in this regard:

> That they call it a "rock resort" has nothin' to do with music. Ha, ha. It's because you can really get into it there—drugs, sex, rock 'n roll, all three at once, whatever. You can smoke your brains out, fuck your brains out, get sexed any way you want, watch sex, get paranoid, fight, watch fights, cut somebody, get high, get killed, whatever the fuck you want.

## Brothels

Although prostitution and trading sex for crack are among the primary activities of many crack houses, in the brothel the owner is a dealer/pimp and the sex-for-drugs exchange system is somewhat unique. The prostitute is a house girl and is not involved in the payment process. For the sexual services she provides, she receives payment from the house man in the form of crack, room, and board.

Several respondents reported having actually lived in a crack house brothel, with many more having visited such establishments. In August 1990, a 26-year-old crack addict with a ten-year career in drugs detailed to me:

> Bein' that I been workin' the streets since I was eleven and don't really mind sexin' a lot of different guys, I thought it would be a real easy deal for gettin' all the cracks [more than one rock] that I needed. So this bond man [drug dealer] that I'd know'd real well takes me in. He says all it is givin' a lot a brains [oral sex]. Well man, I know'd a lot a brains. I probably done more *fellatio* [her emphasis] than any lady on the street.
>
> . . . I really got my self into somethin' bad. It wasn't just brains like he said. It was everything. There was guys pushin' their natures [genitals] everywhere—in my mouth, in my guts [vagina], up my ass; guys gettin' off [climaxing] in my face; one guy goin' down on me with five others watchin' and jerkin' off. Most of the time I just didn't care, 'cause I was gettin' all the rock I wanted. But times I just wanted to be left alone, but I couldn't. One time they raped me man; they raped me, 'cause I wouldn't fuck 'em just that minute. They held me down and beat me and did all kind of terrible things. . . .
>
> And I tried to leave but I was a prisoner there. After the rape I tried to leave, but the man at the door he's got his orders and I can't go. So when I try to get out he slapped me around and they rape me again. They raped me again real bad this time, fucking me in the cunt and the ass at the same time, slapping my face and pinching my tits, and one fuck pissed on me after he was done. An' then to teach me another lesson they hold back on the pipe. . . .
>
> After a while I got sick, and I was all bruised and looked so bad, that they threw me out. They just threw me out like I was just some piece of shit.

In addition to the sexual services available in the brothels, some street prostitutes use them solely as places to have sex with their customers. For example, a 25-year-old woman who had been exchanging sex for money and drugs for eight years reported:

> One of the rooms is for base [crack], the other three rooms are for tricking and one of the first rooms inside the door, that's where the dude sit, that's where the G-man [security man, bouncer] sit. When you come in the house he pat you down. They pat you down, and when you come in you say "date." That means pat you down and let you go and have a date. See anyone was allowed to bring a date, anyone was allowed to bring a trick. When you go in you can bring a date in from the outside and use the room and get money from him and you got to do what you gotta do—five dollars

to use the room, five dollars one hour, they say an hour but they only give you forty-five minutes with that mother fucker. . . .

This would suggest that for some individuals, the primary purpose of the brothel-type crack house is not using drugs but having sex. This notion is corroborated in the statement of a Miami cocaine dealer:

Now in *that* place [a local crack house] something a little different is going on. A lot of the boys goin' in and out are not into crack. Some of them are not even into heavy drugs. What they know is that they can get a blow job from a 12-year old "strawberry" [a female who exchanges sex for crack], which you know ain't too easy to get in most places. Or they know that they can get a lady who will do anything to them, and I mean *anything*, any kind of sex you can think of, and even some ya can't think of, for some crack. So the word is that for a donation to the house first they can get whatever they want. . . . And I'm told too that there's some filming going on in there of some of the stuff that's happening. It's being done with one of those video recorders, and being sold to people who just like to watch.[16]

### Residence Houses

Residence houses are quite numerous in the Miami area and are likely the most common form of crack house. They are houses or apartments where small groups of people gather regularly to smoke crack. The operators are reluctant to call these places "crack houses," because they are used as such only by their friends. However, the activities are the same as those in other crack houses, including sex-for-crack exchanges. The major differences revolve around the payment system. Crack is not sold in residence houses; it is only smoked there. In the more traditional crack house, such as a brothel or resort, payment for using the house can be made with money or crack, although money is preferred. In the residence house, payment is made only with crack. Visitors give crack or more often share crack with the owner of the house or apartment in return for having a place to smoke or turn a trick. There are usually fewer people in these crack houses than in others—five or six compared to fifteen or twenty. They are also the same five or six individuals, whereas in other types there is a greater turnover of people. Finally, whereas the visitors to other types of crack houses are "customers," only "friends" are invited to residence houses.

### Graveyards

The designation graveyards, rooms in abandoned buildings, has an interesting genesis. At the corner of Northeast Second Avenue and Seventy-first Street in Miami stands a housing project, described by a local journalist in this way:

Sure, there always were problems. Its official name is Site 5, Project FL527-B, but residents began calling it The Graveyard years ago. Poverty breeds crime, and crime bred more of itself. But when a tidal wave of cocaine rocks descended on the place two years ago, crime seemed to put The Graveyard in a stranglehold. The pulse of the community grew faint. Residents began moving out of The Graveyard and prospective tenants refused to move in. So basers [crack users and dealers] claimed the vacant apartments for themselves.[17]

In time, the Graveyard's abandoned apartments became overrun by crack dealers and users, so much so that the county government began boarding up the project's vacant rooms.[18] But the name took on a life of its own, and by the end of 1987 every abandoned building in Miami that was used for smoking crack became known as a graveyard. A methadone client and active crack user reported in 1988 that there were "lots of graveyards in almost every part of the city—Liberty City, Overtown, Miami Beach, South Miami—every neighborhood where there's empty buildings and lots of crack. Crack, and lots of crack . . . that's what makes it a graveyard."

According to most informants, no one actually owns a particular graveyard, although there do seem to be turf issues associated with their use, based on squatters' rights. Crack users bring their own crack. Sex for money and/or drugs is performed in these buildings. For example:

It's an empty house, empty rooms. So somebody like go into this room, the first one there. They might put a board you know, you have cloth, you know, a bucket of water to bathe and shit. I did it myself. Put up those boards and shit, sometimes curtains hanging over the door, this room had no doors, no windows, nothing like that.

I know'd this one place off Miami Avenue where this lady set up in a burned out house. She was sort of a whore/crack head/skeezer/bag lady who'd do anythin' for crack and for food for her trick baby [a prostitute's child fathered by a john], her base baby [a child conceived and gestated by a crack-using mother]. For a hit on yer pipe or for some food or money or drugs or cigarettes she'd let you smoke in her digs and she'd suck your prick too.

And finally, somewhat related to graveyards are base cars—abandoned automobiles that serve as places to smoke crack, to have sex, or to exchange sex for crack.

## Organized Crack Houses

Organized crack houses are reportedly few in number in Miami. The environment in these establishments is far more controlled than in any other type of crack house, with the owners more visible and closely monitoring all activities. Violence and general chaos are uncommon. The ambience is described as calm, and children are not permitted. They have more workers than other crack houses, most of whom maintain order inside or watch for police:

> They would have people outside, lookouts. Way up and down the street, like on the corner. And another guy sitting in the yard like he was cleaning the yard or something.
> There would be like a bouncer at the door with a gun to watch to make sure no cops or anything would walk in. Or to make sure that there were no problems within the place itself. Just to make it secure for their sake.

Purchasing crack in organized houses is more structured than elsewhere. Several have specific hours of operation. Upon arrival, a customer is sold crack, seated with a pipe, and strict order is maintained. For example:

> You can't come in the house after 8:00. Other than that he passes it through the window. Before 8:00 you can come in and he lays them [crack and crack pipes] on the table and you can pick what you want. Sometimes you walk in and he's sifting it [cocaine hydrochloride] with the baking soda so he can cook it and tell you to come back in ten or fifteen minutes.
> When you walk in they have a person that pats you down to see if you got any weapons on you, and then you go through the doors then they have a person that brings you a torch. And they set you up to a table and OK when you first walk in the door it's goin' back a little bit you buy your rocks at the door. They have a little stand. They have all the rocks you want from five dollars all the way to a fifty-dollar rock. And you pick out which one you want, whatever your money can afford and then they have someone that escorts you back in the back. And that's where we smoke at. They give you a pipe, they give you a torch, and then you're on your own.
> It wasn't like these abandoned burned-out houses that you see here in the city. This house was very nice, very organized; he had house pipes, torches; he supplied lighters, screens, drugs; everything you needed was right there to prevent so much traffic. Once you get there if you have enough money, you can sit there and use the house pipes and everything. If you only came there to buy a nickel [five-dollar rock] or a dime [ten-dollar rock], you got it and left.

Finally, direct sex-for-crack exchanges do not occur in the organized houses. One prostitute noted that "they let the hookers and skeezers in the door only if they was going to buy crack. The house is for buying and smoking only. They let us cut deals there, you know, but you can't sex there. Got to go someplace else, usually out to the customer's car."

# Study Population Characteristics

> Crack is the last word in empty promises.
> —Miami crack user

Using guidelines developed specifically for this study, systematic interviews were conducted with seventeen men and thirty-five women who had traded sex for crack (or sex for money to buy crack) during the thirty-day period prior to study recruitment. All systematic interviewing was conducted by two experienced interviewers during the period November 1989 through June 1990.[19] Some 62 percent of the subjects ($N = 32$) were interviewed in a local drug treatment facility, having been screened for study eligibility within forty-eight hours of program entry. The remaining 38 percent ($N = 20$) were interviewed at an AIDS outreach office operated by the University of Miami School of Medicine. These latter subjects had been recruited from the streets by an indigenous fieldworker who accompanied them to the outreach office. All interviews were recorded, and subjects were paid forty dollars for study participation.

Although whites, Hispanics, and Asians were represented in the sample of informants, the majority were blacks under age 35 (table 2–1). Less than half had completed high school, and more than three-fourths reported prostitution, drug dealing, theft, and/or street hustles as their primary source of income. On a monthly basis, this income averaged $2,181, with a range of $400 to $7,500.

# Drug Use Patterns

> One is too much and a thousand is never enough.
> —28-year-old Miami head hunter

> Crack is my keeper, my lover, my god.
> —15-year-old Miami crack whore

All of the fifty-two informants had long histories of drug use. They began their illicit drug using careers with marijuana at a mean age of 14 years. Importantly, however, it would appear that for virtually all of these subjects, alcohol and tobacco use preceded marijuana use. As significant proportions of the group experimented with inhalants, hallucinogens, stimulants (uppers), and depressants (downers), almost all began using marijuana on a continuous basis.

Injecting drugs was not uncommon among the study subjects. Overall, some 40 percent had early histories of intravenous cocaine, heroin, speed,

**Table 2–1**
**Selected Characteristics of Fifty-two Miami Crack Users**

|  | *Males* | *Females* | *Total* |
|---|---|---|---|
| *Race/ethnicity* | | | |
| Black | 9 (53%) | 24 (69%) | 33 (64%) |
| White | 5 (29%) | 7 (20%) | 12 (23%) |
| Hispanic | 3 (18%) | 3 (9%) | 6 (12%) |
| Asian | — | 1 (3%) | 1 (2%) |
| *Age* | | | |
| 19–24 | 6 (35%) | 6 (17%) | 12 (23%) |
| 25–29 | 1 (6%) | 15 (43%) | 16 (31%) |
| 30–35 | 9 (53%) | 8 (23%) | 17 (33%) |
| 36–40 | 1 (6%) | 6 (17%) | 7 (14%) |
| *Education* | | | |
| Mean grade completed | 11.5 | 10.6 | 10.9 |
| High school graduate or general equivalency diploma | 11 (65%) | 12 (34%) | 12 (44%) |
| *Primary source of income* | | | |
| Legal | 4 (24%) | 1 (3%) | 5 (10%) |
| Prostitution | 4 (24%) | 22 (63%) | 26 (50%) |
| Drug dealing | 1 (6%) | 1 (3%) | 2 (4%) |
| Theft/bustles | 6 (35%) | 6 (17%) | 12 (23%) |
| None | 2 (12%) | 5 (14%) | 7 (14%) |
| Also receiving AFDC or food stamps | 1 (6%) | 12 (34%) | 13 (25%) |
| *Income (last month)* | | | |
| Range | $400–7,500 | $257–6,000 | — |
| Mean | $2,441 | $2,055 | $2,181 |

and/or speedball (heroin and cocaine). Not surprising was the prevalence of cocaine use within this population. All of the men and all but one of the women had experimented with cocaine (non-IV) during their teenage years, with 75 percent using the drug on a continuous basis. Crack use began for both men and women by age 25.

In terms of current drug use, crack clearly predominated.[20] All of the men and women used the drug continuously, and almost every day. Furthermore, the progression from experimentation to daily use was rapid.

All of the subjects in this sample smoked crack for as long as it was available and they had means to purchase it—with money or sex, stolen goods, furniture, or other drugs. It was rare that someone had just a single hit. It was typical that they spent fifty to one hundred dollars in one period, with binges lasting three or four days. During these smoking cycles, users neither ate nor slept. Some informants purchased crack over two hundred times in the thirty-day period prior to study recruitment, and they gauged how much they smoked by how often, how long, or how much money they spent. It was difficult for them to calculate precisely how many rocks or how much crack they actually consumed.

While many of these crack users binged for several days in a row, over half (58 percent) used the drug on a daily basis. None used crack fewer than ten days of the previous month. A common trend, however, was a three- to four-day smoking bender followed by two days of sleep. For every day they used crack, they were high from as few as three times to as many as fifty times. This would suggest that some were consuming perhaps three to fifty rocks a day, spending up to $250 or more a day on crack. Almost half of this group were high twenty to thirty times each day they smoked.

Once crack was tried, it was not long before it became a daily habit. One-third of the sample used crack daily immediately after first trying it. An additional 27 percent used it daily by the end of their first month. Almost 80 percent of the fifty-two respondents used it daily within six months after their first use. A number of informants reported their crack-smoking patterns:

> When I first started smoking crack I used to smoke every day, seven days a week, and I'd stay up for four and five days at a time.

> I smoked it Thursday, Friday, Saturday, Monday, Tuesday, Wednesday, Thursday, Friday, Saturday on that cycle. I was working at that time. . . . I would spend my whole three-hundred-dollar check. . . . Every day was a crack day for me . . . my day was not made without a hit. I could smoke it before breakfast, don't even have breakfast or I don't eat for three days.

> For the past five months I've been wearing the same pants. And sneakers are new but with all the money you make a day, at least five hundred or six hundred dollars a day, you don't want to spend a hundred dollars in clothes. Everything is rocks, rocks, rocks, rocks, rocks. And to tell you the truth I don't even eat well for having all that money. You don't even want to have patience to sit down and have a good dinner. I could tell you rock is . . . I don't know what to say. I just feel sorry for anyone who falls into it.

> I would make on a weekend up to four hundred or five hundred dollars, 80 percent to 90 percent went to crack. When I was out there bad and then 95 percent. I went to the Brother Community House to eat. I didn't even buy food.

> Sometimes I stayed up the whole week, you know—no sleep, just smoking, smoking, smoking.

## Sexual Histories and Patterns

You're not gonna believe this, but it's the god's honest truth. I swear it. Durin' the last three years, every day, year in an' out, I sexed thirty to forty guys a day, most of it brains. I bet I've given head thirty thousand times easy. I figured it out once, that's about three miles of cock that I swallowed.
—22-year-old Miami house girl

The following quotation, drawn from the transcript of a 28-year-old black female crack user legally employed as a shipping clerk, clearly illustrates a characteristic aspect of the sex-for-crack phenomenon. This woman had been a marijuana user since age 15, a cocaine user since age 18, and a crack user since age 26. In her comments, she details her first exchange of sex for crack and how it came about.

I had my last paycheck, that was $107. That day I went straight from there [work] with a friend guy and copped some drugs. I bought $25—five nickel rocks. I walked up to the apartment, me and the same guy. We drunk a beer, we needed the can to smoke on. So we sat there and we smoked those five rocks and you know, like they say, one is too much and a thousand is never enough. And that's the truth. Those five rocks went like this [snaps fingers], and I immediately, I had maybe about $80 left. I had intentions of takin' my grandmother some money home for the kids. But I had it in my mind you know I was, I was just sick. I wanted to continue to get high so push come to shove I smoked up that—that whole day me and him we smoke up. It didn't last 'til maybe about 8:00 P.M. cause we started maybe about 12:00 that afternoon.

OK all the money was gone, all the drugs was gone. About 9:00 we went and sat in the park. Usually when we set in the park, people will come over and they'll have drugs. Some friends came over, and they had drugs. He walked home. I stayed out because I couldn't give an account for what I had did with the money. My grandmother done thought that I was goin' to pick up my check and comin' back. So I walked around and I walked down this street—you know you got people that will pick you up. So this guy stopped, and I got in the car, and I never did any prostituting but I wanted more drugs. So this guy, he stopped and he picked me up and he asked me: "How much would you charge me for a head?" That's oral sex. And I told him $40. And so he say, how much would you charge me for two hours to have just sex not oral sex? And so I told him $40 so he say: "OK get in," and he took me to this hotel.

He had about six rocks. I didn't want sex. I wanted to get high, so we smoked the rocks and durin' the time I sexed with him. So after I sexed him, he gave me the money, and after the rocks was gone I still wanted to get high. So this man he gave his car and his keys and gave me more money to go get more drugs. We went into another hotel. By that time it was maybe 6:00 in the morning. He ended up leaving me in the hotel. By that time I done spent all my $40. It wasn't nothing I had done wasted the money. So later on that afternoon, my grandmother done let me get sleep and everything. I think later on that day and the next day I went to my godfather's house and I earned $15. I helped him do some work around the house, so he gave me $15.

So I went and stayed home with the kids and waited 'til they got ready to go to bed that night. I went and got three rocks with that $15. I started off smokin' by myself, but when you sittin' in the park, people come to know you and they be tryin' to horn in on what you doin'. So ended up smokin' I think about a rock and a half with somebody that was sittin' in the park. Later on I ended up walkin' down the main strip again, and this guy came by and he say: "Well, how much money would do you want for a head?" So I told him $10. I was really desperate this time around, so I told him $10. He say, "Well, I don't have but $5." I say, "OK. I'll take that; you know I settle for little or nothin'." So we went down the street and parked in this parkin' lot and I gave him a head. And I immediately went to the drug house, and bought a nickel rock.

The individuals interviewed in this study had sexual histories that began early and involved many partners. The mean age of first sexual intercourse was 14 years, with the females initiating sex almost a year earlier than the males (table 2–2). The first sex-for-money exchange occurred at a mean age of 19.8 years and sex for drugs at a mean of 23.2 years.

During the thirty-day period prior to interview, the sexual activities of the fifty-two informants were extensive. Among the seventeen male crack users, more than half had twenty-five or more male sex partners, and five of the seventeen had a hundred or more male partners. In addition, 60 percent of these male crack users had more than twenty-five female sex partners during the same period. Moreover, 42 percent participated in vaginal sex

## Table 2–2
## Sexual Histories of Fifty-two Miami Crack Users

|  | Males (N = 17) Age (% Sample) | Females (N = 35) Age (% Sample) |
|---|---|---|
| Mean age first sexual intercourse | 14.3 (100%) | 13.7 (100%) |
| Mean age first sex for money | 19.1 (94%) | 20.1 (97%) |
| Mean age first sex for drugs | 23.1 (71%) | 23.3 (86%) |

more than twenty-five times; 88 percent participated in oral sex more than twenty-five times, with 25 percent engaging in oral sex a hundred or more times; just under half participated in anal-insertive sex at least once; and 30 percent engaged in anal-receptive sex during this thirty-day period. Finally, 30 percent of these men masturbated other men ("hand jobs"), with one individual providing this service more than twenty-five times.

The women appeared to have many more sexual contacts than the men. Almost 90 percent of the women had a hundred or more male sex partners, and 11 percent had as many as twenty-five female partners. Some 39 percent of these women participated in vaginal sex more than fifty times, 57 percent engaged in oral sex more than fifty times, 20 percent participated in anal sex, and 29 percent provided men with hand jobs, with one woman doing so on more than fifty occasions.

It would appear that most of the sex in Miami crack houses is oral and frequent. At the same time, the majority of the respondents reported performing sexual acts that they would do only while on crack and/or for crack. For example, a 31-year-old male prostitute reported: "As a matter of fact, when you are high on crack you'll do almost anything. We [the respondent and his boyfriend] had sex in front of other people, and one male joined us. Usually I gave the other guy head while we had anal intercourse." Similarly, a male "customer" of sex-for-crack exchanges commented:

> He wanted me to suck his chest while he jerk off. Boy this is a big secret. This other guy he wanted to give me some brain. The next time I ran into this prostitute man dressed like a woman, and I paid her/him ten dollars to have sex. I thought it was a woman. So she bend over, and I got in from behind and, hey, it was just like a woman. And if I wasn't on crack, I'm for sure I wouldn't have been doing that.

A 24-year-old white female who had been a prostitute since age 22 and had used cocaine in one form or another since age 17 noted:

> I've been asked to step on guys' balls for it [crack]. I had a date that wanted me to find a girlfriend that enjoys females. I said sure, I knew a girl that enjoyed females so I got her. We set a date and time where I was supposed to meet this guy, and we did, and it was thirty dollars a piece. Just for him to watch us eat each other out. She ate me for about five minutes, and I ate her for like five minutes. I was tryin' not to do it, but then it was like he wanted to watch. He was like right there on top. So I had no choice but to do it if I wanted my money because I was high at the time. Still high coming, I was coming down, and I wanted to get back out, so I went ahead and done it. But I didn't enjoy it. I like men.

Along similar lines, a 35-year-old black female with a seventeen-year history of drug use, including IV cocaine and heroin, indicated:

I let guys fuck me from my butt. . . . It [crack] had me sellin' my body for rocks, and if a customer came up and say all I got is five dollars, I'd take it and give them a blow job and let him do anything you wanted to do to me for five dollars and I never did that before. I even suck a girl's body, went down on her for rocks.

And finally, although the majority of the sexual activities take place in a separate room, in many crack houses they occur in the common area where everyone else is smoking. In this regard, three informants reported:

Some of them didn't care. Some womens didn't care. They'll suck a guy's peter there or suck a woman's peter [genitalia].

It was like a sex show or somethin' like that. Everybody's sittin' and layin' around smokin' and this lady starts takin' her clothes off, says she's burnin' up. And a guy goes over to her, hands her his pipe in one hand and his meat [penis] in the other. And she starts givin' him a blow job right there.

There was this one place where just nobody cared what they did and where they did it. And let's see, I was giving heads for everybody to see 'cause since they didn't care, so I didn't either. So I givin' heads all around the room for hits. Even another lady. All the mens wanted to see us lickin' pussy. So we was lickin' pussy, and everyone see'd it.

## Sex-for-Crack Exchanges and HIV Risk

I discussed it [AIDS] with my mom, my mom discussed it with me. My mom say, "Don't you think you're fucking with your life? The men are dying." I don't want to hear any of that shit.
—Miami prostitute

The findings of this study suggest that both men and women who exchange sex for crack are at significant risk for HIV infection. In addition to frequent high-risk sexual activities with multiple partners, many of these activities are unprotected. For example, only 23 percent of the women always used condoms during vaginal sex (table 2–3). An even smaller proportion (14 percent) of these women always used condoms during oral sex. Of the seven of the thirty-five women in this sample who engaged in anal sex during the thirty-day period prior to interview, only two of them always used condoms. Although the potential for HIV transmission during unprotected vaginal and anal sex is well documented,[21] clearly placing at considerable risk women who engage in these activities with multiple and anonymous sex partners,

**Table 2–3**
**Reported Condom Use During the Last Thirty Days by Fifty-two Miami Crack Users**

|  | Males (N = 17) | Females (N = 35) | Total (N = 52) |
|---|---|---|---|
| During vaginal intercourse |  |  |  |
| Never | 5 (42%) | 8 (24%) | 13 (37%) |
| Fifty/fifty | 4 (33%) | 18 (53%) | 22 (48%) |
| Always | 3 (25%) | 8 (24%) | 11 (24%) |
| N/A | 5 | 1 | 6 |
| During oral sex |  |  |  |
| Never | 11 (69%) | 16 (42%) | 27 (54%) |
| Fifty/fifty | 3 (19%) | 13 (38%) | 16 (32%) |
| Always | 2 (12%) | 5 (15%) | 7 (14%) |
| N/A | 1 | 1 | 2 |
| During anal sex |  |  |  |
| Never | 3 (27%) | 3 (43%) | 6 (33%) |
| Fifty/fifty | 3 (27%) | 2 (29%) | 5 (28%) |
| Always | 5 (45%) | 2 (29%) | 7 (39%) |
| N/A | 6 | 28 | 34 |

infection risk through oral sex is less clear.[22] However, open sores on the lips and tongues of chronic users of crack are not uncommon, a result of burns and skin ulcerations caused by the heated stems of crack smoking paraphernalia. Given the high concentrations of virus in the semen of men infected with HIV,[23] the potential for transmission of infection under these circumstances is considerable. And similar to the women, only 18 percent of the men always used condoms during vaginal sex, only 12 percent always used condoms during oral sex, and only 29 percent always used condoms during anal sex.

Given their widespread participation in high-risk behaviors, it is surprising that a significant proportion of the respondents were so well informed about HIV and AIDS. A majority understood that AIDS was not a disease that infected only homosexuals, most understood that there is a latency period associated with HIV infection, and only 13 percent believed that AIDS could be spread through casual contact. Moreover, almost all (94 percent) realized that condom use during sex helped prevent the spread of AIDS, and although 48 percent did not know that cleaning needles could reduce the spread of AIDS among intravenous drugs, all of the current injectors responded to this question correctly.

Not surprisingly, 88 percent of the sample had considerable or extreme concern about AIDS, with slightly higher proportions of women than men responding as such. And while 56 percent either started using condoms or increased their use recently, only small proportions changed their types of sexual practices (11 percent), reduced the number of sex partners (17 percent), or were more selective about sex partners (19 percent).

Perhaps most significant about these crack users was their self-reported HIV test data. Some 92 percent reported having been tested for HIV infection, and of these, 19 percent indicated that they were HIV positive. Or stated differently, of those who received their test results, 31 percent of the men and 21 percent of the women reported being HIV positive.

# Discussion

> The crack house is the devil's den.
> —Miami crack user

The primary purposes of this research were to develop some preliminary insights into the attributes and patterns of sex-for-crack exchanges, particularly those that occurred in crack houses; to determine the general characteristics of individuals who exchanged sex for crack or sex for money to purchase crack; to assess the potential impact of sex for crack exchange behaviors on the spread of HIV infection; and to target significant areas for further study.

To accomplish these goals, systematic interviews were conducted with seventeen males and thirty-five females who were regular users of crack and who had exchanged sex for crack or money to buy crack within the thirty-day period prior to study recruitment. These interviews were accomplished with the use of an interview guide that focused on current and past drug use and sexual behaviors, crack use, crack house activities, HIV risk behaviors, and knowledge and concerns about HIV infection. The interviews were conducted during the period November 1989 throught June 1990 on a part-time basis by two employees of an AIDS outreach project who had extensive experience in interviewing on sensitive topics, such as drug using and criminal activities, sexual practices, and HIV risk behaviors. The cases selected for interview were drawn from the street by an experienced outreach worker or from a pool of recent admissions (within the previous 48 hours) to a local drug treatment program.

In addition, during the period September 1989 through September 1990, I completed twenty-two observations in seven crack houses. Furthermore, from project initiation through December 1990, I also conducted unstructured interviews with numerous others who served as key informants, including twenty-two crack users (contacted either in crack houses or on the street), three crack and/or cocaine dealers, and four police officers familiar with the greater Miami crack scene. Additional insights were obtained from numerous contacts with other players in the local street subculture.

Although the sample size and case selection procedures make generalization difficult, the data from both the structured and unstructured interviews clearly suggest that persons who exchange sex for crack are not casual users of drugs. Most had been using illegal drugs for at least a decade, almost half had injected drugs at some point in their drug-using careers, and virtually all were daily users of crack at the time of study recruitment. Similarly, exchanges of sex for money or drugs were not new experiences for these individuals. Some 94 percent of the males and 97 percent of the females systematically interviewed had been exchanging sex for money for an average of seven years. Moreover, 81 percent of these same men and women had also exchanged sex for drugs for an average of four years.

The interview and observational data suggest that individuals who exchange sex for crack do so with considerable frequency and through a variety of sexual activities. The sysematic data indicated that almost a third of the men and 89 percent of the women had a hundred or more sex partners during the thirty-day period prior to study recruitment. Moreover, one of the key informants reported more than thirty thousand anonymous sexual contacts during the previous three years. And finally, not only were sexual activities anonymous, extremely frequent, varied, uninhibited (often undertaken in public areas of crack houses), and with multiple partners, but in addition, condoms were not used during the majority of these sexual contacts. As such, these preliminary data suggest that persons who exchange sex for crack (or for money to buy crack) are at considerable risk of infection with and/or transmission of HIV disease.

A retrospective glance at the interview and observational data reveals several important issues that deserve discussion but cannot be fully addressed by these data: the difference between crack whores and prostitutes, oral and vaginal sex practices associated with crack house sex that increase the risk of HIV infection, and the difficulty of reaching the studied population with traditional AIDS prevention messages. All of these issues warrant further consideration and study.

## *"Crack Whores" versus "Prostitutes"*

There seem to be some interesting differences between women who exchange sex for crack in crack houses and those who hustle tricks on the street for money to buy crack. These latter women were not directly addressed in this chapter, chiefly due to their minimal representation in the sample. However, anecdotal data from interviews and observations suggest that they may be at lesser risk for HIV infection and transmission than their crack house counterparts. This inference is based on their frequency of sexual contacts and their attitudes and practices associated with condom use.

First, it appears that street prostitutes have fewer sex partners, and considerably less frequent sexual activity, than the so-called skeezers and chicken heads who exchange sex for crack in the smoking and freak rooms of neighborhood resorts, brothels, and base houses. Soliciting a trick on the street, negotiating a price, going to a place to have sex, engaging in sex, receiving payment, and then going back to the streets to purchase and smoke crack take time. To a considerable extent, this regulates a street prostitute's aggregate number of customers. Several of the street prostitutes in this study reported an average of three to six tricks each day that they worked, with most soliciting clients fifteen to thirty days during the month prior to interview. Although this, too, results in an inordinate number of sex partners during the course of a year, or even a month,[24] the numbers may be considerably fewer than those of women who exchange sex exclusively in crack houses. Recall, for example, the remarks already mentioned by the women who spent much or all of the day in crack houses, smoking crack and participating in oral and vaginal sex.

Second, it appears that the street prostitutes in this study were more conscious of sexually transmitted diseases and more often insisted that their customers use condoms. The following comments are representative:

> If they don't want to use a condom, they don't go. I will not go, I will not do it. Most instances, there are very, very few where they don't even want to wear a condom, and very few refuse to wear them.

> I just tell them, "Hey, you know I'm afraid of getting AIDS. You don't know that you have it. I don't know if I have it, but you never can tell you know." You know I tell them if you want to make love to me or whatever, you have to put one on. If you don't you can't. And no oral sex either.

By contrast, based on my observations and the reports of numerous informants, condoms are rarely used during the sexual activities that occur in crack house freak and smoking rooms. There are likely several reasons for this difference. There is a socialization process, for example, associated with becoming a prostitute. Would-be and neophyte prostitutes learn the appropriate techniques and safeguards through apprenticeships with pimps and/or more experienced prostitutes.[25] In some cases, there is formal or informal training on how to protect oneself from theft, violence, or disease. For example, in one sociological analysis of prostitution as an occupation, it was found that the recognition of sexually transmitted disease was a specific topic of instruction for neophyte house prostitutes:

> Ann [the madam of a small house of prostitution] accompanies the *turn-out* [neophyte prostitute] and the client to the bedroom and begins teaching the woman how to check the man for any cuts or open sores on the genitals and for any signs of old or active venereal disease. She usually rechecks herself during the turn-out's first two weeks of work.[26]

Furthermore, however loose, unstructured, and transitory they may often be, those who work the streets or in organized houses of prostitution have friendships and peer relationships through which experiences are shared, techniques are traded, warnings are communicated, and knowledge is reinforced.

Concern for cleanliness and signs of sexually transmitted disease were readily apparent among several of the street prostitute/informants in this investigation—for example:

> If there ain't no sink with washin' water and a light and I can see their cock and they got crabs or something and then I gotta inspect them. I've got to darlin'. That's an old, old trick from the trade.

> You know some of thems not clean, you know, like they haven't washed and before I even do something I check them out first. And if I see dirt I say, "No, you gotta wash up first." And even if I put my mouth to it and I can taste like it's not clean I just draw back from it. I say I don't want it, you know, and if I feel like if the taste is not right I give them their money back.

> Ain't no way any cock is goin' into any part of my body without me checkin' it twice. An' even after he pass inspection, then he got to put on a rubber [condom]. That's the rule I tell him. An' if he don't have a rubber I sell him one for a dollar. That's the way it been with me all along, even before AIDS. "Ya don't want to take anything home to yer ole lady," I say, "and I don't wanna take yer germs home to my old man." So now we both safe and sound.

There appears to be no such concern in crack houses. The women who trade sex for crack in crack houses are typically not experienced prostitutes who moved from the streets to the crack house. As one prostitute described a skeezer:

> It's called a girl put in that predicament. They acts like a communist fucked their brain up. She's young and naive right out of high school, and they'll get her started see. They'll give her hits free; you know she's stayin' in there gettin' high for free and she doesn't know why. Now she wants another hit. She doesn't understand you have to do that for that guy to get a hit, you know what I'm saying. He wants you to suck his dick for an hour, and then the mother fucker can't get hard. He's so into that rock you see. They make a person vulnerable like that.

Another street prostitute commented:

> Them chicken heads are bad for business. They don't come off the street; them mother fuckers come from who knows where and start takin' dates

on their knees for a penny rock. I never seen anything like it. Who would do that? Not nobody I know.

And a third reported:

I picked up a date in a crack house once and I didn't believe what I was seein' in there. She was a little girl—19, 18, maybe 17 that's all—doin' stuff like in a porno film. They be doin' anything and everything in front of anyone, and you could tell they were no bitches [street prostitutes]. . . . Yeah, I feel real sorry for 'em. They probably turned a trick now an' then, but they're not experienced girls [prostitutes]. If they was, they wouldn't be on their knees givin' heads all day in crack houses.

And a house girl said about herself:

Once in a while I'd be sitting on a park bench or walking down the street and somebody would stop and ask me if I wanted a ride or go to a party or something. Maybe once or twice a month that would happen and for some sex I'd get thirty or forty dollars. But I wasn't really a hustler. I never did it regular. . . . That was when I had a real job and wasn't doing much crack. . . . But after a while I just wanted to be high all the time, and I saw what was going on all of the time. . . . So I ask the house man one night if I could work for him. He calls in this guy Stoney. He was working "lookout" across the street. And then right there he says, "Sit down on his chair and do Stoney, let Stoney come in your mouth." He wanted me to do it right there, in front of five, six people. And Stoney was real happy, because he was just a green kid, was happy to have me get off his nut [make him climax]. And after Stoney, I did three others in the room, and by midnight I had done thirty more.

A second likely reason for the differences between skeezers and street prostitutes is the role that crack plays in their lives. For skeezers and house girls, crack is at the basis of their sex exchanges, as clearly evidenced in such comments as "I do it for crack" and "crack is my pimp." By contrast, although the use of crack and other drugs is the reason that many women engage in prostitution, their need for crack seems to be somewhat less pressing. For example, one prostitute remarked, "First I tend to business, you know, getting dates, getting money, saving for the rent, you know, and then I go buy a couple of rocks. If another date comes along, I wait to smoke." And associated with this is the prostitute's strong commitment to paying for her own crack. Prostitutes will exchange sex for money but not for a hit:

I'd go out on Biscayne Boulevard, make my money there, and go to the base house.

If I had money I'd get my own drugs. I don't need nobody else. If I really wanted some more [crack] then I'd find someone to have sex with.

The first time [sex was exchanged for crack] I'll tell you was about three years ago. And I made him pay me double in drugs as if it was money. And they did it, and I got it in my hand up front as payment as I would money. I don't do that very often but it was the only way I was going to make anything and I was going to buy crack with my own money anyway and since I doubled the price of the cash that I wanted I went for it. And then I don't, very rarely do that [exchange sex for drugs rather than money].

## Crack House Sex, Cofactors, and HIV Infection Risk

The biological variables that determine HIV infectivity (the tendency to spread from host to host) and susceptibility (the tendency for a host to become infected) are not completely understood. HIV has been isolated from the semen of infected men, and it appears that it may be harbored in the cells of preejaculated fluids or sequestered in inflammatory lesions.[27] Furthermore, it appears that women can harbor HIV in vaginal and cervical secretions at varying times during the menstrual cycle.[28] The probability of sexual transmission of HIV among homosexual and bisexual men through anal intercourse, and to women through vaginal intercourse, has been well documented.[29] However, although there is the potential for viral transmission from female secretions, the absolute amounts of virus in these secretions appear to be relatively low. The efficiency of transmission of male-to-female versus female-to-male is likely affected by the relative infectivity of these different secretions, as well as sex during menses, specific sexual practices, the relative integrity of skin and mucosal surfaces involved, and possibly the presence of other sexually transmitted diseases. Within this context, the character of crack house sex, both vaginal and oral, may facilitate the heterosexual transmission of HIV.

The potential for transmission of HIV from women to men during vaginal intercourse in crack houses is related to one aspect of the cocaine/sexuality connection. Cocaine has long had a reputation as an aphrodisiac, although sexuality is notoriously a playground of legend, exaggeration, and rumor. In all likelihood, much of cocaine's reputation may be from the mental exhilaration and disinhibition it engenders, thus bringing about some heightened sexual pleasure during the early stages of use. At the same time, however, cocaine users have consistently reported over the years that the drug tends to delay the sexual climax, and that after prolonged stimulation, an explosive orgasm occurs. Users also report that chronic use of the drug results in sexual dysfunction, with impotence and the inability to ejaculate the common complaints of male users and decreased desire for sex becoming the norm for both male and female users.[30]

What applies to powder cocaine with regard to sexual stimulation and functioning would also apply to crack cocaine. Male customers, as well as male and female providers, in the sex-for-crack exchange networks report the difficulties associated with ejaculating under the influence of crack. Some report that they can climax only through extremely vigorous masturbation. One house girl commented: "Some of these mens have trouble gettin' it up and keepin' it up, and it's hard to get a limp cock to come, although sometimes even that happens." Others similarly reported:

> The cracks causes problems for men. They can get a hard-on, but they don't come quick like when they're straight. So first they want heads, and when that don't work, they want pussy sex. Then it still takes 'em forever, pumpin' away until his cock gets sore, I get sore, and then I get pissed. But I can't say anything, because he already gave me the cracks.

> One time this Hispanic dude was prongin' my pussy so long that he sees blood and starts yelling: "What the fuck's goin' on with you lady, you on the rag or something?" But it was him that was bleedin' in me. His cock was goin' in and out of me so long that he rubbed it raw.

> I had this guy once who they should've named him "horse cock." He was so big that it really hurt when he pushed it in me. An' he was so hot an' so hard that I figured it'd be over quick. But he don't come. Fuck, fuck, fuck, and he still don't come. Then he starts jerkin' himself off fast, doin' it 'til ya can see his cock bleedin' on his hand. His dick has blood on it an' so does his hand. And then he rams his bloody dick back in me and fuck, fuck, fuck. . . . He never did come.

It is within such a situation that the potential for female-to-male transmission of HIV exists. During vaginal intercourse, the friction of the penis against the clitoris, labia minora, and vaginal vestibule, opening, and canal causes stimulation that can generate copious amounts of vaginal secretions. And as noted, HIV has been isolated from vaginal and cervical secretions. Furthermore, since women who exchange sex for crack in crack houses do so with many different men during the course of a day or night, potentially HIV-infected semen from a previous customer can still be present in the vagina. Moreover, it was reported by one crack house customer that he ruptured the skin on his penis while having intercourse with a "crack house prostitute" while she was menstruating:

> I really didn't think much about it. I was high, and I had been high most of the night, and porking a crack house prostitute while she was on the rag

was something I had done more than once in my time. . . . She was bleeding, and I was bleeding, first from a bad blow job and then from too much sex. . . . After a while, the blood, hers, got too much, so I turned her over and put it in her chute [anus].

Although vaginal and anal intercourse often occur, much of the sex that occurs in crack houses involves women performing oral sex on men. To date, however, evidence for an oral route of HIV has been unconvincing. In most of the investigations of homosexual practices where a full range of sexual activities were carefully considered, for example, the risk from either insertive or receptive orogenital contact was uncertain, although regarded to be quite low.[31] The data concerning heterosexual spread of the virus by oral sex are also limited. For example, in one study of the spouses of AIDS patients, HIV seropositivity among spouses was higher for couples who practiced oral sex in addition to penile-vaginal sex, as compared with couples who practiced only penile-vaginal sex.[32]

There is an accumulating body of evidence that impaired host immunity, as well as concomitant sexually transmitted diseases, and particularly genital ulceration, may potentiate the transmission of HIV by increasing both infectivity and susceptibility.[33] In addition to these, there is another cofactor apparent in crack house oral sex that may be affecting the spread of HIV: the open sores on the lips and tongues of crack users as the result of burns and other epidermal trauma caused by the heat in the crack pipe stem. Because most women who perform repeated acts of oral sex in crack houses refuse to swallow a customer's semen as it is ejaculated, the potential for HIV transmission from infected semen becomes apparent. For example, the 22-year-old who claimed to have engaged in more than thirty thousand episodes of oral sex commented:

I may have swallowed a lot of cock in my time, but I don't swallow nobody's come [semen]. Ya can tell when the man is gonna come, so ya try to get his cock out of yer mouth so it ends up somewhere else. Most of the time it ends up on yer face, hair, chest. . . . Either that or he surprises me and I end up with a mouth full of jizz [semen]. So I wait 'til he's done pumpin' and then I let it out all at once.[34]

Another house girl reported:

Yeah, I really don't want to swallow any of it. I don't like that, not at all. I hold it, see, in my mouth. Some times it dribbles out while he's still workin' in an' out of my face. But when he's all done I don't fuck the dog [waste time]. I get rid of it quick. Spit it out.

Interestingly, and not surprisingly, street prostitutes not only disdain swallowing a customer's semen, but most of those interviewed in this study avoided having semen enter their mouths:

I don't like them to climax in my mouth. A man will push my head because they want it deeper. And I'll tell them, I'll give them one warning: "Get your hand off my head. I know my job, you know." I hate that, to push my head and I'll give them a warning and then I'll get out quick.

They'll just come in your hand. I won't let them come in my mouth.

## Sex, Crack, and HIV Prevention Messages

The only reported experiences with AIDS prevention efforts in the drug-using community relate to intravenous users. Injecting drug users, in addition to being the second highest risk group for HIV and AIDS, also represent a population that has been difficult to affect with routine AIDS prevention initiatives. The potential for HIV acquisition and transmission from infected paraphernalia and "unsafe" sex is likely known to the majority of these drug users. Yet most are accustomed to risking death (through overdose or the violence-prone nature of the illegal drug marketplace) and disease (hepatitis and other infections) on a daily basis, and these generally fail to eliminate their drug-taking behaviors. For these reasons, warnings that needle sharing or unsafe sex may facilitate an infection that could cause death perhaps five or more years down the road often have had little meaning. Moreover, there appears to be little relationship between engaging in high-risk behaviors and perceptions of risk for acquiring HIV infection.[35]

It appears that what has been said about injecting drug users also applies to crack users, and perhaps even more so. The apparently more compulsive nature of crack use suggests that effective prevention and intervention efforts would be difficult to implement, particularly those not undertaken within the context of intensive residential drug treatment. Moreover, although long-term follow-up studies of crack users in treatment have yet to be conducted, anecdotal reports from clinicians in the field suggest that patient attrition and relapse rates are high. All of this suggests that crack users in general, and those who exchange sex for crack in particular, represent a problem population for which specially focused prevention and outreach initiatives must be designed.

# Notes

1. In the street argot of the Miami crack scene, a "chicken head" is a woman who trades sex for crack in a crack house, so-called becaus of the continuous up-and-down movement of her head while engaging in oral sex.
2. *Newsweek*, June 16, 1986, p. 15.
3. See *New York Times*, May 16, 1986, p. A1; *Time*, June 2, 1986, pp. 16–18; *Newsweek*, June 16, 1986, pp. 15–22, June 30, 1986, pp. 52–54; *New York Times*, August 25, 1986, p. B1, September 13, 1986, p. 1; *USA Today*, June 16, 1986, p. 1A.

4. Cited in James A. Inciardi, "Beyond Cocaine: Basuco, Crack, and Other Coca Products," *Contemporary Drug Problems* 14 (Fall 1987): 469.
5. James N. Hall, "Hurricane Crack," *Street Pharmacologist* 10 (September 1986): 1–2.
6. James A. Inciardi, "*Crack*-Cocaine in Miami," National Institute on Drug Abuse Technical Review Meeting on the Epidemiology of Cocaine Use and Abuse, Rockville, Maryland, May 3–4, 1988.
7. For example, see, *Newsweek*, June 16, 1986, pp. 15–22; Arnold M. Washton, Mark S. Gold, and A. Carter Pottash, "Crack," *Journal of the American Medical Association*, August 8, 1986, p. 711; *New York Times*, September 13, 1986, pp. 1, 8; Victor Cohn, "Crack Use," *NIDA Notes* (December 1988): 6–7.
8. See Ron Rosenbaum, "Crack Murder: A Detective Story," *New York Times Magazine*, February 15, 1987, pp. 29–33, 57, 60; *Newsweek*, February 22, 1988, pp. 24–25; *Time*, March 7, 1988, p. 24; *Newsweek*, March 28, 1988, pp. 20–29; *Newsweek*, April 27, 1988, pp. 35–36; *Time*, May 9, 1988, pp. 20–23; *New York Times*, June 23, 1988, pp. A1, B4; *Time*, December 5, 1988, p. 32; *New York Doctor*, April 10, 1989, pp. 1, 22; *U.S. News & World Report*, April 10, 1989, pp. 20–32; *New York Times*, June 1, 1989, pp. A1, B4; *New York Times* (National Edition), August 11, 1989, pp. 1, 10; Andrew C. Revkin, "Crack in the Cradle," *Discover* (September 1989): 62–69.
9. James A. Inciardi, "The Crack/Violence Connection Within a Population of Hard-Core Adolescent Offenders," National Institute on Drug Abuse Technical Review on Drugs and Violence, Rockville, Maryland, September 25–26, 1989.
10. *Miami Herald* ("Neighbors" Supplement), April 24, 1988, pp. 21–25; James A. Inciardi and Anne E. Pottieger, "Kids, Crack, and Crime," *Journal of Drug Issues*, Spring 1991: 257–270.
11. *Crack/Cocaine: Overview 1989* (Washington, D.C.: Drug Enforcement Administration, 1989).
12. See "Sex for Crack: How the New Prostitution Affects Drug Abuse Treatment," *Substance Abuse Report*, November 15, 1988, pp. 1–4; "Syphilis and Gonorrhea on the Rise Among Inner-City Drug Addicts," *Substance Abuse Report*, June 1, 1989, pp. 1–2; "Syphilis and Crack Linked in Connecticut," *Substance Abuse Report*, August 1, 1989, pp. 1–2; *New York Times*, August 20, 1989, pp. 1, 36; *New York Times*, October 9, 1989, pp. A1, A30; *U.S. News & World Report*, October 23, 1989, pp. 29–30; *Newsweek*, September 25, 1989, p. 59; *Miami Herald*, October 22, 1989, pp. 1G, 6G; James A Inciardi, "Trading Sex for Crack Among Juvenile Drug Users: A Research Note," *Contemporary Drug Problems* 16 (Winter 1989): 689–700; Mary Ann Forney and T. Holloway, "Crack, Syphilis and AIDS: The Triple Threat to Rural Georgia," *Georgia Academy of Family Physicians Journal* 12 (1989): 5–6; Robert T. Rolfs, Martin Goldberg, and Robert G. Sharrar, "Rick Factors for Syphilis: Cocaine Use and Prostitution," *American Journal of Public Health* 80 (July 1990): 853–857.
13. Dale D. Chitwood, James A. Inciardi, Duane C. McBride, Clyde B. McCoy, H. Virginia McCoy, and Edward J. Trapido, *A Community Approach to AIDS Intervention: Exploring the Miami Outreach Project for Injecting Drug Users and Other High Risk Groups* (Westport, Conn.: Greenwood Press, 1991).
14. In the Miami crack scene, "kingrats" are crack house owners. Owners are also known as "rock masters" and "house men."

"Pay masters" are male crack house customers who purchase sex. A "scrug" is a man who tries to get sex for free.

"Gut buckets" are women who trade sex for crack in crack houses, while "guts" refer to a vagina.

A "slow neck" is oral sex during which the penis is sucked very slowly, as compared to a "fast head," where the intent is to bring the customer to a climax as quickly as possible. "Slow necks" typically cost more than "fast heads."

A "penny" is a single hit on a crack pipe, typically in exchange for sex.

A "freak" was originally a crack whore who would engage in oral sex with another woman. However, "freak" now refers to anyone who trades any type of sex for crack, and the "freak room" in a crack house is the locus of most of the sex.

"Rock monsters," also known as "base heads," "base whores," "crackies," "crack whores," "head hunters," "rock stars," "skeeter heads," and "skeezers," are women who trade sex for crack.

A "blood sucker" is a type of female freak who will engage in oral sex with a woman who is menstruating.

"Stems," "skillets," and "tools" refer to crack smoking paraphernalia.

15. In the greater Miami area, crack houses are known as "cribs," "huts," "jungles," "rock farms," "rock stalls," and "gravel pits." There are also specific types of crack houses.
16. See Inciardi, "Trading Sex for Crack," p. 696.
17. Lynne Duke, "The Graveyard," *Miami Herald Tropic*, April 5, 1987, pp. 12–28.
18. See *Miami Herald*, April 9, 1987, pp. 1D, 2D; *Miami Herald*, April 22, 1987, p. 12–28.
19. I conducted additional interviews and observations through the end of 1990.
20. "Current" drug use is defined as any use during the thirty-day period prior to interview.
21. For a comprehensive treatment of HIV transmission patterns, see, P. T. Cohen, Merle A. Sande, and Paul A. Volberding (eds.), *The AIDS Knowledge Base* (Waltham, Mass.: Massachusetts Medical Society).
22. Thomas A. Peterson, "Facilitators of HIV Transmission During Sexual Contact," in Nancy J. Alexander, Henry L. Gabelnick, and Jeffrey M. Speiler (eds.), *Heterosexual Transmission of AIDS* (New York: Wiley-Liss, 1990), pp. 55–68.
23. Giora M. Mavligit, Moshe Talpaz, Flora T. Hsia, Wendy Wong, Benjamin Lichtiger, Peter W. A. Mansell, and David M. Mumford, "Chronic Immune Stimulation by Sperm Alloantigens: Support for the Hypothesis That Spermatozoa Induce Immune Dysregulation in Homosexual Men," *Journal of the American Medical Association* 251 (1984): 237–241; Robert R. Redfield, Phillip D. Markham, Syed Zaki Salahuddin, M. G. Sarngadharan, Anne J. Bodner, Thomas N. Folks, William R. Ballou, D. Craig Wright, and Robert C. Gallo, "Frequent Transmission of HTLV-III Among Spouses of Patients with AIDS-Related Complex and AIDS," *Journal of the American Medical Association* 253 (1985): 1571–1573; Jay A. Levy, "The Human Immunodeficiency Viruses: Detection and Pathogenesis," in Jay A. Levy (ed.), *AIDS: Pathogenesis and Treatment* (New York: Marcel Dekker, 1989), pp. 159–229.
24. During the past decade, a number of studies have focused on the prostitution and other criminal behaviors of drug-using women in Miami. However, the

samples were exclusively narcotics-using women, populations that typically engage in a variety of criminal activities, of which prostitution is but one. As a result, comparative data on women for whom sex was the primary source of income for obtaining drugs are limited and inconclusive. For example, see, James A. Inciardi, "Heroin Use and Street Crime," *Crime and Delinquency* (July 1979): 335–346; Susan K. Datesman and James A. Inciardi, "Female Heroin Use, Criminality, and Prostitution," *Contemporary Drug Problems* (Winter 1979): 455–473; James A. Inciardi, Anne E. Pottieger, and Charles E. Faupel, "Black Women, Heroin and Crime: Some Empirical Notes," *Journal of Drug Issues* (Summer 1982): 241–250; James A. Inciardi and Anne E. Pottieger, "Drug Use and Crime Among Two Cohorts of Women Narcotics Users: An Empirical Assessment," *Journal of Drug Issues* 16 (Winter 1986): 91–106; James A. Inciardi, *The War on Drugs: Heroin, Cocaine, Crime, and Public Policy* (Palo Alto, Calif.: Mayfield, 1986), pp. 156–169.

25. There is a wealth of literature on this topic. For example, see Charles Winick and Paul M. Kinsie, *The Lively Commerce: Prostitution in the United States* (Chicago: Quadrangle Books, 1971); Paul J. Goldstein, *Prostitution and Drugs* (New York: Lexington Books, 1979); Hilary Evans, *Harlots, Whores and Hookers: A History of Prostitution* (New York: Dorset Books, 1979); Marsha Rosenbaum, *Women on Heroin* (New Brunswick, N.J.: Rutgers University Press, 1981); Arlene Carmen and Howard Moody, *Working Women: The Subterranean World of Street Prostitution* (New York: Harper & Row, 1985); Eleanor M. Miller, *Street Women* (Philadelphia: Temple University Press, 1986.)

26. Barbara Sherman Heyl, *The Madam as Entrepreneur: Career Management in House Prostitution* (New Brunswick, N.J.: Transaction Books, 1979), pp. 115–116.

27. Margaret A. Fischl, "Prevention of Transmission of AIDS During Sexual Intercourse," in Vincent T. DeVita, Samuel Hellman, and Steven A. Rosenberg (eds.), *AIDS: Etiology, Diagnosis, Treatment, and Prevention* (Philadelphia: J. B. Lippincott, 1988), pp. 369–374.

28. M. W. Vogt, D. E. Craven, D. E. Crawford, D. J. Witt, R. Byington, R. T. Schooley, and M. S. Hirsch, "Isolation of HTLV-III/LAV from Cervical Secretions of Women at Risk for AIDS," *Lancet* i (1986): 525–527; M. W. Vogt, D. J. Witt, D. E. Craven, R. Byington, D. S. Crawford, M. S. Hutchinson, R. T. Schooley, and M. S. Hirsch, "Isolation Patterns of the Human Immunodeficiency Virus from Cervical Secretions During the Menstrual Cycle of Women at Risk for the Acquired Immunodeficiency Syndrome," *Annals of Internal Medicine* 106 (1987): 380–382; C. B. Wofsy, J. B. Cohen, L. B. Hauer, N. Padian, B. Michaelis, J. Evans, and J. A. Levy, "Isolation of AIDS-Associated Retrovirus from Genital Secretions of Women with Antibodies to the Virus," *Lancet*, i (1986): 527–529.

29. See, for example, Pearl Ma and Donald Armstrong (eds.), *AIDS and Infections of Homosexual Men* (Boston: Butterworths, 1989); Judith B. Cohen and Constance B. Wofsy, "Heterosexual Transmission of HIV," in Levy, *AIDS: Pathogenesis and Treatment*, pp. 135–157.

30. Lester Grinspoon and James B. Bakalar, *Cocaine: A Drug and Its Social Evolution* (New York: Basic Books, 1976), pp. 104–108; Roger D. Weiss and Steven M. Mirin, *Cocaine* (Washington, D.C.: American Psychiatric Press, 1987), p. 31.

31. Richard A. Kaslow and Donald P. Francis, *The Epidemiology of AIDS: Expression,*

*Occurrence, and Control of Human Immunodeficiency Virus Type I Infection* (New York: Oxford University Press, 1989), p. 98.

32. M. Fischl, T. Fayne, S. Flanagan, M. Ledan, R. Stevens, M. Fletcher, L. La Voie, and E. Trapido, "Seroprevalence and Risks of HIV Infection in Spouses of Persons Infected with HIV" (paper presented at the IV International Conference on AIDS, June 1988, Stockholm).

33. Anne M. Johnson and Marie Laga, "Heterosexual Transmission of HIV," *AIDS* 2 (Supplement 1, 988): S49–S56.

34. This particular woman also reported having an open sore on the inside of her lower lip, which she assumed was from a crack pipe.

35. Duane C. McBride, Carolyn Y. McKay, Clyde B. McCoy, and Dale C. Chitwood, "The Relationship Between HIV Risk Behaviors and Perception of Infection Risk Among IV Drug Users" (paper presented at the VI International Conference on AIDS, San Francisco, June 20–24, 1990).

# 3

# Crack Cocaine and the Transformation of Prostitution in Three Chicago Neighborhoods

*Lawrence J. Ouellet*
*W. Wayne Wiebel*
*Antonio D. Jimenez*
*Wendell A. Johnson*

From our seats by the window, we could see Billie rapidly walking north on Sheridan. Her pace was surprising because this area is a prostitution stroll, she sells sex, and these were business hours. Certainly the forty-degree weather on this January 1992 evening was not a problem, not in Chicago. We signaled to Billie, inviting her to join us in the fast-food café. Billie is an experienced but youthful-appearing prostitute who has worked this area for years. By local standards, she is attractive and well groomed, and she consistently manages to maintain both her appearance and heroin use. Billie accepted our invitation and, as usual, was talkative. At one point, Ouellet asked her, "Are you still working over on Lincoln?" Her reply said much about the impact of cocaine, especially crack cocaine, on the conduct of street-level prostitution in Chicago:

> I ain't hardly workin' at all anymore. There ain't nothing out there anymore. . . . Those rock stars [females who habitually smoke crack], whatever they call themselves, with them you can't make money anymore. Any decent 'hoe gonna ask for twenty dollars, but these girls, they'll give head for five dollars. Half-and-half, ten dollars! [sarcastic laugh] Can you believe it? . . . Now these johns comin' up and that's all they want to pay.

Street-level prostitution probably always has had rate cutters, in-kind bartering, sellers able to exercise only a minimum of control over their transactions, or drug-addicted practitioners who neglected most of their other needs (Goldstein 1979). However, in Chicago's lower-class neighborhoods, the ascendance of cocaine to a dominant position in street drug markets appears to have accentuated these particularly negative facets of commercial sex transactions. Compared to periods when heroin dominated these inner-city neighborhoods, prostitution now seems even more desperate. Evidence of this change is found in reported increases in trades of sex for drugs, erratic sex-selling patterns, decreased prices for sex, less control over sex acts, and instances of extreme degradation. In Chicago, the arrival of crack cocaine intensified these trends, all of which have significant implications for the transmission of the human immunodeficiency virus (HIV). In this chapter, we examine exchanges of sex to acquire cocaine, with an emphasis on sex transactions linked to crack cocaine.

## Data Collection

Forty cocaine users were interviewed: thirty-six by the authors, and four by a female outreach worker under Ouellet's supervision. The authors and outreach workers are members of the AIDS Outreach Intervention Project—Chicago, an effort funded by the National Institute on Drug Abuse to understand and slow HIV transmission among injection drug users (IDUs) and their sex partners.

The project uses a multimethod approach that combines the basic principles of medical epidemiology with those of community ethnography (Wiebel 1988). A key feature of the project is its targeting of social networks of active, on-the-street IDUs as opposed to individual IDUs who are being processed by an official institution of some sort—typically a drug treatment program, hospital, jail, or prison.[1]

By early 1988, the project established storefront field stations in three areas of Chicago that varied from one another in their ethnic and community characteristics: the mostly African-American South Side, ethnically mixed North Side, and largely Puerto Rican Northwest Side. Gentrification is underway in the North Side and Northwest Side neighborhoods, and, as a result, their lower-class inhabitants experience considerable residential instability. South Side neighborhoods selected for study also house many poor people, but there is little gentrification, and existing housing is relatively stable. At each site, three social networks of IDUs were targeted to receive AIDS education and HIV prevention materials. Further, network members were invited to join a panel study that focused on changes in HIV high-risk behaviors.

Field stations in these neighborhoods are staffed by interviewers, ethnographers, and indigenous, ex-IDU outreach workers. (Three of the authors are ethnographers at these field stations.) Besides serving as research sites, field stations are drop-in centers for local IDUs, and one station offers medical services. From these field stations, outreach workers and ethnographers go into the neighborhoods and congregation sites of IDUs (e.g., drug-copping areas) to do AIDS education and individual risk assessments, pass out bleach and condoms, provide referrals to appropriate social and medical services, and conduct research.

To launch this study of sex-for-cocaine transactions, we used contacts known to us from our AIDS intervention work among IDUs. Because in 1989 there were in Chicago relatively few individuals with street reputations for smoking crack, we began our explorations with cocaine users who either injected or snorted the drug. As our study progressed, we came into contact with people who smoked, bought, and/or sold crack cocaine, and they were added to our sample. Thus, although this study focuses on exchanges of sex associated with crack cocaine, it also discusses such transactions in conjunction with other forms of the drug. The interviews with sample members followed a general guide but were open-ended and exploratory. Each interview was audiotaped and transcribed.

The ethnographers collected other qualitative data while on the streets through informal discussions, listening to the conversations of others, and direct observation. Information also was provided by cocaine smokers, most often female, who came into the field stations to get condoms.

## The Sample

All but two of the forty subjects formally interviewed for this study live and use drugs in one of the three areas served by the project. Despite geographic and ethnic variations, the sample is nearly homogeneous in its socioeconomic dimensions, with most subjects occupying statuses commonly associated with the lower class or lower working class. (One exception that provided a fruitful contrast is a female whose drug use takes place within upper-middle-class social circles.) The sample is 60 percent female, has an average age of 36 for males and 33 for females, and is 60 percent African-American, 28 percent white, and 13 percent Puerto Rican (table 3–1). Residential instability was reported by the majority of subjects, with 20 percent calling themselves homeless and 47 percent having spent less than six months in their current residence. However, almost all of this transience occurred among those from the North Side or Northwest Side. Only 43 percent of the sample completed high school, and almost none reported full-time, legal employment. Instead, public aid (53 percent), part-time jobs and legal hustles (39 percent), and prostitution (42 percent of females) are the most commonly reported sources of income.

All subjects use or have a recent history of using cocaine more often than any other illicit drug. Smoking is the primary route of cocaine administration for 62 percent of our sample, and another 15 percent engage in a mix of smoking and intravenous use (table 3–2). The remaining subjects exclusivly shoot (18 percent) or snort (5 percent) cocaine. While only 33 percent of subjects were active IDUs when interviewed, 74 percent injected

**Table 3–1**
**Sample Profile**

|  | North Side | Northwest Side | South Side | Total |
|---|---|---|---|---|
| **Sex** | | | | |
| Male | 5 | 9 | 1 | 15 (38%) |
| Female | 8 | 5 | 11 | 24 (60%) |
| Transsexual | - | - | 1 | 1 |
| **Age** | | | | |
| Male | 34 | 35 | 54 (n = 1) | 36 |
| Female | 34 | 30 | 34 | 33 |
| Range | 24-49 | 25-47 | 27-54 | 24-54 |
| **Race** | | | | |
| African-American | 4 | 7 | 13 | 24 (60%) |
| Hispanic | 1 | 4 | - | 5 (13%) |
| White | 8 | 3 | - | 11 (28%) |
| **Residence** | | | | |
| Homeless | 4 | 1 | 1 | 6 (20%) |
| Current ≤ 6 months | 5 | 9 | - | 14 (47%) (n = 30) |
| **Education** | 8 | 8 | 5 | 21 (57%) |
| <12 years | | | | (n = 37) |
| **Income** | | | | |
| Legal | 4 | 6 | 5 | 15 (39%) |
| Public aid | 3 | 7 | 10 | 20 (53%) (n = 38) |
| **Prostitution** | 4 | 2 | 4 | 10 (42%) of females) |

**Table 3–2**
**Cocaine Use Profile**

|  | North Side | Northwest Side | South Side | Total |
|---|---|---|---|---|
| **Primary route** | | | | |
| IV | 6 | 1 | - | 7 (18%) |
| Pipe | 5 | 8 | 11 | 24 (62%) |
| Pipe and IV | 1 | 3 | 2 | 6 (15%) |
| Snort | 0 | 2 | 0 | 2 (5%) (n = 39) |
| Ever IV (any drug) | 9 | 8 | 9 | 26 (74%) (n = 38) |
| **Days used during** | | | | |
| last thirty days | 21 | 16 | 24 | 20 |
| Daily use | 10 | 5 | 10 | 8 |

drugs at some time in the past.[2] In the thirty days prior to the interview, cocaine was used an average of twenty days, and on those days it was used an average of eight times. For the most part, those with the highest rates of daily use were smokers of crack cocaine.

After each ethnographer completed two interviews, we decided to reject as subjects those who had not recently engaged in sex. Further, male candidates rendered asexual by cocaine also were barred from the sample. Given the many people who reported that cocaine extinguishes their sexual desire or impedes their sexual performance, we felt these screens were necessary to avoid ending up with a largely asexual sample. It is important, therefore, to understand that this exploration is not of cocaine's effect on sexual activity. Rather, we mostly investigated cases where cocaine plays a role in provoking or shaping sexual activity.

## The Evolution of Cocaine Smoking in Chicago

With sales of crack cocaine, known locally as "ready rock" or "rock," either absent or uncommon in its lower-class neighborhoods, Chicago before late 1989 and early 1990 was an anomaly compared to major coastal cities such as New York and Los Angeles. City officials claimed Chicago largely was crack free, and police statistics seemed to support them. In 1988 only 148 grams of crack were seized by Chicago police. As of July 1989, in spite of the formation by police of a Crack Task Force, this figure still amounted to a mere 97.5 grams (Cooper 1989). By the end of 1989, police confiscations of crack increased significantly but still amounted to less than a kilogram (Blau 1990). A threefold rise in 1990 of the amount of crack seized by police suggested that 1989's increase was not a fluke, but still this amount was minuscule compared to confiscations of cocaine hydrochloride (powdered cocaine).

The relative absence until 1990 of rock cocaine for sale did not mean no one smoked it. Historically, Chicago's rock users prepared the drug themselves, and most of those we interviewed had the same explanation for this trend: ready-rock manufactured for sale is inferior in purity to homemade rocks. As these people saw it, making rock cocaine presents an opportunity for further adulteration of the drug; thus, they would rather buy cocaine in its hydrochloride form and do their own "cooking." As one man related, "I told him that anything that I can't cook myself, I don't want it. . . . I didn't trust him. I wanted to see how good the cocaine was when you cook it and bring it back. . . . You can tell how potent it is."

By no later than mid-1990, street sales of rock became plentiful in poor African-American neighborhoods on the South Side and West Side. In Puerto Rican areas on the Northwest Side sales of rock were rare, but as 1991 unfolded we began to hear of such transactions. Street sales of ready rock in the North Side's poor white and ethnically mixed neighborhoods were more frequent than on the Northwest Side but much less likely than on the South Side and West Side.

By January 1992, the preparation of rock cocaine by its users became the exception, not the rule. The rise in seizures of rock cocaine beginning late in 1989 proved prophetic, and now sales of ready rock are widespread in Chicago's lower-class neighborhoods, including Puerto Rican areas of the Northwest Side. In most of these places, rock is the dominant form of cocaine sold in street drug markets. Thus, it appears that Chicago's experience with crack cocaine is anomalous in comparison to the other cities in this study only in the later onset here of massive street sales.

When this study began, most users of rock cocaine prepared the drug themselves. Now most rock users buy the drug ready-made. In the following discussion we refer to users of rock cocaine without distinguishing between these two modes of obtaining rock except when the difference is important.

## Marketing Ready Rock

Street sales of rock cocaine appear to be conducted almost entirely by African-Americans, most of whom are young and reputed gang members. However, older males are reported to be supplying and directing these street vendors.

In early 1990, ready rock usually was sold in ten- and twenty-dollar bags. When the kilo price of cocaine doubled later in 1990, street prices remained stable, but reports from users suggested the increases were passed to consumers through product adulteration. Currently, prices for a bag of rock begin at around five dollars, with ten-dollar bags the most common unit. Quality is said to be good.

It was uncommon in 1990 to see ready rock sold through mass marketing at well-known intersections of major thoroughfares. Instead, sales of ready rock in the neighborhoods where it was most prevalent were spread out and often made on smaller streets and by numerous vendors. Clearly, this strategy made it more difficult for the police to control sales. Now, both forms of selling exist. When street sales of ready rock exploded on Chicago's North Side in the summer of 1991, they centered around a single building and dominated one street. Sales were obvious, drive-up sales did a brisk business, and all this took place at or near a busy intersection. Dealers stood in the street holding rolls of money, and few bothered to disguise their activities. Heavy attention from the police and other officials forced offenders out of the building and led to decentralized, lower-profile selling. Still, according to local rock users, "You can buy rocks on every street in the neighborhood."

In 1990, the decision to purchase ready rock rather than do one's own freebasing was most likely when the user was outside his or her neighborhood or otherwise on the move. However, some smokers preferred to buy their rocks no matter what the situation, and the recent proliferation of ready-rock sellers suggests that this attitude is not uncommon. One South Side user explained:

> The ready rock is already cooked up and the only thing you have to do, you can be riding down the street and—if you got your pipe in your hand— put you a little grain and throw it right on the pipe and just go on and throw on down, go on and smoke. Now if you got the powder, you got to go through all that shit of having your tools and cooking it up, getting you some soda.

## Rock Smokers: Age and Sex Profiles

Several general comments can be made about those who smoke rock cocaine. Across the neighborhoods we studied, rock smoking is not restricted to any age group. However, it appears that young people find injection a relatively undesirable method for administering illicit drugs; therefore, when using cocaine, they typically snort or smoke it. While our sample is weighted toward middle-aged users—probably an artifact of our primary connections with IDUs—rock smokers on the whole appear younger than IDUs. Further, since those who sell ready rock on the street typically are youths in their teens and twenties, these young people are, by the fact of their immediate contact with the drug, in a position where experimentation is likely.

Women are more plentiful among rock smokers than among IDUs. Whereas our sampling of IDUs for the AIDS Outreach Intervention Study indicates that women constitute about 25 to 30 percent of this group, reports from cocaine dealers and users suggest that at least 50 percent of those who smoke rock are women.

Regarding these descriptions, we wish to underline that since this study focused almost entirely on inhabitants of poor, inner-city neighborhoods, most of our observations are limited to this social and economic stratum.

## Ethnic and Intracity Variations of the Use of Cocaine

Until mid-1991, rock smoking appeared most popular among African-Americans and whites and not at all popular among Puerto Ricans on the Northwest Side. Puerto Ricans who smoke rock typically were initiated by African-Americans or whites and continued on in the company of members of one or both of these groups. In the beginning, we found no networks or cliques of smokers composed wholly, or even predominantly, of Puerto Ricans. On the other hand, social cliques of rock smokers are found among whites and African-Americans. It is not clear what accounted for these differences, but they are starting to disappear. Increasing numbers of Puerto Ricans smoke rock cocaine, and we are now aware of emerging networks of Puerto Rican rock smokers.

Ethnic and intercity variations also were seen in the distribution of "smoke houses," places where rock cocaine is smoked and perhaps purchased or—until recently—cooked by patrons. Until mid-1991, smoke houses were most likely to be found in the city's South Side and West Side African-American neighborhoods. Now numerous smoke houses also exist on the city's North Side and are increasing in number on the Puerto Rican Northwest Side.

## Onset of Drug Use

The people we formally interviewed typically experienced alcohol or an illicit drug for the first time while in their preteenage or teenage years. Their ages at this event ranged from 8 to 21 years old, with a mean of 14.8. Alcohol was the most common introductory substance, followed by marijuana; together these drugs accounted for almost 90 percent of first experiences (excluding cigarettes).

The age of initiation into cocaine use varied widely among interviewees, ranging from 15 to 41 years old, but 75 percent tried cocaine by the time they were 25 (mean = 21.9). Chronic use (three or more uses per week for more than a month) began within one year after initiation for 60 percent of them and in less than two years for 75 percent.[3] Those who took more than two years before becoming chronic users almost always were introduced to the drug eight or more years before the interview, that is, either prior to the current cocaine epidemic or during its early stages when cocaine was less available and far more expensive. This delay in the onset of chronic use suggests that market factors, as well as users' personal characteristics and the drug's pharmacological properties, affect the likelihood of chronic use.

Interestingly, a number of those we interviewed, particularly those who originally were heroin users, reported not enjoying their introductory use of cocaine. For these people, it took at least several more experiences with the drug to define its use as pleasurable.

Of the thirty-eight interviewees who reported the route of administration when first trying cocaine, 50 percent said they took it intranasally, 28 percent injected it, and 19 percent smoked a rock. This pattern showed considerable variation between areas of the city; initiation through rock smoking was much more common among South Siders. This difference is consistent with other indicators in 1990 that suggested smoking rock cocaine was most common on the South Side.

Only three of the forty interviewees were introduced to smoking rock cocaine through the solicitations of a dealer, and two others were dealers and heroin addicts who were encouraged by customers to try it. The remainder first experienced rock through a friend, lover, or family member. For example, a 36-year-old, South Side, African-American woman explained:

I was trying to give up shooting drugs, firing drugs up. So my sister showed me. . . . I was cramping. I was hurting so bad this particular day. I guess I had a lot of blood clots in my system from all the shit that I had been doing. And I was hurting so bad that I came to the kitchen and I was crying. She was sitting at the table. . . . I asked her did she have some aspirins. She asked me what was wrong. I said, "I'm hurting so bad I'm ready to cry." She said, "Hit this pipe." So I hit the pipe. I said, "That didn't do me no good." I made it on to the bathroom. I come back out of the bathroom, I said, "Yeah, that shit really works. I don't have no more pain." And I went back to bed. I left her and her girlfriend there and went back to bed and went to sleep.

Candy, a 36-year-old South Side, African-American transsexual also began smoking with a relative:

I went to California. I stayed there for about four weeks. . . . I didn't know what smoking was about. I went to LA because my cousins and all of them were there, and they were doing it. That was like 1980 and [smoking cocaine] was what they were doing. They introduced me to it and I really liked it. I really, really liked it. I came back here and come to find out I had four friends here that was doing the same thing, and I never knew that they were doing it. We would get together every day and get high. Here one of them, she was selling it and she would just like us to be around her for the company. She was an older lady, and just liked us to be around her. She would give it to us.

A 33-year-old, white, North Side woman explained, "Well, I was using dust [PCP] a lot, and my friends were starting to use cocaine a lot, so I tried it."

Four people first smoked cocaine in California or Florida. In all these cases, the initiation took place during the late 1970s or early 1980s, and two people noted that during this period smoking cocaine was not common in Chicago.

Contrary to some predictions, only five of sixteen women reported being introduced to rock cocaine by a man, and in only one case did the desire for sex appear as a motive behind the man's offer. Reasons for trying cocaine were numerous, but most had to do with experimentation with drugs in general, curiosity about its use by a significant other, and/or using it as an alternative to another drug, particularly heroin. Regarding the latter motive, a self-described "cocaine addict," told us, "[I prefer] coke, any day . . . because you don't be sick like you would be sick off of heroin." It was not uncommon for cocaine users to note that in the 1980s cocaine was more readily available than heroin or pharmaceutical opiates and that it delivered a greater "bang for the buck" than Chicago's low-quality heroin. Both factors led these people to try cocaine and continue its use. A 49-year-old, white North Side woman described this situation:

I went to jail, so that took care of my Dilaudid and morphine habit. When I came out I started doing coke. . . . that is what Wilson Avenue was about then. . . . The good connects [dealers or doctors who wrote desired prescriptions] that we had . . . they weren't around. . . . [Cocaine] was all that was up there. There wasn't nothing [heroin] and it ain't nothing around here still [heroin quality remains poor].

## Continued Cocaine Use

Although smoking rock cocaine usually began in the company of someone socially close to the initiate, habitual smokers appear rather isolated. As the desire to use cocaine increases, users increasingly organize their lives around this urge. For some, fulfilling this desire becomes their overriding concern each day, often to the exclusion of people with whom they once were close. Over and over, smokers and injectors told us how their craving for cocaine led to the loss of all their material goods and to the destruction of human relationships they valued. Eventually, many of these users fell into a world peopled mostly by predatory "associates." Leroy, a 44-year-old, North Side, African-American male recalled:

I started smoking like a wildman. Before I know anything I was damn near broke. I just barely had my head on top of the water. Like, I see a lot of my partners—they sunk, they lost their cribs, their cars, their wife, they sold everything out from their house and all that kind of shit. I wasn't at that stage yet . . . but I could see it coming. I guess it might have been for the best that I got busted.

Sarah, a 31-year-old, South Side, African-American female, described the people with whom she smoked cocaine:

And don't lay your purse down. They can be real good friends of yours, but don't lay your purse down. And especially don't go to the bathroom. You know how you can buy a package [of cocaine] and come in and lay it on the mirror and say, "I got to go to the bathroom"? You can't do that. You got to take your shit to the bathroom with you. Now that is pitiful, ain't it?

Sarah went on to describe an encounter that occurred the day prior to the interview and one that she said is common among cocaine smokers:

He said, "Well, I put three fucking dollars on there and you ain't [put] shit on there [he contributed money to buy the cocaine they were smoking, but she had not]. How the fuck you think you are going to get more when I had a hit sitting there and I turned my back and it was gone?" I said [to myself], "Let me get the fuck away from these niggers." I mean, it wasn't comfortable at all. What killed me is that one of the guys was my brother, and I just shook my head and said, "Damn!"

Angie, a 33-year-old, white North Sider had this to say about her drug use, which primarily consists of cocaine and alcohol:

> It's done nothing but bring me down. It's having me stay in shelters and sleeping in the streets, being in the cold and waiting on this and that. Trying to do all crazy things to survive where I could just be doing something and living a regular life and not even have to go through all this stuff.

Richard, a 31-year-old, Northwest Side African-American described relationships with his family and past girlfriends:

> I turned my whole family against me, man. I got eight sisters and two brothers, one of them passed [died]. Don't nobody want to deal with me no more. They seen track marks on my arm. I got sisters that are nurses and stuff like that. They see me rollin' up marijuana cigarettes with stuff in it, with cocaine in it and everything else. I got to the point sometimes where I didn't care about them, and I would go smoke in their bathroom or something. They were like, "What is this I smell?" We just grew apart. Ain't no love lost, but I don't think they would try to help me unless they really knew I needed some help, because they think I'm going to take their money and go right and get some cocaine, which I probably would. So we just are apart from each other. . . . I ain't got no girlfriends. I done run all of them off.

José, a 34-year-old, North Side Puerto Rican who was just released from jail spoke of his relationship with his girlfriend, for whom he often expressed love. "But once I do that cocaine that's it. The gorilla pimp, the gorilla pimp. I mean I was awful, and I feel sorry for her, too." Speedy Bob, a North Side, African-American male familiar with both heroin and cocaine use compared the experiences. "You know how you'll do some lowdown things when you be using stuff [heroin]? Taking shit from your family, your loved ones, people you know? With cocaine, multiply that by ten."

Not all respondents described their relationships in such depressing terms. In fact, half reported no serious relationship problems. This is not to say that cocaine posed no such difficulties for these people. More often than not, those who reported few problems were longtime drug users who years ago had organized a life that included few or no close ties to family and friends. That is, these people appeared to have adjusted to a life devoid of close social ties and thus no longer identified this situation as particularly problematic.

The presence or absence of disrupted social relationships was not evenly distributed among the cocaine users we interviewed; habitual smokers of rock cocaine were the most likely to report such problems.

## Smoke Houses

"Smoke house" is the most common term for organized places where cocaine smokers can get the privacy and paraphernalia needed to smoke and often, in the recent past, to cook their cocaine. Smoke houses may also sell cocaine, and by January 1992 they were most likely to sell it in its rock form. However, by choosing to sell cocaine, smoke house proprietors greatly increase their risk of being targeted for arrest by the police.

The social organization of smoke houses ranges from dictatorial to near anarchy, but all have at least some rules. At a minimum, the user is expected to "take care of business" upon entry, which means paying the proprietor (we have heard the term "house man" for this position, but we are not sure what term is used when a woman occupies it). Payment almost always is a taste of one's cocaine. One person explained this form of exchange: "Some people runnin' a shooting gallery be about money, but the person runnin' a smoke house, they be about cocaine. That's why they runnin' the place."

In the more anarchical smoke houses, which appear to be the most common type, people freely wander about, beg for "hits," engage in sex—often as a trade for cocaine—steal from one another, "tweak" (bizarre or annoying behavior induced by cocaine) without restraint, and generally respect only strength. One respondent described such a place:

> I saw her date every man in the place for some coke. . . . She was giving one head, the other was fucking her from the back. . . . If it's ten niggers in there it doesn't make a difference. [*Later*] We be all in the same room and you look up and a nigger just done jumped up and busted him in the head and you wonder what for, and going in his pocket and taking his money. And then take his money and make him sit there while he smoke his money up. . . . Then when the nigger get the pipe he be even more vicious. The nigger gets to running and then gets to pulling out his pistol and all that shit. . . . He slapped this nigger the other day and took his money and smoke it up and then beat this girl up and ripped her clothes off and smoked her money up. . . . [The other people in the house were] just doing what they were doing and saying, "This muthafucka is acting fool again." . . . He had a tendency to pick on the weaker.

A North Sider offered this description.

> What's a smoke house like? It's nuts. OK, around here, most of the fuckin' girls that get high they get paranoid. Like my cousin, her mother fuckin' locked her in closets when she was little, so now she's scared to death of the dark. When she gets high she goes through the house and turns on every light there is, I mean every light. And then she will walk back and forth from every door to the bathroom, back and forth, back and forth. . . . My other cousin gets a thing about rats. . . . a smoke house is worse than a

shooting gallery. You see people everywhere. You see people smoking, you see people laid out from smoking too much. And you see someone who just got up from smoking the pipe and goes and stands in the corner, and someone will go and lock themself in the goddamn bathroom. It's just crazy.

Like this North Sider, several other people suggested that, compared to shooting galleries, smoke houses were more likely to have sex, stealing, bizarre behavior, begging, and/or violence. "Fiending," the willingness to do just about anything for more of a drug, also is more often attributed to smoke houses than to shooting galleries.

Not all smoke houses were described as anarchic. Jimmy's smoke house was highly organized and dictatorially governed by its proprietor. This house was unusual in that it was one of only two known to us where entrants are charged money (five dollars). The proprietor also sold cocaine and consequently did not allow customers to bring any of their own with them. When asked about house rules, a respondent said:

> You can't talk to anyone you didn't come in with. . . . [The owner] goes by my rules to be left alone [by others in the house]. . . . You can't bring anything in with you; he has it all. . . . You have to buy a certain amount; there's no ten- or twenty-dollar bullshit. . . . You can't move around from room to room. . . . You can't give a hit to someone you didn't come in with. . . . You got to keep the pipe he gives you, you can't let someone else use it. . . . You can't recook the stuff that's left in the pipe. . . . There's no hangin' around when you're done . . . no sex.

This smoke house was very attractive to the respondent because she was able to smoke cocaine and not worry about being bothered by people freeloading or tweaking, or worry about her drugs or belongings being stolen. Further, since the house provided everything she needed, she felt she did not have to worry about being arrested. The proprietor had five to ten people guarding the inside and outside of the house, and she believed that—in the event of a raid—she would have enough time to rid herself of cocaine, and she believed only the house man would have to "take the heat."

Besides security, this smoke house proprietor offered a "ladies day" twice a month on Sundays, when women were given a discount on the cost of cocaine. The house man occasionally gave his better customers a free bag of cocaine. The respondent claimed that, in contrast, most house men give nothing away for free, no matter how much money customers spend. "This is stupid," she said, "because you piss these people off after they done spent all their money and they be putting the police on you."

Smoke houses appear more necessary for smokers who need to hide this activity from those with whom they live than are galleries for IDUs in a similiar situation. As a South Side woman explained, "I haven't ever went to no shooting gallery. I can do that at the house. I can lock my door and do that, but it's a little different with smoking." Mothers, in particular, were drawn to smoke houses for the privacy they offered, because they did not want their children to know they smoked cocaine.[4]

## Cocaine and Sex

### Cocaine as an Aphrodisiac

Nine of the forty users interviewed reported that cocaine produces sexual stimulation. A South Side woman described an enjoyable sexual experience that took place in her early days of smoking rock cocaine:

> Anyway, [my sister] took me over to the coke man's house and his friend was over there. They let us smoke as much as we wanted to, and it turned me into a super freak. I mean freaky like a muthafucka, and I loved every minute of it. . . . [It was] a lot of oral sex, that is basically what it was. It was oral sex. . . . I was scared the way the 'caine did me. The whole time I kept saying, "What is wrong with me?" I said, "You want me to suck your dick again? What is wrong with me? Ooh baby, I got to suck your dick again." I was out of control, out of control. . . . Anyway, this showed me it wasn't that bad. So what if you flip a nigger; you're high, and it feels kinda good. It wasn't that bad as somebody told you, you know, sucking dicks for a hit. This ain't so bad, but it still bothered me.

Another South Side woman described her reaction to cocaine: "Cocaine makes me freaky. . . . It makes me feel good. . . . Hell yeah, I used to do cocaine and it used to be so good your stuff [vagina] start dripping. It used to make me come on myself." Of the nine people who found cocaine sexually stimulating, three said this was a temporary response confined to the early days of their use. One of the three attributed this change to the inferior quality of cocaine currently available, while the other two suggested that it was an effect of intensive use.

Men appear more likely than women to find that cocaine enhances their sexual desire (four of twelve versus two of nineteen, respectively). And when asked to recount instances where cocaine sexually stimulated people, respondents who knew or observed such people usually described only one such woman but multiple men. That is, respondents had seen only one or a few women but numerous men who reacted to cocaine in this manner. Women subjects especially were convinced that cocaine was a sexual stimulant for men; however, social conditions may convene to produce this impression. If men who want sex are drawn to places where cocaine is used—because such places often present readily available sex in a wide variety of forms—then it is likely that women offering sex in these places will see men, in general, as being sexually stimulated by cocaine.

Women largely agree that while cocaine tended to excite at least some men sexually, most were rendered nearly incapable of orgasm, at least within a period of time the women deemed reasonable. Men frequently were reported to be desirous of sex but unable to get an erection. A South Side woman complained, "It won't budge, it won't get hard, it won't do nothing. It just lay there. . . . It be like they want to do it in their mind, but the body won't let them do it."

Numerous women grumbled about having to "give head" (fellate) for periods as long as an hour to a male recipient high on cocaine. A South Side woman said, "You be sucking on their cock and sucking and sucking and nothing happen. They can go an hour and still nothing happen while you done wore yourself out." A North Side woman and operator of a shooting gallery that caters mostly to female cocaine injectors noted this problem and cited how women exchanging sex for cocaine are further exploited:

> These girls out here that are 20, 21, 22 years old and they go home with anybody who's got coke, for a bag. They will turn a trick with a man, man picks up the bag, and they shoot half the bag and let the man shoot half the bag, and then he's going to fuck them for an hour or two hours or something. . . . A man [who is high on cocaine] his dick will get hard, but he will fuck you forever and can't reach a climax.

She claimed that this situation was so common that women were "wising up" to men when trading sex for cocaine by demanding and consuming the drug prior to sex:

> So now these broads, they going to shoot the stuff [before having sex] and then put on an act, or if it ain't an act, and they are going to be paranoid or something to get out of it [having sex for an extended period of time]. He stuck with a hard dick, and they done got high and split. . . . [Otherwise] by the time he tries to get a nut, he done wore your high off anyway, so [the women] are not doing it that way anymore.

Several subjects—all female—indicated that cocaine use led to an extension of their sexual repertoire. Two separate motivations provoked this change: sexual pleasure and economic necessity. In the former instance, cocaine intoxication led to sexual experimentation for fun, but this was very short-lived. One woman reported acting out her curiosity about group sex, and three were more inclined to have sex with another woman (though not necessarily more likely to desire sex). Another woman told of greater pleasure in performing oral sex on a man, and one man claimed that women were affected in this manner. (In the latter case, this observation may have more to do with his possessing cocaine than with anything inherently sexual.) Finally, one woman said she was introduced to cocaine during an orgy at college, but the orgy was underway prior to the use of cocaine. At the time of their experimentation, these women appeared less concerned with safer sex than otherwise.

Women appear to engage in sex acts beyond their normal repertoire most often in response to the demands of men from whom will come the next round of cocaine, either via money or a direct trade. While the following example is an exception to these gender roles, it nonetheless illustrates the craving rock cocaine produces in some people. One woman told us that she performed oral sex on her adult daughter; though she found this act appalling, it was the price her daughter set for a bag of cocaine.

The men who reported being sexually stimulated by cocaine did not suggest that cocaine led them to broaden the content of their sexual activity. One subject noted that he was a "freak," but this condition seemed to predate his use of cocaine. Instead, the men seem to indulge already existing appetites that previously had been acted upon. When under the influence of cocaine, these men appear less likely to practice safer sex. However, since their preferred form of sex while high on cocaine is oral passive, it is not clear whether cocaine use makes the men more careless or that they feel this type of sex is not dangerous. Contrary to the men we interviewed, several female respondents claimed that cocaine not only excites men but also makes them "freaky"— that is, having a greater desire for having oral sex performed on them, a desire to perform oral sex, licking cocaine off a woman's genitals and erogenous zones, anal sex, and wanting their nipples sucked.

For twenty-two of thirty-one interviewees, cocaine never acted as a sexual stimulant. A typical assessment came from Sally, a 29-year-old North Sider:

> When I'm high on cocaine I can't stand to be touched. That's why I drink so much Bacardi. . . . I've had sex while I'm high, but I hated it. If the cocaine has a lot of speed on it, I don't even want to have sex with my boyfriend. If it's mostly cocaine, then it's OK [to have sex] with him [but she went on to express a preference for foreplay to the exclusion of coitus]. . . . It's real hard to turn dates [when I'm high on cocaine], that's why I drink.

In response to the question, "At any time in your life did cocaine turn you on sexually?" another North Side woman replied, "It makes me not want to." A North Side African-American male answered, "Cocaine kills my sex drive," and a Northwest Side African-American male responded, "I don't get turned on sexually. . . . I don't have thoughts of sex when I'm on cocaine. In fact, I'm totally the opposite; I don't want to be bothered." A North Side Puerto Rican male said, "When I shot cocaine, that [sex] was the last thing I wanted to do—I wanted to get out there and get more money to get more cocaine." This man offered his estimation of women who appear to be sexually stimulated by cocaine:

It's cold sex. Usually the girls that smokes that shit would just fuck you or suck you for another hit on the pipe. That is conditional love. In other words, they are not really being turned on by you, that's for sure. I don't know if the cocaine is really turning them on. I think what is really turned on is the dog in them. Now they got to get some more, or do whatever they got to do. So they will play that role like, "Yeah, let's go and have some sex." Just make sure you got that drug handy.

Taken together, these reports and the many asexual and impotent cocaine users we encountered suggest that most people either do not find cocaine to be sexually stimulating or find this effect to be fleeting. In particular, the great majority of women found that cocaine produced feelings antithetical to sex—a desire not to be touched, often fueled by paranoia. Paradoxically, their appetite for cocaine pushed many of these women into prostitution, and several mentioned alcohol as an antidote for their abhorrence of physical contact.

## Cocaine and Prostitution

Cocaine use clearly leads to much sexual activity, most of which is—for the women we contacted—prompted by the financial demands of repeated cocaine use. For a variety of reasons, few lower-class cocaine users are likely to buy a large quantity of cocaine all at once and then settle in for a binge. Instead, cocaine, like other illicit drugs, typically is purchased in small amounts that quickly are used up. Use produces an immediate desire for more cocaine. William Burroughs (1959) described the experience of injecting cocaine: "You smell it going in, clean and cold in your nose and throat then a rush of pure pleasure right through the brain lighting up those C connections. Your head shatters in white explosions. Ten minutes later you want another shot. . . . You will walk across town for another shot" (p. 19). Among the oral histories collected by Courtwright, Herman, and DesJarlais (1989) was a similar observation by May, a prostitute who briefly used cocaine in 1949: "The only thing, though, with cocaine, the more you get that sensation, the more you want it. But you never get the sensation more than once [in an episode of multiple use]. . . . So then all our money was going for cocaine (pp. 162–163).

Rudy, a North Sider, emphasized this desire for cocaine by comparing it to heroin: "Cocaine is different, you are greedy. You don't want to give nothing away. You don't want to give it to your woman, even, you know? . . . Heroin was cool. Heroin is different. Heroin you can share. You are not a dog. Heroin, you do one shot, maybe two shots. . . . Cocaine, as soon as you do one shot, you want another one."

Rock cocaine produces a desire for repeated use at least as strong as that reported by cocaine injectors. A 22-year-old male North Side gang member who smokes rock cocaine recently told us: "If I don't have any money I'm cool. But if I get, say, two hundred dollars in my pocket—you might not believe this, but I actually get a cramp in my stomach, a craving for those rocks. So I say to myself, 'I'm gonna get me one bag.' But ain't no way you can smoke just one bag. I end up spending everything I got." The problem then becomes how to finance another purchase and as quickly as possible. After more of the drug is bought and used, the cycle repeats itself.

Prostitution provides a solution to maintaining this cycle of drug use. Selling or trading sex can be done episodically, quickly, and twenty-four hours a day with a fair degree of control over its scheduling, and it usually pays enough per episode to finance cocaine in the amounts marketed on the street. Even more quickly, sex can be traded for cocaine. It appears that given this intoxication profile and the lack of resources among the urban poor, cocaine use and prostitution merge into a symbiotic relationship: one begets the other. Rudy, the North Sider, explained:

> I see a lot of broads, they run all night, man, because they shoot all night. Fast as they turn a date, then they get themselves a bag of dope. The next muthafucka might turn her on and get her high for a piece of pussy. When she get through with that, run right back up and get another date and buy her another bag of coke. It's all night long until she damn near pass out.

An interview with a female, upper-middle-class cocaine smoker illuminated the relationship of class status, prostitution, and cocaine use. She admitted that there were times that if she had to "suck a dick" for cocaine, she would not have hesitated but noted that her finances and social contacts were such that she never had to do this.

The extensive use of cocaine in lower-class neighborhoods appears to have qualitatively changed street-level prostitution. No one we talked with who had a first-hand knowledge of prostitution as it existed before the ascendancy of cocaine in the 1980s believed otherwise. Old-timers were unanimous in describing cocaine-driven prostitutes as generally out of control and the prostitution scene as having ever less dignity. One North Side oral historian put it this way: "To me, cocaine has made women a mess. How should I say it? It has did a woman so bad that you really don't have no respect for them, the women that use cocaine. Heroin didn't do that. . . . I've seen women just do anything for some cocaine."

Several respondents, both female and male, asserted that prostitutes during precocaine days were more likely to set aside money for living essentials, nice clothes, and personal hygiene, whereas now almost all of a habitual cocaine user's money is spent on the drug. A male respondent with a long history of pimping said:

> Heroin . . . a girl or prostitute may have a habit, but I guarantee you she would have kept money. She would be cleaner and she would care a little

about herself. Where a prostitute on cocaine, that's it. Every penny that girl will make will go to that cocaine dealer, every penny. She don't care about eating. She don't care about dressing. She don't care about bathing. She don't care about living or housing herself. All she wants to do is that drug, that drug, that drug.

A North Side woman involved with drugs and prostitution in this neighborhod for over twenty years said:

Things have changed in the last five years. A woman was out here on the streets making money for herself or whatever, a woman had a pimp or whatever. The broads out here now, the coke is their pimp, the coke is their life. They won't get no clothes, they won't have an apartment. A woman has got to have a place. They won't have a crib over there, they won't have nothing but another bag of coke. They won't even stay out there long enough to get a half a gram or something together. They make enough to get one fifteen-dollar bag [of powdered cocaine], and the shit ain't nothing, and they do it and run right back out there. It's some speed so it scares them to death, they run out there to get another date and get another bag, or turn a date with somebody who has got some coke. They don't have a man, no apartment, no clothes, no nothing.

Over and over, old-timers disparaged the practice of trading sex for drugs, which they associated with cocaine. A 44-year-old North-Side, African-American male said:

Back when I was coming up most of the prostitutes mainly if they got high, they got high because of all the different type of tricks they had to deal with. They had to kind of motivate themselves to deal with all them different types of tricks that are around at night. See back then it, back when I was coming up, back in the sixties, it was for the money, man. Now, man, it's for the high. You still got some decent whores out there that will turn that cocaine down and want the cash. But the majority of the whores now, they are pipeheads. That's all they want. You tell them, "Say, baby, I have a quarter bag of cocaine." And don't say you got a sixteenth, goddamn, she is going to jump on top of your head.

As Carol put it, "I was brought up that you don't bring your pussy to the dope man. You bring money." A male South Sider said, "Prostitutes used to be about money; now they're about drugs."

Several people thought the practice of trading sex for drugs was especially foolish, because, as Carol put it, "the man end up using half of what he gives the girl." Note that even the choice of words Carol used suggests the inferior position of women who trade sex for cocaine. Rather than being "paid" for her services, which infers that she has earned the payment and has a right to it, the man "gives" her cocaine, an exchange that suggests less status and honor and fewer rights on the part of the recipient. A South Side woman described such a transaction: "My brother . . . he has dated her for a ten-dollar bag of cocaine and has smoked damn near all of it up, where she has got one hit. And she had fucked, sucked, and everything. I have seen it with my own eyes."

Longtime prostitutes were unanimous in complaining that cocaine use has driven down prostitution prices. One woman told of performing oral sex for three dollars, the amount she was short for a bag of cocaine, and others complained about being propositioned for as little as five dollars. On numerous occasions we were told by observers, some of them prostitutes, "These girls now have no self-respect."

Finally, several people called the streets "meaner." One woman said that cocaine-using prostitutes are more likely to rip off tricks, and another noted that "cocaine has made pimps more desperate, more selfish and stupid . . . girls with black eyes earn less money." Similar evidence came from a prostitute who entered our field station one day and asked for information on local strolls. She explained that it was no longer possible to make decent money at her West Side locations, because "them pipeheads be ripping off the tricks, both the girls and their boyfriends. It's stupid, 'cause now the tricks staying away; they be afraid to go to them places."

Some skepticism about these accounts seems prudent. Are the old-timers painting the past through rose-colored glasses? Past descriptions of prostitution and/or drug scenes in periods not dominated by cocaine (Hall 1973; Reckless 1969 [1933]; Hughes 1977; Rosenbaum 1981; Fiddle 1967; Courtwright, Herman, and DesJarlais 1989; Goldstein 1979) present a mixed picture. All show street-level prostitution to be a grim activity marked by predatory relationships. Most of these studies cite rate cutting among practitioners, variations in their ability to control sex transactions, and prostitutes who are destitute—whether due to their drug use or for other reasons. Is there any evidence that these aspects of prostitution are more pronounced now than when cocaine did not dominate street drug sales?

Regarding prices, evidence suggests that current averages are low. A New York City prostitute describing streetwalking in the early 1940s claimed that ten dollars was the minimum amount for a sex act (Courtwright, Herman, and DesJarlais 1989: 168). Kim, a streetwalker featured in Hall's 1973 profile of New York City prostitutes, derides the prostitutes working in Times Squares, calling them "cheap ten-dollar and twenty-dollar girls." Street prices for sex in New York City in the early 1980s were estimated by Johnson and colleagues (1985) to average at least twenty dollars. Estimates for Chicago in the late 1970s to early 1980s, provided by two old-timers— one an ex-pimp and another an ex-prostitute—mirror those of Johnson and colleagues: fifteen to twenty-five dollars per sex act. Currently, street-level prostitutes in Chicago charge approximately ten dollars for oral sex and ten to twenty dollars for vaginal sex. When adjusted for inflation, current prices are notably lower than the estimates for previous years. Note, too, that it is not uncommon to hear of sex being sold for as little as five dollars, and sometimes even less. The reason for such seemingly absurd prices appears to be tied to unit prices of rock cocaine; rocks, unlike heroin, can be purchased for these small amounts of money.

Comparisons in levels of destitution and self-neglect between current cocaine-era prostitutes and their past heroin-era counterparts are difficult to make. For example, past studies such as Goldstein's and Rosenbaum's describe as rather common the presence of heroin-addicted prostitutes who have lost virtually all their material belongings and seem to care little about maintaining their personal appearance. On the other hand, virtually all the old-timers we contacted feel that this sort of destitution is more common among today's cocaine users as compared to yesterday's heroin-addicted prostitutes. Our observations of street-level prostitutes support the notion that compared to those using heroin, the cocaine users are in more desperate straits, as judged by homelessness, self-reported financial problems, and personal appearance. A definitive answer here is impossible; we are content to note that the decline suggested here is not improbable.

Of greater interest for our purposes are the bartering of sex for drugs and control over the content of commercial sex transactions. Among the studies cited, only Goldstein's work discusses the bartering of sex for drugs— in this case, by heroin users. And none of these studies describes the extremes of sexual degradation we, and the other authors in this book, regularly found among habitual, lower-class, cocaine injectors and rock smokers.

The fact that most researchers did not discover or overlooked the bartering of sex for drugs suggests that it is less common among street-level prostitutes of previous years than among today's cocaine users. It is impossible to imagine a current, cocaine-era researcher of prostitution or drug use not observing this phenomenon. Further, even if the old-timers who provided us with these comparisons tended to paint an overly favorable picture of the past, it is hard to ignore the consistency and certitude of their depictions. Consider the 43-year-old ex-prostitute who told us:

> These [cocaine-using] girls now, they are an embarrassment. They give prostitution a bad name. Anymore, I'm embarrassed to say I ever worked the streets. Fuckin' a trick for ten, five dollars. For a lousy rock. For a hit off a pipe! It's pitiful! And look at them. They don't keep themselves up. All they can think about is that damn coke. . . . And the way the men talk about them. Sure, men would say so and so is a whore, but now, "skeezer" [a woman who will do almost anything to get rock cocaine]. It's terrible the way men talk about these girls: "I wouldn't fuck her with someone else's dick." These girls don't have a clue; they don't know what they're doing out there.

Goldstein's discussion of "bag whores" makes it clear that the bartering of sex for drugs is not exclusively associated with cocaine use. These women were heroin users who traded sex for the drug. A Chicago old-timer admitted that this practice existed when heroin reigned supreme, an act he labeled as "lowlife." The difference between then and now appears not to be that sex-for-drug bartering was nonexistent during heroin-dominated periods but that it is more pronounced among today's cocaine users. And it seems likely that sexual trades in kind are least likely among prostitutes who are not drug users, seemingly a more common situation in years past. The following comment supports the notion that sex-for-drug bartering is close to a norm among cocaine injectors, especially rock smokers. The speaker is a male polydrug user in is mid-forties who addressed Ouellet on a summer night in 1991 as they stood in the middle of a North Side rock-copping area and prostitution stroll:

> Larry, I want you to try something, just for the sake of it, just so you can see what I'm talking about. Go get ya a couple of rocks. You can see that's no problem. Get ya a bag of rocks, and then go hold it in front of any of these girls around here. Black, white, Chinese, brown, Indian, it don't matter. Just show 'em that bag of rocks, and you can have any one of them. I'm not kidding. Try it. You'll see I'll telling you true. It's a fuck'n shame, but its true.

Certainly even Goldstein does not suggest that the bartering of sex for drugs was the norm for the heroin users he examined, but something close to that seems to be the case for habitual cocaine injectors and rock smokers, particularly the latter. In the following observation, a 44-year-old male implies this norm by identifying its converse as an exception. He addressed Ouellet during the summer of 1991 as they walked along a rock-copping area and prostitution stroll. The man's comment came spontaneously; it was not prompted by a question.

> You see that 'hoe [whore] over there, the nice-looking one? She's been out here all day and now going on all night. That's a skeezer. [*pause*] You know, I really shouldn't call her that. I saw her up at [a dealer's] crib earlier and she put down $130 cash money. The shit's [cocaine] all gone now, she done smoked it up. But, you know, she taking care of business. You got to give her credit for that. She ain't like most of them, you know, anything for a rock. She's out here makin' her own money and gettin' her own rocks. . . . And she's lookin' good, you know; she's clean, she takes care of herself. You got to give her credit.

Finally, the typical pattern of cocaine use suggests that it is more likely than other drugs to lead users to the bartering of sex. Injected and rock cocaine characteristically are experienced as an intensely pleasurable rush that subsides quickly and is replaced by unpleasant feelings and a craving to repeat the experience. Injectors who also have smoked rock cocaine generally contend that the desire for more of the drug recurs the soonest when smoking rock. For a prostitute on a cocaine binge, this cycle may mean returning to the street hourly, perhaps in even less time. Binges commonly are reported to last two to three days. For at least two reasons, then, prostitutes may be inclined to forgo prostitution for cash and instead engage in direct exchanges of sex for cocaine. First, by bartering directly for cocaine, the intense and overriding desire to repeat its rush can be satisfied more quickly than by first getting money and then copping the drug. If, indeed, rock smoking produces the shortest cycle between the rush and the craving to repeat it, then rock smokers may be the most likely to trade sex for the drug.

The second reason cocaine use may encourage sex-for-drug trades is found in the hazards of street-level prostitution. The quickly recurring need to return to the street to earn the money needed to sustain a cocaine binge (hundreds of dollars as compared to the twenty to seventy dollars needed to sustain a heroin habit for a day) increases the woman's exposure to arrest and threats from customers unknown to her. During Chicago's winter, the physical discomforts of hustling on the street also are considerable. By trading sex for the drug, she minimizes the likelihood of arrest, avoids the discomforts of harsh weather, and, if she knows the person offering the cocaine, eliminates the dangers and hassles of dealing with a customer who is a stranger. Further, if she does her bartering in a smoke house where she knows people, she may feel somewhat safer than selling sex in a stranger's car.

Thus, the major trends in cocaine-era prostitution appear to be a more monomaniacal fixation on procuring the drug of choice, an increase in the trading of sex for drugs, perhaps an increase in sexual activity in return for drugs or money for drugs, and a greater desperation that is reflected at the least in decreased prices for sex. These trends, while pronounced in those who inject cocaine, appear even more extreme in rock smokers.

These prostitution patterns, according to most of those with whom we talked, result in the degradation of the women caught up in them. Of particular note, the practice of trading sex for drugs appears to render women less able to control the transaction and is symbolically demeaning. In this situation, the woman is put in the position of being given a gift (cocaine) rather than of earning her money. She is denied the ability to claim engagement in an occupation (prostitution) that is loosely governed by norms that can be called upon to gain control of sex transactions. For example, most tricks are reported to understand that the prostitute expects to be paid up front, that she has the right to deny them certain acts (e.g., kissing, anal sex), and that prices vary with the acts performed. To illustrate both the level of degradation commonly reported to us and its relation to sex-for-cocaine exchanges, we offer one more instance. The speaker, a male in his forties, is describing a recent visit to a West Side smoke house that also serves as a shooting gallery (generally an organized setting that, for a price, offers IDUs the privacy and, perhaps, paraphernalia to inject drugs):

> I was up in Jay's place, I went up there to take off [inject], and I saw this woman I went to high school with. I was surprised to see her, man, because she always was a real straight person. In high school, man, she wouldn't even go out with you if she knew you be smoking marijuana. No way, wouldn't have nothing to do with you. So I was shocked to see her up there. My family knows her family, and I be knowing her for years. Anyway, man, she was down in front of this guy sucking on him. Didn't even seem to care other people were around. And dig, he was one of these guys with a mean streak in him. So he tells her, "If you want some of this [rock cocaine], I want you to bark like a dog." And, man, she started barking like the moon was out. It broke my heart to see that.

## Cocaine Use and Risks for HIV Disease

The intense, overriding urge to repeat the use of cocaine clearly leads to unsafe sex. Although some of the women who spoke to us insisted they would not sell or trade sex under any circumstances where the customer refused to wear a condom, most reports suggested the opposite. In their candid moments, prostitutes often admit lapses in condom use when trying to acquire more cocaine and encountering a customer unwilling to use a condom.

Trades of sex for cocaine, as opposed to sex exchanged for money, are reported to be more likely to lead to sex acts beyond the provider's normal repertoire and to unsafe sex. Carol, who allowed her house to be used by prostitutes, told us,

> Because as soon as you do a shot of cocaine, you want another one. You want it and it happens to be there and if there's no rubbers, no nothing—and I've seen them in my own bed—[they say to themselves], "Fuck it, I ain't got a rubber. At least I got a shot and it's right there, and I don't have to go out in the streets."

The greater risk of sexual transmission of HIV when trading sex probably has to do with the greater likelihood that these trades are consummated where cocaine is being used. When such a trade is struck, users are at the height of their desire to repeat the drug's rush and more willing to accommodate a partner's demands. It also seems plausible that men view as weakness any craving for cocaine sufficient to trigger trades for sex and see these trades as symbolically degrading to women. In turn, this definition of the situation may permit men to demand sexual acts they otherwise would forgo.

An emerging concern is the convergence of shooting galleries and smoke houses. In our most recently completed round of follow-up interviews ($N = 678$) with the project's original panel of IDUs (finished in April 1991), 25 percent of those whose last injection took place at a shooting gallery also identified the place as a smoke house. This overlap concerns us because smoke houses are reported to be sites of much sexual activity, sex is a mode of transmitting HIV, and Chicago IDUs have a moderately high rate of HIV infection. Based on blood testing done by our project, we estimate that approximately 30 percent of Chicago's IDUs are infected with HIV (Ouellet et al. 1991). Given the fewer HIV risk factors and generally younger age of rock smokers, we believe their rate of HIV infection to be much lower than that of IDUs. Thus, smoke houses constitute a likely setting for the sexual transmission of HIV into a population whose risk otherwise is comparatively low. This is particularly distressing when one considers the many females of childbearing age who smoke rock cocaine and are prone to using a smoke house for that purpose. Consider the following exchange between Ouellet and a 22-year-old male rock smoker:

> *Ouellet:* Have you ever been in a smoke house and seen someone shooting drugs there?
> *R:* Ya, I saw that not long ago. There was a guy shooting up.
> *Ouellet:* Do you know if he had sex while he was there?
> *R:* Ya. He had sex with one of the skeezers.

## AIDS Prevention

Until recently, our efforts at addressing HIV disease in Chicago were directed at IDUs and their sex partners. When this study began and we directed more of our attention to rock smokers, we found them to be far less aware and concerned about AIDS than were the IDUs. IDUs describe our program as having a considerable impact on the consciousness and drug-using practices of those with whom they shoot drugs. The awareness of AIDS exhibited by rock smokers is reminiscent of what we found among the majority of IDUs at the project's inception—a sort of secondhand relationship to the disease. That is, non-IDU rock smokers know about HIV disease and may even know people that are infected by HIV, yet the threat of infection does not seem to be taken seriously. A young rock smoker recently told us: "People, my friends, they listen to stuff on TV about AIDS, but, really, they don't think it can happen to them. . . . Behind them smoking rocks, they don't see that they have to worry about it."

We suggest that the same fundamental strategies employed by our project would go a long way toward changing the high-risk behaviors of rock users. Briefly, we suggest using ethnographic and epidemiologic methods to target high-risk neighborhoods and then employing indigenous outreach workers to teach and encourage behavioral changes. Rock smokers and those who have promiscuous sex within these social networks should be taught to assess their own level of risk and then be offered a range of alternatives to high-risk behaviors. In our own experience, people are the most willing to initiate condom use in the very sort of situations that have been described in smoke houses: random sex with casual partners. Attempts at risk reduction by rock smokers should be reinforced and further reduction encouraged. Indigenous advocates for risk reduction should be developed and encouraged. Smoke houses could be stocked with condoms, and both proprietors and patrons could be educated about the health risks inherent in smoke house activities. In addition, drug treatment programs better suited to cocaine abuse need to be implemented.

Finally, nearly all the rock cocaine smokers we spoke with said that ready rock is different from crack in ways that make it (rock) less harmful, either physically, psychologically, or spiritually. This belief suggests that public health messages aimed at crack smokers are reaching Chicago's rock smokers but then are being dismissed as inapplicable to their own drug use. As an alternative, campaigns and programs that target users of cooked cocaine should take care to localize their language and also focus more precisely on the form itself.

We conclude with a caveat. In making comparisons between past and present exchanges of sex for drugs and sex for money, the predominance among drug users of cocaine or heroin is not the only variable. For example, during the 1980s, as huge amounts of cocaine moved from other parts of the world into Chicago's inner-city neighborhoods, the reverse was happening with jobs that were open to relatively uneducated people and that paid enough money for self-support and perhaps support of a family. An assessment of street-level prostitution or any other means of earning an income in these neighborhoods is incomplete if it does not examine broad economic patterns. In a similar vein, inner-city neighborhoods undergoing gentrification are very disruptive of the lives of its lower-class residents and may affect their legal and illegal work patterns, drug use, mental health, and so on. In sum, this chapter suggests that the dominance of cocaine in lower-class Chicago neighborhoods may have an impact on the commercial sex transactions that take place in these areas, but we do not claim to have told the whole story of such transactions.

# Notes

1. For a more complete description of our sampling strategy see Wiebel (1990). Watters and Biernacki (1989) also describe a sampling scheme that, with minor differences, is very much like what we used.
2. The fact that IDUs were our original contacts for locating cocaine smokers probably acted to increase the proportion of smokers who had injected drugs.
3. Subjects were asked for their age when they first used cocaine and when they first used it three or more times a week for more than a month. While most subjects indicated a very quick progression from initiation to chronic use, our indicator does not allow for a precise measurement. For example, if a subject began use at 15 years old and chronic use at 16 years old, the elapsed time between these points could range from a matter of hours to almost two years. In such a case we use the conservative figure of "under two years." However, most subjects with a one-year difference in age between initiation and chronic use suggested that the elapsed time was closer to a year or less.
4. For a comparison to Chicago's shooting galleries see Ouellet et al. (1991).

# References

Blau, Robert, 1990. "Going Inside a Crack Smokehouse: It's a $2 Tour." *Chicago Tribune*, February 25, 2:1.

Burroughs, William S. 1959. *Naked Lunch*. New York: Grove Weidenfeld.

Cooper, William. 1989. "The Emperor's New Blows." *New City*, August 3, p. 7.

Courtwright, David, Joseph Herman, and Don DesJarlais. 1989. *Addicts Who Survived: An Oral History of Narcotic Use in America*. Knoxville: University of Tennessee Press.

Fiddle, Seymour. 1967. *Portraits from a Shooting Gallery*. New York: Harper & Row.

Goldstein, Paul J. 1979. *Prostitution and Drugs*. New York: Lexington Books.

Hall, Suzanne. 1973. *Ladies of the Night*. New York: Triden Press.

Hughes, Patrick H. 1977. *Behind the Wall of Respect: Community Experiments in Heroin Addiction Control*. Chicago: University of Chicago Press.

Johnson, Bruce D., Paul J. Goldstein, Edward Prebble, et al. 1985. *Taking Care of Business*. New York: Lexington Books.

Ouellet, Lawrence J., Antonio D. Jimenez, Wendell A. Johnson, and W. Wayne Wiebel. 1991. "Shooting Galleries and HIV Disease: Variations in Places for Injecting Illicit Drugs." *Crime and Delinquency* 37:64–85.

Ouellet, Lawrence J., Antonio D. Jimenez, Wendell A. Johnson, Patricia Murphy, Charlene Pyskoty, and W. Wayne Wiebel. 1991. "Shooting Drugs in Chicago: Settings and Their HIV Risks. Poster presented at the Seventh International Conference on AIDS, Florence, Italy, June 16–21.

Reckless, Walter. 1969 (1933). *Vice in Chicago*. Montclair, N.J.: Patterson-Smith.

Rosenbaum, Marsha. 1981. *Women on Heroin*. New Brunswick, N.J.: Rutgers University Press.

Wiebel, W. Wayne. 1988. "Combining Ethnographic and Epidemiologic Methods in Targeted AIDS Interventions: the Chicago Model." *Needle Sharing Among Intravenous Drug Abusers: National and International Perspectives*, pp. 137–150. Research Monograph 80. Edited by R. J. Battjes and R. W. Pickens. Rockville, Md.: National Institute on Drug Abuse.

————. 1990. "Identifying and Gaining Access to Hidden Populations." *Collection and Interpretation of Data on Hidden Populations*. Research Monograph 98. Edited by E. Y. Lambert and W. W. Wiebel. Rockville, Md.: National Institute on Drug Abuse.

# 4

# Exorcising Sex-for-Crack: An Ethnographic Perspective from Harlem

*Philippe Bourgois*
*Eloise Dunlap*

C rack cocaine burst onto the streets of New York City in late 1985 and subsequently swept through much of America's inner cities, causing a toll of social disruption that attracted remarkable media, political, and social science attention (cf. two special issues on crack of *Contemporary Drug Problems*, Winter 1989 and Spring 1990; *Editor & Publisher* 1989; Johnson et al. 1989). In the short run, the only way to obtain accurate and urgently needed information on the dynamics of a new, illegal phenomenon such as sex-for-crack is through intensive, participant-observation ethnographic fieldwork among crack addicts on the streets and in their homes. Living and immersing oneself in the world of crack is a frightening and personally draining experience. Ethnographic techniques oblige the researcher to confront in person a great deal of suffering individuals. Participant-observation methodology, therefore, risks distorting a researcher's analytic process when it is undertaken in the polarized social settings that contextualize crack use in Harlem because of the intensity of the human pain encountered (Bourgois 1992a).

In our day-to-day interaction and documentation of the most intimate facets of the lives of crack users and crack sellers, we have witnessed extreme examples of violence, personal self-destruction, and victimization. To the street ethnographer, the effects of crack appear overwhelming. Ironically, the media's sensationalist portrayals of sex and violence in the crack scene often seem tame in comparison to what we witnessed (Massing 1989; *New York Times* 1989a, 1989b; *Newsweek* 1988, 1991; *U.S. News and World Report* 1991).

---

Dr. Joyce Wallace and the Foundation for Research on Sexually Transmitted Diseases did the HIV and syphilis blood testing reported in this chapter.

The worst-case perspective that researchers often adopt when they live immersed in the crack reality needs to be contextualized and balanced with a historical perspective (Morgan 1981; Reinarman and Levine 1989). Every new drug that has entered U.S. society during periods of economic and social strain has invariably been portrayed as the "worst ever." The dramatic new waves of substance abuse that periodically plague America are always presented by politicians, the press, and the affected communities as harbingers of imminent social breakdown. In fact, however, an "even worse" drug inevitably surfaces in the future. Today, for example, we bemoan the "good old days of heroin," while simultaneously developing amnesia about the initial horror that angel dust inspired at the height of its epidemic in the 1970s (Feldman, Agar, and Beschner 1979; Musto 1987).

The demonization of crack in both the media and popular consciousness on inner-city streets obfuscates the political economic context and history that defines substance abuse and victimization in urban America. Consequently, to analyze the sex-for-crack phenomenon adequately, we have had to repress the painful—and often righteous—emotions that arose during our fieldwork, such as when we witnessed child abuse or a pregnant addict smoking a crack pipe. In order to keep from being consumed by an ahistorical, Pollyannaish despair or anger, we have attempted to contextualize our experiences of human horror and cruelty. It is only when we step back from the tortured reality of addiction in the street that we can begin to appreciate the fact that the pharmacological properties of crack are largely irrelevant to the devastation it has wreaked on so many inner-city communities. Crack is merely the latest medium through which the already desperate are expressing publicly their suffering and hopelessness.

The 1980s and early 1990s saw a dramatic polarization in the concentration of wealth and poverty in the United States (*New York Times* 1992; Phillips 1990.) This immiseration was exacerbated by reductions in public sector commitments to social programs. The virulence of crack in the inner city is an expression of these large-scale political and economic transformations.

This chapter, therefore, although focused on the details of social relations around crack use, proceeds from the assumption that all drug use patterns may be understood within historical and social-structural contexts. At the same time, a great deal can be learned about larger social-structural contradictions from a close examination of inner-city substance abuse, because the complex processes of social marginalization are magnified in the drug world. Similarly, precisely because crack prostitution is an exaggerated caricature of hostile male-female interaction, a close examination of its logistics offers a window into gender relations in the larger society and culture.

## Research Methodology

We worked as a two-person team in Harlem, selecting respondents from streets saturated by crack use and sales and where prostitutes congregate. One fieldworker (Dunlap) concentrated on central Harlem, which is primarily African-American. The other (Bourgois) worked primarily among street-level networks of Puerto Rican crack dealers in East Harlem (Bourgois 1989, forthcoming). Dunlap is an African-American female engaged in a long-term ethnographic study of crack dealing, focusing on how black families survive in the context of extreme poverty (Dunlap 1991, 1992a, 1992b). Bourgois is a white male who lived with his wife and son for five years in the neighborhood where he undertook full-time participant-observation field research.

We purposefully worked as a team in order to explore the different types of responses accessible to us through our distinct races, genders, ages, class backgrounds, personal attitudes, and theoretical orientations. Dunlap was able in a very short time to establish extremely trusting and intimate individual relationships with African-American women and men. She was also able to accompany prostitutes on their "missions" (crack binges). She was invited into their homes and attended family gatherings. In many cases she became a confidante. Several women wept on her shoulder. At times she became as much a street psychotherapist to the crack addicts as she was an ethnographer to the study. This enabled her to elicit the subtleties, inconsistencies, and deeper meanings of the actions, behaviors, and attitudes of her respondents. An excerpt from her fieldwork notes reveals the intensity of her research encounters:

> Sharon runs a crack house. It is apparent that she gets some customers from this business, but when first talking of this she cries. She feels very guilty, and I try to comfort her and make her feel better. I may have done a good job because before she leaves she hugs me and tells me that it was good to talk to someone who understands.
>
> Sharon smokes crack every day; her apartment is a crack house—people come there to smoke crack. They get her high and pay to come in. She charges two dollars to come in; she tricks when she does not have money to get crack.
>
> It is hard for her to talk about her crack house prostitution business. She cries while talking to me and blames herself for being hooked on crack. . . . She talks of never having feelings of remorse (meanwhile she is crying) and that she does not cry over it. Sharon talks of rebuking a friend who tried to kill herself once for crying. She feels that when you cry you have to stop or try to stop. "Why cry when you are going to do it tomorrow?" She asks this while crying all along.

Dunlap also had the ability to merge into the midst of the crack-using streetwalkers. This allowed her to document the dynamics of street prostitution, which differ substantially from the statistical portrait gleaned from our interview questionnaires. For example:

> Eventually a man comes up and Rose tells him that I am her stepmother and starts talking to him about "licking" her "pussy": "You know you like to lick my pussy, what you want to do today? I want you to take me to a hotel."
>
> The man looks as if he is stoned out of his mind—he is acting slow and his eyes are wide open. He finally says to her that he likes me and would like to "eat" both our "pussy" and we can "freak" for him.
>
> Rose slaps him and kicks him in the legs and begins to curse him out. She calls him many names—"motherfucker, cocksucker, son of a bitch"— she tells him, "Don't talk like that to my mother, didn't I tell you who she was."
>
> He is saying, "I'm sorry, baby, excuse me." He is not fighting back but moving back and forth out of her path of kicks.
>
> I tell Rose to be cool, that, "It's OK." I pull her back over to the car where we are sitting and say, "I want another beer. Please! Walk with me to the store." Rose is hot tempered, and I don't see how she has lasted this long in her life. The man walks across the street and she calls out to him that she will see him later, meaning she'll take care of him later, and we walk back up the street toward the store.

Although Bourgois also interviewed dozens of female crack prostitutes, he spent most of his time with male crack dealers and addicts, collecting data on the male perspective toward the sex-for-crack phenomenon. He was able to collect accounts of rape and abuse from the perspective of the perpetrators. Given the extreme polarization of ethnic and class relations in the inner city, his outsider status as a white introduced tensions in his research. Bourgois was cut off from important dynamics in the community and excluded from some personal relationships. At the same time, this outsider status worked in his favor in many instances by providing access to dimensions of community and personal interaction off-limits to an insider. It also played a central role in physically dangerous moments when he was confronted with violence on the streets late at night. On one occasion, his Puerto Rican companion was beaten up by two muggers, but the assailants refrained from attacking Bourgois, fearing he might be an undercover police officer. Although the personal relationships Bourgois formed were overwhelmingly positive, he was acutely conscious of how his own ethnic and class markers might be a factor in altering social interaction around him and in influencing his data collection.

A note of caution on the representativeness of our sample of crack-using women is necessary. Most of the more than forty women who answered our questions and agreed to participate in the extended, tape-recorded, life-history interviews were self-identified streetwalking prostitutes. Professional prostitutes who insist on a cash payment for their services therefore are overrepresented in our sample of participants in the sex-for-crack scene. Nevertheless, through our extended participant-observation research in the community, we were also able to access the men and women who represent the hidden iceberg of the sex-for-crack phenomenon.

The craving for crack has created cohorts of closet prostitutes, part-time prostitutes, acquaintance prostitutes, female gigolos, and out-of-control, manic-depressive bingers. These freelance providers of sexual services define the sex-for-crack scene as much as do the professional prostitutes. This mass of desperately addicted women has allowed the crack street scene to become infused with greater levels of violence and cruelty.

## The Neighborhood

East Harlem, also referred to as *El Barrio* or Spanish Harlem, is a 200-square-block neighborhood on the Upper East Side of Manhattan in New York City. Although the population is between 40 and 45 percent African-American, it is considered by both its residents and outsiders to be New York's quintessential Puerto Rican community. In this community, most of the individuals with whom we interacted were second- or third-generation New York–born Puerto Ricans.

According to the 1980 census data, 29 percent of the population of East Harlem exist at 75 percent of the poverty level, 48 percent endure at 125 percent of the poverty level, and 68 percent of the population survive at 200 percent. In other words, if one were to adjust for the exorbitant cost of living in New York City, well over half of the population of East Harlem would fall into the ranks of the working poor. One in three families in East Harlem is dependent on public assistance, and approximately half of all households are headed by women. The schools in the neighborhood are reputed to have the highest dropout rate in the country (New York Department of City Planning 1984). The neighborhood is visibly poor. Abandoned buildings, vacant lots, and rubbish-strewn streets are the rule rather than the exception. When Bourgois resided in East Harlem, he could get heroin, crack, powder cocaine, hypodermic needles, methadone, valium, PCP, and mescaline within a two-block radius of his apartment (Bourgois 1992b).

Despite this active street scene and the visible social and economic crisis it reflects, the majority of the adult population of East Harlem abhors drugs. Most heads of households work nine-to-five plus overtime at entry-level jobs and shun illegal activity. Unfortunately, this majority, mainstream working-class and working-poor sector is in retreat. Many residents, especially the elderly, live in terror; they venture outside only during daylight hours, and they bemoan the deteriorated quality of life in the neighborhood (Bourgois 1991).

Central Harlem's statistics are virtually the same as those for East Harlem (New York Department of City Planning 1984). Perhaps the best way of conveying the personal experience of the larger forces impinging on the neighborhood is the following quotation from Dunlap's field notes in which she describes one of the streets where she conducted interviews:

> This area is close to a ghost town, with abandoned buildings and crack users living in and around the area. The people in the area look like life has been very hard; they sit on stoops and broken chairs. The building in which I conducted the interviews was situated on a block in which all the buildings were abandoned; it is the only building on this block in which people are living. The area is dilapidated and a crack haven. Many of the prostitutes in this group come from this area. The apartment in which the interviews were conducted was a typical apartment in that it was in need of repair.

## The Logistics of Crack Use and Prostitution

Since 1985 there has been an explosion of new prostitutes onto the streets of Harlem. This flooded market is reflected concretely in lowered prices for sexual services. Intercourse and fellatio now cost as little as three dollars, the price for a small vial of crack in the neighborhood. On one occasion a high school girl grabbed Bourgois by the arms in a housing project stairwell sobbing hysterically and begging him, "Please! Please! Let me suck you off for two dollars—I'll swallow it. Please! Please! I promise!" The intense craving and binge behavior often associated with crack use has dramatically increased the number of vulnerable prostitutes, allowing for greater violence, degradation, victimization, and personal suffering.

Most crack use follows a pattern of binges. Unlike the "righteous dope fiend" (heroin addict) who maintains self-respect so long as he or she injects the required amount of the drug to stay "healthy" (Biernacki 1979; Finestone 1957; Sutter 1966), the "thirsty crackhead" typically goes on massive nonstop binges that can last up to seventy-two hours. In contrast to heroin addicts, crack addicts never ingest "enough" of their drug. They always crave more, never "nod out," and rarely die of overdoses. On the contrary, crack is an intense stimulant, which keeps its users wide awake and on the move, searching for more. A crack smoker constantly seeks to replicate the euphoric ecstacy that is achieved for only a few minutes after each inhalation. The intensely compulsive craving that accompanies the binging behavior of crack addiction therefore allows for extreme degradation.

Novice crack smokers are often unable to pace their use, and they can fall apart rapidly, losing dozens of pounds of weight in a matter of weeks and/or spiraling into nervous breakdowns. This is especially true for women exchanging sex for crack who have access to relatively large supplies of the drug and often lose control of their life-sustaining activities:

In the beginning of Rose's crack days she turned her apartment into a crack house and tricked. This enabled her to get a great deal of crack and stay high most of the time. The longest she has been high was three days, after which she began to "bug out." She began to accuse people of things; it was her son, who was 17 years old at the time, who informed her that she was "out of it." (Dunlap field notes)

None of the women on the street could estimate accurately how much crack they had actually consumed each day. Virtually all of them said they smoked every day and "as much as possible." Indeed from our participant-observation fieldwork, which entailed spending entire days and nights on the streets while accompanying prostitutes who were constantly getting high, we saw that it would be impossible for anyone to keep track of how much they smoked and how many customers they had when they were on a binge.

There are several different patterns to smoking behavior. Often crack vials are shared. In a typical crack house or crack smoking scene, people beg hits from one another and take turns sharing what they are smoking. At the same time, many people run off on their own to avoid sharing. Generally the longer-term smokers tend to become more isolated and behave in a more paranoid and erratic manner. Novice or occasional users often share their crack generously. In fact, most people are introduced to crack through this sharing process, which frequently follows a gender dynamic. The pattern is for women to be initiated into crack by their boyfriends, relatives, close friends or neighbors. Sometimes there is a sexual dimension to the initial crack experience. It is frequently offered to women by men attempting a seductive ploy.

In New York City, the crack pipe is called the "stem." Users are not full-fledged crack addicts until they own a stem. Smokers often have a very intense personal relationship with their stem. There is even a pharmacological basis for this intense relationship because resin accumulates along the sides of the stem and in its screen. When a crack smoker runs out of money and crack, he or she can continue getting high by scraping the resin off the side of the stem and reheating the screen. Crack smokers spend hours hunched over their stems obsessively eking out the last residues on which to get high. Often they end up bursting or cracking their stem in their frantic search for a vestigial high.

The term "stemmer" or "being on the stem" refers to being a hard-core "crackhead." Full-blown addicts do not leave home without their crack pipe, and they depreciate one another for having a chipped or broken stem. Many people do not share stems, claiming that it is an AIDS vector. Their stem becomes their best friend.

Some users differentiate themselves from crackheads by asserting that they never smoke out of a stem. Many start using crack in combination with marijuana rolled in a joint known as a "woola." They talk about falling apart only when they started smoking crack directly from a stem. Users describe the woola high as qualitatively different from the stem high. One crack smoker drew an analogy relating stemming to woola smoking the way "mainlining" (injecting into primary arteries) is related to heroin snorting.

Almost half of the women were high school graduates. Most had worked briefly at entry-level service jobs, such as fast food cashiers, home attendants, or file clerks. Several respondents objected to being labeled as prostitutes. They call their sexual activities "getting busy" and refer to their customers as "dates." Some of them see their regular customers more or less as friends, if not as lovers. Others compare themselves to male gigolos:

> Like I said . . . I had special friends, like male men. I don't really be calling it prostituting. Whenever I need some money—or whatever—I call them up, and they give it to me. They might want something and they might don't want nothing. I don't really call it prostituting. I never really stood out there on a corner or nothing like that. I didn't have to. And it is not every day. (Interview with Jessie)

Most of the women we interacted with, however, explicitly consider prostitution to be a job that is a safer and more ethical way of earning money than stealing or drug dealing. On the average, the prostitutes estimated that they have sex five to ten times a day, but observations of their behavior indicated they had sex significantly more frequently. Indeed, this inability on the part of the participants in the sex-for-crack scene to estimate adequately their volume of sexual activity points once again to the necessity for a committed ethnographic approach if accurate data are to be collected. After one particularly successful day of fieldwork, we finally understood in a more realistic manner what a "mission" implies and why the expression "getting busy" is used by the prostitutes:

> Today I met Rose and she said that she was going to show me firsthand what was happening. She always kids me about my being a "big square." [Rose] . . . is nervous and shaking. . . . She [lit up] fifteen minutes ago and thinks it was *ice* instead of crack. [She complains] she is coming down and not really high.
>
> As we are walking, another woman named Joy called out to Rose from across the street. Rose began to curse Joy calling her different kinds of "bitches" because the night before last Joy had thrown a bottle that almost hit Rose. Rose had begun to fight Joy, and the police had broken up the fight. During the fight Rose had lost her wig and eyebrow pencil.
>
> Joy has some money. We walk back to 209th Street and buy a bottle of Thunderbird. We go to the park across the street on the Avenue, and Joy and Rose drink the wine. In the Park there is a dealer; they decide to get some crack together. . . . We meet another one of Rose's friends. She has a customer with her; we try to talk to her, but she tells us that she is

"busy." She is going in the hallway with him to "suck his dick." She tells us she will see us later, that it will not take long because "this nigger ain't goin'a last." When Rose and I come back, Joy has *copped* [bought crack], and they go to smoke in a building. . . .

As we are walking, a man is coming towards us; Rose tells me "watch this." When we get to him, we stop and she starts talking to him. The interaction goes like this:

"Hey, nigger, you want me to suck your dick? You know how good it is, I can lick you all over, put some wine on it 'cause I like to suck it when it is bitter. What you want?"

Man responds: "OK, baby, you want to do that now?"

Rose to me: "Wait for me in the park. I will be right back."

They walk back up to a building near us and I continue down to the park. When I get there, I meet a few of the prostitutes that I have interviewed. I also meet Danielle's mother. She is with her daughter, who is 21 years old. They are both high and picking up tricks.

At this point I am amazed. I am in the middle of a lot of action going on: the dealer selling in the park; the prostitutes picking up tricks; and people getting high smoking crack and drinking Thunderbird wine. It seems that everyone is busy. To look at them, though, it would appear that they are just ordinary people sitting in the park, standing around, and sitting on cars and stoops on a nice day. The mother [Lilly] asks a man, "What's you got?" He tells her he has "want she want," and they leave together. The daughter goes over to a car that drives up, gets in, and they drive around the corner.

The prostitutes are *busy*. They talk about their tricks; there is so much talk of sexual acts I can't believe it. There is no shame. They talk freely about what they do, but none of them talk of anal sex. This seems to be out of the bounds of their sexual behavior.

As we sit talking, people are passing, and we are talking to many people on and off. No one can stand and talk for long; everyone is doing something. The "something" that they do doesn't take long because they are back and forth all the time. . . .

Wally, Jim, and Ronney go into the stairway to smoke crack, and rose and I go back to the corner and sit on another car. Rose picks up another man, and they talk—she will "fuck his brains out," she will give him the "best fuck" he ever had; she is "ready"; it will be "better than ever"; "how much money you got?" He says he doesn't have much. She calls him a few "mother-fuckers" and tells him that she knows he has money. She knows he has "25 for a good fuck." They leave. I sit there and I am alone—but not for long because Ronney and Jim return. . . .

Everyone decides to get more crack. They go to get the crack, and I go with them. Rose goes somewhere else. We come back to the block. I sit on the car on the corner while they go to smoke. As I am sitting there Rose returns. She is very loud now and is getting more out of control. By this I mean that she is cursing and not talking sensibly. When Wally, Ronney, and Jim return, she curses them about everything. She is just difficult to get along with. (Dunlap field notes)

## Customers

Bourgois' fieldwork notes from East Harlem convey the same activities described in Dunlap's field notes except that they are from the perspective of the customers rather than the prostitute:

7/89: Wiwi points out closet crack prostitutes to me as they walk by the crack house he is working security for. He shouts out so they can hear, "There goes my mouth [pronounced 'mouf']." He points to one who still owes him a blow job, explaining to me that he gives crack on credit to desperate women.

6/89: Papo was up at Lester's [a sex-for-crack house] a month ago. He says there was this "gorgeous girl" who had just starting smoking and looked great. He claims she was 18. He had sex with her for $5. He says he could not believe how beautiful she was and that she just wanted to "get next to" him. He was not worried about AIDS because she "looked good" and had "just started smoking." He says that now she is a *Cambodian* [i.e., emaciated and hideous] and that he would not touch her ever again.

9/89: Hanging out with three Mexican men on a stoop. Two Puerto Rican women come by and ask for someone in the building. Then they take two of the Mexicans into the building and ask them if they want blow jobs for $3.

2/90: At a bodega [local grocery store] with a Dominican owner a Puerto Rican man is offering the store owner a blow job from a woman who is standing there dejectedly in the entrance. She is black and in cocaine psychosis. The guy says she can do it in the back of the store. She will do whatever he wants. The owner says no way, he is married and does not want to bring some disease back to his wife and kids. This all happened in front of customers going in and out. The guy advertising the woman wanted us to overhear so that maybe we would take the girl.

10/90: Julio brings up the story of the *skeezer* [crack whore] he and Carlos ripped off for a two-for-one five-dollar blowjob two months ago. He brags to me about how pathetic the girl sounded as she screamed after them while they ran off, threatening to tell their boss, Big Petee, on them. This was in the project stairwell. She is now a *Cambodian* but used to be very beautiful. I later found out that Big Petee, their crack dealer boss, paid the woman for fear that she might *drop a dime* (call the police) on his crack sales outfit if he did not pay her for her "rape" by his employees.

10/90: Pedro and Carlos run off with a woman who comes in the crack house to get a "low-budget blow job"—two for the price of one—in the project stairwell across the street. Afterwards, Carlos says the discounted blow job was "good for the deficit." They all laugh.

Although African-American and Puerto Rican men constitute the bulk of the customers of the Harlem-based prostitutes, the women made sharp ethnic distinctions around the ethnicity of their clients, especially their white customers. These categories inevitably translated into dollars and cents:

In talking of her customers Jennifer feels that the white customers are stupid because they ask her what she wants to do. They generally take her to a cheap hotel and give excuses of why they are picking up a prostitute. Generally, they claim they are having problems with their wives. Jennifer dislikes this because [she says] she doesn't care what types of problems they are having because she is having problems, too, and that is why she prostitutes. She charges them more and feels that she has to because they are dummies. She charges the whites $150 for straight sex and for oral sex, too.

Most want oral sex. She relates that the white customers are generally satisfied with what they get, but the black customer wants everything and does not want to pay for it. If she attempts to charge the black male as much as she does the white male he tells her "bitch, I'm not going to pay that much," so she compromises. The black males want "everything, even in the ass," but she won't do that. (Dunlap field notes)

The prostitutes also constructed important distinctions around the age and sexual desires of their customers. Some of the most enterprising prostitutes develop specialized niches of expertise at hustling certain types of men who are willing to pay more and yet require fewer sexual services. Other women develop more casual relationships with elderly men, preying on them strategically in order to minimize the sexual interaction:

I always get them elderly men. You know, them elderly men? You know them elderly lonely men and shit that don't mind giving up the money. And you give them a story and some of them they give it to you. Really all they want to do is just have a nice time, just fuck. You know, drink, go to a hotel, drink and talk and then you just fuck and they give you money. . . . You will give them a sob story and then you get more. That is how I have been getting mine.

They want . . . they just want to fuck, most of them, and some of them just want to sit there. Most of the time I don't even have to go to bed. I just keep them company and stuff. Especially if I get them high, I don't have to do nothing. Just get them high. Yep, and they just sit there; we talk, and then they can't do nothing. . . .

What do you expect for them to do? They old. They can't do nothing. That is why I like older men because they can't do nothing. [Interview with Soso]

A pattern beginning to emerge is that of prostitutes in their late twenties and thirties who focus their attention on lonely men over 50. There is a cohort of aging men in the inner city who find themselves living alone as a consequence of the street-oriented life-styles of their youth. Upon reaching late middle age, they begin to desire stable, household companionship. Many of these men, ironically, were successful on the street's underground economy in their youth. Others pursued legal jobs but never rooted themselves in a household. When they retire from their jobs (e.g., postal service, transit authority), they have modestly secure incomes for their old age, but they are alone. This growing cohort of single, lonely, aging men serves as a point of stability for many of the crack prostitutes. The men provide the younger women with an apartment in which they can store their clothes, eat, bathe, and otherwise recover from missions. Sometimes, they even contribute small sums of money to the prostitutes' crack use. In return, the women keep the apartment clean, provide sexual services, and, most important, act as a companion or girlfriend. Many of these aging men are rarely sexually active. They are so desperate for the companionship of a woman in a household setting that they are willing to tolerate their girlfriend's crack binges. Indeed, the power differentials are often ambiguous in these cross-generational and cross-gender relationships. Sometimes the older man violently opposes his girlfriend's substance abuse and beats her regularly. In other cases the men are treated by the prostitutes as vulnerable victims to be preyed upon ruthlessly.

## Crack Houses as Social Institutions

The social settings for substance abuse span just as wide a range of social contexts as do the prostitute/client relationships. Some crack houses are organized like bars with a cover charge. They have tables, torches (lighters), and pipes for rent. These were disappearing in Harlem, however, due to police enforcement. Others—perhaps most—are merely abandoned buildings or housing project stairwells and roofs.

Many of the women specifically associate the term "crack house" with the type of place where sex occurs. Almost all talked negatively about these kinds of locales:

> Basically, the majority of them don't have lights. They do, but they don't have most of the appliances; they've been sold. They don't have a phone. They don't have no TV; they sold them. And it's messed up. It depends, if it's a base house—base houses are just for basing, you know. The room got a bed in it, just in case a person want to do what they gonna do.
>
> But there are other people who base, who got their house and smoke, and they got a decent house and everything. Just like a regular person, they take care. And they use that, as far as letting people come in when they want a hit or whatever. [Interview with Cora]

> It is the kind of place where there's room for having sex. It cost five dollars a half-hour. You bring your own crack and the person who owns it is called "house master." You can go get crack and smoke it there or you can send him out to get it for you. You give him a bottle.
>
> My friend Ron has a place like that, and he does it all on the sneak tip

when his mother is working. When she home, he don't let nobody in. [Interview with Gloria]

The women tended to differentiate between crack houses that cater primarily to addicts who wanted to smoke versus those that specialize in providing sexual services to nonaddicts. Nevertheless, even the most broken-down, addict-oriented crack houses also sport side rooms or couches for sexual activity.

Bourgois regularly visited one pool hall crack house in an abandoned building that was primarily a sales point. On a typical weekday evening, it could have been mistaken for a day care center. On one occasion there were three teenage mothers standing in the crack house next to their strollers carrying newborn babies. No one seemed to think it unusual that these young girls and their newborns should be "relaxing" at the crack house. Significantly, these girls were not (yet) crack users. They merely wanted an exciting place for socializing and "conversating" that was air-conditioned in the summer and heated during the winter (Bourgois 1991).

For the younger generations growing up on the street in Harlem, the crack house has emerged as one of the only energetic and attractive social centers in the neighborhood. A large proportion of the generation coming of age in the late 1980s and early 1990s is at risk of accepting the use of crack by their peers as a routine part of life.

## Intergenerational Drug Use

Socialization into crack use is not solely through the institutional settings provided by the neighborhood. Most women were introduced to alcohol and drugs through their families long before crack existed (Dunlap 1991). Many of our life-history tape recordings sound like skipping records. They repeat over and over the same sad tales of the intergenerational transmission of substance abuse in families. Often they begin with the premature death of one or more parents, with abusive stepparents, or with one or both of the parents abusing alcohol or heroin. Virtually all the stories document repressive relationships with state-run institutions (mental, juvenile detention, detox) or at the very least demonstrate unsatisfactory relationships with public educational institutions. Most of the respondents also endured negative experiences with entry-level jobs, survived economic deprivation in their earliest childhood, and suffered lack of love and respect through most of their lives.

Perhaps the best way to portray what many of these prostitutes lived through as children is the following field note from a visit to the home of one of the older prostitutes Dunlap befriended. The pathologies of substance abuse and alcoholism occur side by side with the partially successful attempts to provide the essentials of a clean, nurturing household. Ultimately, however, the children are taught that adulthood and love involves substance abuse.

> I am in Bessie's apartment, which is in New Jersey. Bessie is a nice-looking woman who has kept herself up very well. She is a person who is afraid to think about the consequences of her actions. She talks of this at the end of the interview. I have come here with another prostitute (Glo) who is a friend of Bessie's. The apartments are arranged in a semicircle. They are small, attached, two-story family units. Many of her children are home, along with other children of family and friends. They are in and out of the apartment.
>
> The door is open; the sun is shining; and young males sit around on cars outside the apartment. One of these is her son. All the children are dressed well. They seem to be well kept. Adults and children are in and out of the apartment. Bessie's ex-husband came by. He is a crack dealer. He talks of having sold $900 worth of crack that day. He has AIDS. The adults are drinking wine and using drugs while the children are in and out of the house. It is as if everyone is having a party. There is an air of festivity but without any food—just drugs and liquor.
>
> The adults and the children are interacting on various levels. When the adults want to hear "their" music, the children have to change the tape. Consequently, the children are playing tapes, dancing, and running in and out of the apartment.
>
> One little girl, about 10 or 11, mixed the wine and beer for an adult. The attitude of the adults was one in which it was acceptable for her to mix and serve the drinks, but she was not allowed to drink any.
>
> In this little girl, I saw many of the prostitutes I have talked with who began to take their parents' liquor and drink it secretly. There is also an adolescent female about 15 years old who is pouring herself a drink every now and then. Bessie related that this is her son's girlfriend, and that she "works" him by "running behind him all the time."
>
> "Friends" are coming in and out, and everything is happening fast to me. There is so much going on that the interview is interrupted in various ways. I have to stop the tape recorder several times while Bessie's brother gives her a hit on this crack stem.

Although substance abuse is clearly a family affair in this household, it would be inaccurate to limit our understanding of the crisis of the inner-city family to its internal dynamics. The family is not held together solely by values or cultures; it is an institution that responds to political and economic constraints, as well as to a history of gender-based inequality (Baca Zinn 1989; see also special issue of *Signs* 1989). For example, many—if not all—of the families of the crack prostitutes had undergone extraordinary hardship ranging from migration, job loss, or housing loss, to the premature death of one or both parents.

# Pregnancy

Trauma often starts in the womb (Haller 1991; Dunlap 1992). Several of the prostitutes were born addicted to heroin. The future promises an even larger cohort of survivors of neonatal substance abuse. For example, without making any effort to find pregnant prostitutes, six of our sample of forty were pregnant. Some of these expecting women were able to capitalize on their pregnant status to increase their consumption of crack. Standing on the corner in midwinter, Lorie, one of the respondents, was opening her coat to display her distended belly as a sexual enticement to potential customers. When we interviewed her, she explained that she was eight months pregnant and that she received benefits from people on the street for being pregnant: food, protection, and free hits of crack. She also noted specifically that some men were sexually excited by her visibly protruding womb:

> Some of the tricks you have a certain relationship with them, they don't want to do nothing but they still come anyway and they give you money.
> Others, like it. I've gotten a few new dates—mostly whites really—because they like pregnant pussy. That's what they say. They say "pregnant pussy the best" for them. That's how they say it: "pregnant pussy." [Interview with Lorie]

On the street, pregnant addicts are usually condemned for smoking crack, but at the same time most people will get high with a pregnant woman if she is treating: "When they real high they start to preaching. But any other time if I'm the one that has crack and I'm giving it to them it is a whole different story. Then afterwards, they say 'I don't know why she does it.' " [Interview with Lorie]

Attitudes on the street toward pregnancy are extremely inconsistent. Few addicts or dealers practice what they preach when it comes to children. For example, Big Pete, the owner of three crack sales points in East Harlem, considers abortion to be murder. He calls it a "capital sin" punishable by God. Nevertheless, he defends his right to sell crack to pregnant women: "If they don't buy it from me, they will get it somewhere else."

Among the mothers, there is a great deal of straightforward denial about the damage crack does to their bodies. Most of the pregnant women, for example, claim they are taking care of themselves and protecting their fetuses:

> When I be smoking it don't make it [the fetus] move around. It moves around just like any other; it will move sometimes and then sometimes it don't. When it's hungry I know it. Anytime I feel any type of hunger I go and eat. I don't just put it off and go take another hit, and then that kills my urge so I don't feed it. Anytime my stomach starts feeling I always go

eat. I grab something to eat, anything, just a little hamburger for a dollar or a dollar fifty, you know something. Get some bananas from the store back there, something. Buy me a can of fruit cocktail, go to the store, something like that, no expensive thing. If I don't make no money, I go to the little Spanish store on the corner right before they close up and I'll get food for him and me [patting her stomach]. They know I'm pregnant. [Interview with Rita]

This same woman knows that there is a good chance her fetus is being damaged. In response to the question, "Who is going to take care of your baby?" she answered, "It depends how bad the baby turns out." This was her second pregnancy as a crack addict.

Another woman who was interviewed in a crack house known for its sexual activity described how two years earlier she gave birth to her son on the same bed that she was sitting on during the interview. Scrawled on the wall in one of the bedrooms of this crack house was the notification, "$5 for each half hour." This woman claimed that her 2-year-old son who was born on the crack house bed was "perfectly normal" and "very smart." He was taken away from her by the court and given to her sister who is also a crack addict but has no legal record.

Virtually all the pregnant women claimed their pregnancies were progressing healthily. One woman explained that she was careful never to smoke when her fetus was sleeping. Others claimed that they were protecting their fetuses by reducing their intake:

Sharon is 32 years old and is homeless. She sits very quietly while she talks. She is dressed relatively clean in jeans and large shirt. She is now pregnant and has two other children—one with the father and one which she signed over to her mother. Her pregnancy now keeps her tired and sleepy. She went to sleep several times while we were talking.

She had her first child when she was 19 years old and in the 11th grade. She had to drop out of school in order to take care of the baby. I must admit it was very painful talking to this woman. She has not been for any prenatal care. She tries to take care of the baby by eating "good," which translates into eating a little more than before and drinking juices and milk. It seems that this attitude is one that permeates most of the crack women who get pregnant.

Sharon relates that the baby sleeps a lot. She refers to the baby as "lazy." When she takes a hit from the crack pipe the baby starts kicking. She says that the baby feels "the same vibes" that she feels when she is smoking. She relates that she smoked with the other babies but no drugs came out in their system. Her oldest child is 17 and the next is two.

Although she is six months pregnant she says she works all day around the clock prostituting and she smokes all day. I think that she has been taking drugs so much and so long that she is not very sure of some of the questions I ask her. On a normal day she smokes about $100 worth of crack.

She was 30 before she first tried crack. She saw her brother smoking crack in her son's bedroom and decided to try it. (Dunlap field notes)

In New York City at the time of this research, only two of twenty-four state-funded treatment centers accepted pregnant crack users (*Newsday* 1990). Social service institutions in the United States are still not offering adequate outreach or treatment to substance-abused fetuses despite the national moral outrage over the tragic toll of crack babies (*New York Times* 1987). In interviews with treatment center administrators, we were told that pregnant women were refused admission because of "insurance complications": they fear possible legal suits should babies be born damaged on their premises.

## Surviving Early Childhood Rape

From a personal perspective as ethnographers, it was depressing to witness the destructive actions and life-styles of our pregnant respondents. Just as painful was listening—for hours at a time—to the early childhood reminiscences of these same child-abusing mothers. Traumatic experiences in early childhood were the norm rather than the exception. Most of the prostitutes experienced psychological and physical abuse at the most vulnerable moments in their lives and often at very tender ages. In many of their families of origin, there was little, if any, compassion for their plight as rape survivors.

The following verbatim testimony from Nadine who was raped for the first time at the age of 11 years and again at the age of 15 portrays poignantly the terror many of these prostitutes endured as young children. As she was talking into the tape recorder, Nadine jumped up and down, pacing the room, unable to sit still. She also repeatedly referred to her behaviors and feelings derisively as if her life were a joke. Notice how she skips from one terror-stricken memory to another as if free-associating on a therapist's couch:

> My mother, you know, she was on the run because my stepfather used to beat her up. And I had to take care of my brothers and sisters. They used to stay hungry all the time. That's why I learned how to cook and stuff like that. . . . I can't stand to see nobody hungry. My mother was . . . on the run and my stepfather used to beat on her, beat on my mother. Bein' by ourself in the house, I didn't know what to do. I just stand on the chair by the stove and took whatever I seen, 'cause my sister hollerin' and cryin' . . . and a man knowed that we was in there and he was hidin'. I don't know how he got in the house, he was hidin', and he raped me. I used to see him all the time. I was scared to tell her . . . 'cause I tried to hide [it from] her. . . . That's when I told, 'cause I couldn't sit down, that's why. I couldn't sit down. And she said, "What's wrong with you?" And that's when she took me to the doctor . . . but after that, you know, I used

to stay out of my mother's way . . . I miss my mother. . . . I got raped after that, her best friend's old man tried to rape me. About 15.

I know it now. I see it why because the way I looked and my mother used to call me a little old lady when she used to sneak out of the house all the time. . . . I had to be in the house by dark. My mother's best friend's old man tried to rape me. It was my brother who helped me. . . . He just walked in the house and everything, and my mother and them were sittin' outside. And I tried to run, you know, he grabbed a knife and tried to stab me with it and my mother and her best friend. . . . I told her, they fell out, 'cause her best friend didn't believe that he did somethin' like that. And my brother was [saying] "that's right". . . . My mother and her best friend fell out and he didn't come 'round no more. . . . I was born down South, my mother didn't want me, she did want me to live . . . down there. . . . I seen my mother get beaten so bad and my mother used to be in the house, it's a shame what. . . . He used to come in drunk and beat on my mother, and I was the oldest, my nerves, that's when [my] nerves got bad then. I couldn't go to sleep [at] night cause I knew that man was gonna come in and jump on my mother. . . . Yes, my mother used to suffer injury from my sister's father who used to beat on my mother and he used to act just like a . . . give her black eyes. [Interview with Nadine]

In a classic punish-the-victim scenario, several of the prostitutes were institutionalized in juvenile delinquent facilities or mental wards following their childhood rape traumas:

I was raped when I was a kid, 7 years old. . . . My father's friend was sleeping. . . . We went down in the basement . . . and I ran upstairs and got my father and he came downstairs and then he got the police and I had to go to the hospital. He went to jail.

I felt nasty. It just hurt really. It just left me with a lot of aches. I went to the psychiatrist and stuff like that. And then I went to [state mental institution] 'cause I got worse; it got bad.

I used to fight all the time. My foster parents . . . they beat me all the time cause I was bad . . . fighting in the school. I was 10 when they put me in the mental institution. I went to Bellevue first, stayed a year, and then went upstate until I was 17. [Interview with Mary Jane]

## Rape in Current Life

Many of these victimized women are reexperiencing their traumatic childhood experiences in their lives as adults. As street prostitutes, they endure violence as a daily fact of life. Rape is banal. One prostitute, an immigrant from Columbus, Ohio, was raped three nights in a row in a project stairway by three different men. The frequency of these extreme forms of violence leads these women to interpret their abuse as "nothing" or "no big thing."

Oh, last year . . . [I was raped. He] took me in the hallway with a knife. He followed me here and he followed me all over with a knife. I said [raising her voice to feign incredulity], "You gonna kill me over some pussy?" I said, "You can *have* some pussy!" I wasn't gonna get killed for it. No! And he raped me . . . nothin' happened. Later he let me go. We went to the projects and he raped me. That was last year, 'round November. [Interview with Glo]

Once when I was about 20 I was raped again. I was in the Bronx and I was drunk. I was living in the Bronx and a dude came and pushed me down when I was goin' in the building. Came down and tore my clothes off and then he raped me. He hit me on the face, my face was all swollen. It was a middle-aged guy. [Interview with Mary Jane]

Prostitutes often nonchalantly, or even proudly, point to scars on their bodies and recount tales of violent rape:

Yeah, that's why I got this scar right here. Well, a young boy tried to rape me, that was when I first started messin' around, about 29. He took me to the roof, he told me he had some crack, he had a whole bag full of bottles that was filled up with peanuts.

So when I told him I wasn't goin' for it, he pulled out a razor and told me to take off all my clothes. I told him I wasn't doin' nothin' and he cut me in my face, then he started cuttin' my clothes off me, then he put on a condom, then he got what he wanted and he ran, and I called the police.

He had took all my clothes and put them in an incinerator, and I had to walk outside butt naked.

He told me, he said, "How do you want to go? You want me to throw you off or you want to jump off?" I said "You ain't throwin' me off and I ain't jumpin' off. That razor ain't makin' me jump no 14 flights; you gotta be crazy; you better get out of my face. You got what you wanted; you ain't makin' me jump off no roof." [Interview with Jennifer]

In addition to straightforward rape, the low-budget street prostitute scene, which is the only one readily available to broken-down crack addicts, also attracts violently sexually perverted clients:

I had went off with a friend of another guy, one of my regular dates that I usually go out with, I had went out with one of his friends and we had went to his apartment and we was sniffin', and gettin' high and everything and he had brought me some base and I was smokin' and he asked me to, you know, to get into it, to get busy with it.

So I was prepared, but then all of a sudden he pulls out some handcuffs, and when I told him no, he started jokin', he tried to joke around with me until he like got my hands and he locked me to a bedpost and started pullin' my hair and tellin' me to do all these different kinds of positions if I wanted to get out of the cuffs. So I did the positions, and then he let me go. [Another man wanted me] to smoke and take a hit, and he wanted me to let him cut me with a razor, across my stomach. Yes, he wanted me to lay back in his car, in the back seat of his car while he watched me take a hit off my stem and cut me. He said not [a deep cut] just, you know, slightly, across my stomach.

No, I didn't do it. It would hurt. That's what he said, "a small incision." He said, "It would be a small incision across your stomach and I'll give you $100." I said, "No."

So we got into a little fight. But I used [my knife]—I'm not supposed to, ain't nobody supposed to carry a weapon, but I carry a knife, and when he went to pull out his razor, I just stuck him in the hand before he got the razor to me. And I had already had my pants halfway down, so I just kicked one leg off and tried to get out the car the best way I could. And I just ran down the street with my panties and my top on. He drove off. [Interview with Mitu]

The violence engulfing these women is not limited to sexual abuse. All aspects of the street woman's life is governed by violence. What is most obvious to everyone on the street is that "crack whores" are easy victims. Regardless of whether they are prostitutes, women residing in Harlem are mugged, beaten, and terrorized more than any other residents, with the possible exception of the elderly. At the same time, women, especially when they are sexually violated, are often blamed for being victims. In fact, women themselves tend to subscribe to blame-the-victim interpretations of their neighbor's plight:

I remember once, I lived on the first floor and in the basement behind my window they raped this girl and she's gay now. Maybe that's why.

They all stood on the line outside and we were like little kids, and we were all nosey asking like, "What are you all doing?" They were like, "Mind your own business," and they shooed us away so I ran to my house and I was looking out the window and you could hear her screaming and they were all going, one by one. I was thinking that they were fucking her. But when she came out I thought that she enjoyed it. She didn't tell anyone, she didn't tell the cops. So I said, "Damn, she must have enjoyed that." But that's why now she's gay.

You couldn't say it was a scream from pain, it wasn't a scream like if she was getting raped. I don't know how to explain it; it's like I could hear it now and it's not a scream for rape because she wasn't screaming "rape." She was just screaming because maybe it hurted and when she came out it was like, "Oh, I got to get out of here." It was not a run, it was just, "I gotta get out," and she walked out.

I would have ran and called the cops. She didn't do any of that. She was crying but not a vicious cry. [Interview with Jackie]

In addition to being extremely violent, street culture is profoundly sexist. It is commonly accepted in street culture that vulnerable women deserve to be victimized. This misogynist "common sense" can be documented in the spontaneous gangs of local youths who patrol their neighborhoods and prey on local prostitutes. Crack whores are beaten up and humiliated for the "good" of the neighborhood. Significantly, these bands of teenagers in Harlem, unlike the formal gangs of Los Angeles, Chicago, or Detroit, are spontaneously organized (Sanchez-Jankowski 1991; Taylor 1990; Vigil 1988). Their violent actions simply reflect their neighborhood's reality. In one particularly violent crack prostitution area, these youths are referred to as "Gremlins":

> The Gremlins run in little packs like little groups of them. We call them Gremlins and they will come and walk up on you, "give me a dollar." And they seen you come out of a car, but you don't know that. "I ain't got a dollar." "What?" They will beat you up and take all your money. They will say, "We just see you get out of that car."
>
> Even if you try to avoid them, they have no respect. You have to stop them before they take from you because then they can tell they own you and they will always take yours. That is what happened last month. They beat two girls down. I went over there and they had left her and beat her down, hit her with a jack in her head. She died two days later. They prey on the female. [Interview with Lorie]

## Violence

Once again, it is important to place the sexual harassment and degradation associated with the sex-for-crack phenomenon within the context of large-scale social trauma enveloping the entire community. For example, gangs of youths have always been raping vulnerable girls irrespective of what drug happened to be in vogue in that particular historical era.

Bourgois collected dozens of accounts of gang rapes that occurred ten or twenty years ago, long before crack existed. In these oral histories of sexual violence, women were beaten, abused, and sexually objectified just as violently as they are today. Often the rape survivors are portrayed as deserving their fate. The only difference is that a mental deficiency rather than an omnipotent addiction to crack is said to have been the cause:

> . . . and I'm hanging out by myself, nobody's in the block, I'm wandering down the street, the block is quiet. The bar's here, the corner's up here, on the last floor they had an apartment.
>
> I'm standing on the corner. Ramon looks out the window and yells, "Julio, you wanna eat?" I thought he had like a pie, a pizza, or something. I said, "You bet!" When he said that, I got the munchies real quick. But when he looks out the window, he goes like that, with his cock out the

window, and I'm like, "Oh shit, motherfucker." So I say, "I'm going up; I'm going up." So they threw the keys down; I went upstairs; it was Sapo, Ramon, Henry, Shorty, and probably Negro—five or six guys there. And that girl.

She was naked in the room. She was naked there with a beer in her hand; a big 40-ounce, getting boned and laughing. When I went in she was getting boned. I opened the door and she was getting fucked by Shorty. . . .

After that he left, since he wasn't used to hanging out with us anyway and he couldn't concentrate. When he left it was just the fellows. We locked the door, turned on the light, she was there, free meat.

She didn't give a fuck. She just ain't nothing, everybody was there with their cocks. Not me! They wanted me to do it. I said, "Fuck that! I don't want you niggers' leftovers. Don't want to catch no fucking gonorrhea, herpes."

She was already fucked up. She was already a woman, she wasn't a virgin. She's a piece of meat. She was 17 years old. She had a nice body, man. She was great, but I didn't want someone with . . . shit like that.

She was there like a hole, man. She was tight. I put my thumb in her ass. . . . They were holding her there, when I put my thumb in her ass, and like two fingers in her cunt . . . it was like crazy man. I washed my hands after that. But it felted good though. . . .

She was crazy, the bitch was crazy. She had some mental problem or something. I don't know. She was bugged, the girl was crazy.

Wherever she's at now, man, I know she's living wrong. She was 17 years old. [Interview with Julio]

Reminiscences like this one contextualize the contemporary pain that crack prostitutes are living. If we maintain historical blinders, crack easily assumes a demonic or even specifically misogynist character. Significantly, the prostitutes and addicts themselves talk about crack in even more sensationalist terms then do the media. They assign it an omnipotent pharmacology. In fact, however, it is the desperate violence that governs all of street life in the inner city that drives the crack experience rather than vice versa. When we comprehend the wider role that terror plays in the logic of street survival, the excesses in the sex-for-crack scene appear more understandable. Drug dealers, for example, must engage in public displays of violence if they are to maintain their credibility and ward off potential muggers (Bourgois 1989).

Terror seeps into the fabric of the inner city, impinging upon its residents—including the majority of the population who work in mainstream jobs at just above poverty-level wages. The culture of terror is experienced by anyone who spends time on the street. Obligatorily, a street frequenter will be exposed to the violence of the underground economy even if he or she does not participate in it. For example, during the first thirteen months of residence in Spanish Harlem, Bourgois witnessed: (1) a deadly shooting of the mother of a 3-year-old child outside his window by an assailant wielding a sawed-off shotgun; (2) a bombing and a machine gunning of a numbers joint by a rival faction of the local "Mafia," again, within view of his family's apartment window; (3) a shootout and a police car chase in front of a pizza parlor where he happened to be eating a snack; (4) the aftermath of the firebombing of a heroin house by an unpaid supplier around the corner from where he lived; (5) a dozen screaming, clothes-ripping, punching fights; (6) almost daily exposure to the sight of an intravenous drug-user mother with visible tracks on her arms walking down the street with a toddler by her side or a pregnant woman entering and leaving a crack house; (7) dozens of broken-down human beings, some of them in fits of crack-induced paranoia, some suffering from delirium tremens, and others in unidentifiable pathological fits screaming and shouting insults to all around them (Bourgois 1989).

Perhaps the most poignant expression of the pervasiveness of the culture of terror was the comment made to Bourgois by a 12-year-old boy in the course of an otherwise random conversation about how the boy was doing in school and how his mother's pregnancy was progressing. The youth told Bourgois he hoped his mother would give birth to a boy, "because girls are too easy to rape." He was both sad and bragging when he said this matter of factly. It was as if he were asserting his adulthood and realistic knowledge of the mythical level of terror on the street that he was growing up in. Incidentally, this boy's mother is a recovering crack addict who had earned money for her habit by juggling a retinue of "boyfriends" whom she recruited at a local after-hours social club. Following a violent confrontation with one of her jilted boyfriends, her son came to me complaining, "I keep telling my mother to only have one boyfriend at a time. That way she won't get hit."

Violence is a part of an accepted and effective mode of functioning for adults who participate in street life. In fact, teaching effective violence to the younger generation is the responsibility of a mentor:

> Jim talks about being a big brother to Ronney whom he has known since he was a teenager. He tells how he taught him to fight. One day he came home from school, beat up, and crying. Jim questioned him and learned that he had been beaten by some guys. Jim then beat him up to teach him how to fight. The next day Ronney went to school and beat up one guy, and others left him alone. From then on Ronney fought for himself like a man. (Dunlap field notes)

Similarly, men brag about their scars and near misses with death. The public sporting of the ravages of survived violence is a badge of self-respect:

> They plan to get more crack. As we sit there Jim tells me about one of his episodes of getting caught up in a robbery and getting shot. He loaned his friends his gun to rob an "A-Rab" [Arab] store, but went with them so he could keep up with his gun.

They went in to rob the store, but they did not know what they were doing. He was at the door nervous because he did not want to get caught with them. He could tell they were amateurs once they started robbing the store because everything began to go wrong. It ended up with the store owner getting the one gun they had, his buddies running, and him left alone.

The owner shot at him, but he moved his head in time and the bullet hit the side of his face over his eye. He dove through the window and ran. He tells the story demonstratively, and we are laughing at what happened. (Dunlap field notes)

These public displays of the glories of violence are channeled into gender-specific domains. Bullet wounds, for example, are defined as masculine, whereas razor-slash scars on the cheek are feminine. Violence is part of growing up; it is a rite of passage on the street. This imbues violence with the mundane quality that makes it part of a hegemonic "common sense." Hence, many women accede to the brutalization committed against them by their men. In fact, they brag about it, implying that a violent man is a caring man:

One of Rose's friends comes by, and they begin to laugh and talk about last night—how her [the friend's] boyfriend became angry with her because her skirt was too short; how he began to beat her (and she laughs the whole while); how he wants her to go back to Ohio with him; how she is not going anywhere; how he got married on the very day she was giving birth to their daughter (whom I have met during the course of the day—she is about 10 or 11 years old); how he threatens to kill her if she does not return with him; how he is a very tall and big man.

While this is going on, Ronney and Jim are talking to Lee. Lee is smoking angel dust and offering it around. No one wants any. (Dunlap field notes)

Many street people organize their personalities around reputations for violence. This acted-out rage is considered a legitimate way of being:

Rose is really high now. After Lee smokes he walks over to us and asks Rose for the money she owes him. Rose begins to curse him and tries to kick him. He is moving out of her way and laughing; everyone is watching. Jim is sitting on the rail, Ronney in the wheelchair against the stone, and I am sitting on the stoop. Wally is standing beside Ronney leaning against the wall.

Ronny tells him, "Man why you messing with Rose—you know how she gets." Lee tells Rose he is sorry. She gets tired and comes and sits by me. But Rose is so high she curses almost everyone who passes. Everyone seems to know one another or everyone is high everywhere. . . .

She is very loud now and is getting more out of control. By this I mean that she is cursing and not talking sensibly. When Wally, Ronney, and Jim return she curses them about everything. She is just difficult to get along with. Jim is very patient with her; he tries to calm her down. (Dunlap field notes)

In several instances, we documented expressions of sadistic brutality, such as igniting pigeons drenched with lighter fluid and mutilating pet animals. Faced with this grotesque cruelty, the ethnographer can only hope that the social network with which he or she has developed a relationship is a pathological exception. Unfortunately, these incidents of gratuitous brutality are participated in by relatively wide networks, and usually no one intervenes to stop the abuse. In one case, the animal being tormented was also the object of affection:

Rose goes and gets the dog out of the apartment. The dog is shaking very hard; he is a very small dog. I ask, "What is the matter with the dog?" Rose tells me that Ronney beat the dog for some reason. Then they all start laughing and I ask why.

I find out that they have pulled the dog's teeth out, two of the teeth. I ask them why they pulled the dog's teeth out; I say, "No wonder the dog is shaking so much."

Rose puts the dog under her sweater with his head sticking out to stop him from shaking. They laugh and talk about pulling out the dog's teeth. Rose slaps the dog's head that is sticking outside the front of her sweater telling him to stop shaking. We sat for a while longer and walk back to the corner. Everyone continues to drink from the last bottle of wine. While we were walking I take the leash of the dog while Rose drinks her portion. . . .

Eventually Rose staggers back to the apartment in order to take the dog back in. She does not return. (Dunlap field notes)

This violence is much worse when it is directed at humans. Dunlap witnessed an enraged man viciously beating a 4-year-old boy, who was crying hysterically. The boy's mother watched passively as her son, who was apparently being punished for being incapable of pronouncing some phrase, cried so hard he could hardly breathe. When Dunlap asked the mother to intercede, she shrugged her shoulders; "I don't know why he just won't say what his stepfather wants to hear."

## Changing Gender Relations

A casual walk through Harlem's side streets will reveal dozens of young, emaciated women milling agitatedly around crack-copping corners. In a series of ten random surveys undertaken at a network of three crack houses in East Harlem, females represented just under 50 percent of the customers (see also

Deschenes 1988; Greenleaf 1989). This contrasts dramatically to the estimates of a 20 percent female participation rate in the street heroin scenes of the 1970s (Rosenbaum 1981).

Why are so many more young girls addicted to crack than ever were to heroin? This is a frequent subject of conversation in the inner city and is generally explained by moralistic, macho-essentialist, or lecherous street theories: it is due to a breakdown in family values, it is because of a female phobia of hypodermic needles, or it is because of the mythical aphrodisiac powers of crack cocaine. In fact, however, greater female involvement in crack addiction is one of the ways the growing emancipation of women that is taking place throughout all aspects of America culture is expressing itself concretely in the crack-using street scene (Bourgois 1989:643–645). Women—especially the emerging generation that is most at risk for crack addiction—are no longer as obliged to stay at home and maintain the family as they were a generation ago. They no longer so readily sacrifice public life for their children and spouse. A visible documentation of this is the presence in crack houses of pregnant women and of mothers accompanied by infant children and toddlers. Perhaps the insights provided by feminists studying mothers who protect themselves by allowing their weakest progeny to die in infancy in settings of extreme poverty in the Third World might shed light on the actions of desperately addicted pregnant mothers in Harlem (Scheper-Hughes 1985).

On the national level, statistics document an increased female participation in the legal labor market (Wilson 1987:76–77). By the same token, more women—even if a small minority—are also resisting exploitation in the entry-level job market and are pursuing careers in the underground economy. They are seeking self-definition and meaning through participation in street culture. It is not as easy as it formerly was for men to beat their daughters, sisters, and wives into submission when they attempt to socialize or to generate income on the streets. In one instance, Dunlap watched a prostitute publicly threaten her husband for expecting her to behave according to traditional gender norms:

Jim tells Rose he is hungry and asks her to go home and cook him something to eat; she tells him, "kiss my black ass, nigger. If you want something to eat, you better cook the shit your damn self. I ain't goin' to cook you shit. Who the fuck you think I am, your god-motherfuckin'-damn maid or something? You better get the fuck out-a here."

Rose begins to talk to me about Jim. "Can you believe this motherfucker? What the fuck is this shit? He must be mad, asking me to cook him something to eat. Motherfucker! I'll kick his fuckin' ass."

This goes on for awhile, with Rose cursing Jim, and Jim more or less egging her on by telling her that she is supposed to cook for him; that she is his woman. This conversation ends with everyone laughing when Rose asks him, "Does a chicken have lips?" (Dunlap field notes)

Ironically, the breakdown of traditional patriarchal gender relations may be taking place at a faster rate on inner-city streets than in middle-class suburbs. The ultimate proof is that aggressive women, such as Rose, comprise a rising share of the crack-addicted population and are the fastest-growing segment of the population being arrested for street crimes in New York City (*New York Post* 1989; *New York Times* 1989c).

Although women are using crack and participating intensively in street culture, traditional gender relations still largely govern the street's underground economy. Most notably, women are forced disproportionately to rely on prostitution to finance their habits. For example, of the thirty crack sellers who have worked at the crack houses frequented by Bourgois over the past four years, only two have been female, and neither of these female dealers maintained their positions for more than six months.

The flooding of women into the sex market has undercut the price of sexual services and resulted in an epidemic rise in venereal disease among women and newborn babies in the inner city (Althaus 1991). Women who used to support themselves through prostitution prior to the proliferation of crack complain that their profession has been decimated by the flood of nonprofessional, freelancing youths who are scrambling for a vial of crack. Contradictorily, therefore, the underlying process of emancipation that has enabled women to demand equal participation in street culture and to carve out an expanded niche for themselves in the drug-world economy has led to a greater depreciation of women as sex objects. The promiscuity and low cost of what is derisively termed a "crack whore" is a frequent subject of conversation on the street. Desperate women being publicly humiliated sexually is a more common sight today than in the past. A "thirsty" (crack-craving) woman will tolerate extreme levels of verbal and physical abuse in her pursuit of a vial of crack. Some men celebrate their lecherous machismo by publicly ridiculing women who offer their services on crack-copping corners.

The abuse of crack-addicted women assumes an especially violent dimension when men high on crack are unable to function sexually. These cocaine-flushed men crave sex but cannot maintain an erection or achieve an orgasm. This sexual frustration often leads to voyeuristic behavior that involves the violent humiliation of vulnerable females. Many of the men fly into a macho rage and blame their sexual dysfunction on the woman's failure as a sex object:

The place it was in had no door there, and the curtain was sheer so you could see through, like beige or something. And we watchin' in the next room and the girl was tellin' him that she didn't want to. She was sayin' she been here for about two hours and he could have his money back 'cause she don't want to have sex with him because he can't get hard and she was gettin' tired of suckin' on him. And then he punched her in the mouth, started slappin' her and she cried for a little while and attempted to leave. He made her sit down.

We didn't do nothing, 'cause most of all, when they rent a room like that . . . most of the people who rent out those rooms in crack houses, no matter what go on, they'll just make the other party of people ignore it; they'll just make them leave. [Interview with Mercy]

The degradation of such a large cohort of women who are so conspicuously visible on the street is not neutral ideologically. Although addicted street women represent only a tiny proportion of inner-city females, they are extremely visible publicly since they are aggressively spending time on the street. This has a strong negative effect on the community's—and on mainstream society's—perception of minority women. It may ultimately reinforce a more generalized ideological depreciation of females.

Many men complain about the degradation of women since the arrival of crack. This is the case with Julio, an East Harlem crack dealer who humiliates his female customers and righteously bemoans the fact that many women are losing their value as sex objects:

Back in the days, bitches used to look good, and now they look like shit. And some of them are dying of AIDS. And they're just all fucked up. And back then you probably wished you had them, but now you don't even want them, and they want you for some crack. . . .

Ooh! One night in the club, there was this lady—20 something. We knew her when we were young . . . and this guy came in. . . . He had been in her grade in high school; she was about a grade or two higher than me. So she was just sitting there, this bitch. . . . She was like that [legs spread open] . . . and I was standing up, and all of a sudden, out of nowhere, he said, "Damn man, I remember back in the days, when you used to look good and I wanted you, and you used to diss me, and you told me I was ugly. Bitch! Now I know I could *have* you because of the way you look. Man! You look like shit! You look all fucked up! And I know—here I'll give you a coupl'a dollars. It's there [reaching out his hand]. Get high! Fuck it, cause I don't want any of what you got!"

And I was saying, "That's true, right! Back in the days, bitches used to look real good." And right around this time that other one that Pedro had sex with the night before, walked in to buy some shit, and she still had some weight, like she could still look good, but she's a piece of shit now. [Interview with Julio]

One way of interpreting the virulence with which many men abuse vulnerable women in the crack scene is as a frustrated attempt by traditional, patriarchally oriented men to stave off the challenge to gender roles posed by the growing public presence of addicted women. In short, men on the street are not accepting the new roles that women are attempting to carve out for themselves in the world of substance abuse. Instead, males are lashing out at females, and they are desperately striving to reimpose violently the gender order of the previous generation. According to their repressive, patriarchal logic, submitting a woman, or even a teenage girl, to violent sex or gang rape is justifiable since "she wasn't acting like a lady." Bourgois was frequently told "she got what was coming to her" when he argued with gang rapists that they had caused unconscionable trauma to their victims.

Regardless of the deep underlying structural and ideological dynamics involved in gender-based violence on the street, many young men take special pleasure in ripping off crack prostitutes and brag about it to one another. Pedro, for example, claims he is "teaching the bitches a lesson'" when he has sexual relations with a prostitute and then refuses to pay for her services. The crack-addicted women experience Pedro's "lessons" as rape:

> We saw this particular freak with big lips, and we told her exactly what we was gonna do to her. Pop knew her, I didn't know her. She said "gimme you' money." So then I told Pop, "Let's go to your building; get two empty vials; and fill them with Scott tissue, or something." So we did that.
>
> Then we show up with the girl—the one with the big lips. So we went upstairs, and she started parlaying it; started shellacking it; taking the varnish off it. So then she stripped it; she was putting water bead on it; surveying my toilet closet. What she finished doing was an actual act to my southern hemisphere!
>
> I dropped the *jums* [vials of crack] on the floor and I kept walking, and she said, "Wait a minute." I said "Yeah, smoke it! I'm outta here."
>
> Pop was not there; he had left. So I started running and laughing, and she started screaming. I heard her screaming, and she ran downstairs.
>
> She said "You son-of-a-bitch . . . I know you! I know where you're from! I'm gonna tell Big Petee."
>
> And I was like, "shit!" [grinning]. So every time I see her, I used to laugh. I wanted to teach her a lesson, like: "Don't do that kind of nonsense in the street because one day you're gonna get jerked." What if I was a maniac and I would have cut her throat? [Interview with Pedro]

## AIDS

The vulnerable and abusive life-styles that prevail in the settings where sex is exchanged for crack create a host of potential AIDS vectors. The compulsive context and the frequency with which the sexual acts occur mitigate against any rational calculation about the danger of contracting the AIDS virus. In fact, some women get high just to forget that their crack-smoking episodes have made them highly vulnerable to contracting the deadly disease. For most women and men on the street, AIDS is a phenomenon associated with real faces. They have lost friends, acquaintances, and family members to the epidemic. The intense craving associated with a full-blown crack addiction, however, can drive a woman to accept virtually any customer in return for a puff on a crack pipe or for a few dollars. To make matters worse, frustrated males who are unable to reach an orgasm because of the dysfunction caused by cocaine sometimes resort to physically abusing their sexual partners. Violence in the sexual act increases the potential transmission and absorption of HIV-bearing body fluids.

Most of the prostitutes claimed they protected themselves by "checking out" their customers before having sex with them. They thought they could determine whether their customers carried the AIDS virus by talking to them and observing their physical cleanliness. Virtually everyone on the streets is aware that the AIDS virus can be transmitted both sexually and by sharing intravenous needles. Many also recognize that anal sex is a high-risk activity. The vast majority of women on the street vehemently claim they shun customers who demand anal sex—"boodie bandits." Ironically, this is because the act is culturally taboo rather than because it is dangerous for their health. Significantly, almost none of the nonintravenous, drug-using prostitutes knew that bleach kills the AIDS virus in contaminated hypodermic needles. Virtually all the drug-injecting women, however, were aware of the benefits of bleach.

Condoms were recognized as useful for preventing HIV transmission, even if they were infrequently used. Most of the women interviewed would prefer to spend their last dollar on crack rather than on a condom. Perhaps more important, negotiating condom use with customers is a complicated procedure that requires power. The degraded, vulnerable condition of crack whore precludes being able to insist upon using condoms or to refuse relations with intravenous-drug-using men (Worth 1989). Condom use is not a technical operation; it is a social assertion of power, control, and self-respect that most of the women we interacted with on the street were unable to maintain with any consistency.

The customers of the crack prostitutes are not likely to protect themselves against HIV infection given their life-styles. Many are regular crack bingers or alcoholics and petty street hustlers. Nevertheless, the customers would probably be more receptive to AIDS prevention outreach than most of the crack-addicted prostitutes, who tend to be more desperate and compulsive in their substance abuse. Most men in the sex-for-crack scene claimed that they used condoms even when they had oral sex, but they were probably not telling the truth. Participant-observation data revealed that several of the same men who had claimed on interview forms that they "always used condoms" in fact regularly engaged in unprotected sex. Despite the frequency of unprotected sex on the street, virtually all the men were educated enough on the danger of AIDS and other sexually transmitted diseases to know that they were supposed to lie or exaggerate when asked about condom use.

Repeatedly we learned that it is only through intensive, participant-observation ethnographic investigation that accurate data on the details of sexual practices can be collected. The formal interview context is an almost useless forum for obtaining a genuine understanding of condom use or for documenting the specifics of sexual practices. For example, almost all women claimed they used condoms "most of the time." Most women, however, had no condoms in their possession when we asked to see them. We also questioned all the women who claimed they "almost always used condoms" if they ever lost money because of their insistence on condom use with recalcitrant customers. Because only one or two women answered that they lost money due to their insistence on condoms, we believe few women are really using condoms consistently in practice when it threatens their income.

> In talking of condoms, Janet relates that some customers do not like to use them and some customers have their own. When men do not want to use them she will have the sex anyway, especially if she needs the money. Many men feel they want "the real thing" and refuse to use condoms.
>
> To her, drug users are scary, especially when she sees the scars on their arms. Even though she may need the money she will not have sex with them because she fears AIDS. This does affect her business. She relates how a lot of them put flavor condoms on and she will give them oral sex. This is OK, as long as they have the condoms.
>
> Janet is extremely concerned about AIDS and she uses condoms more to make herself safe. She was tested in April 1990 and the results were negative. (Dunlap field notes)

Despite this negative scenario, condoms are being used more today than in the past, usually at the customer's initiative. On two occasions we saw men hawking condoms on the same street corners frequented by strolling prostitutes.

Another possible AIDS vector in the sex-for-crack scene is the "turning out" of cohorts of women who in the past might have either escaped prostitution or matured out of it if crack were not so plentiful, inexpensive, and socially accessible. A number of young women from relatively stable households were swept unsuspecting into the crack tide to become "crack whores" almost before they were aware of what they were doing. This was especially true during the early years of crack's advent, before local social controls had evolved to regulate and define the dangers and limits of its use. Similarly, a surprisingly large number of the women in the sex-for-crack market were over age 30. Many had quit using drugs and stabilized themselves following turbulent careers as heroin prostitutes in their youth. Crack—like heroin before—ripped them out of their households once again. Crack, therefore, created a second—even sadder—cycle that sent these survivors of opiates into another grueling round of unwanted pregnancies and social distress. Most of these returnees to the street had achieved a ten-year hiatus without unwanted pregnancies. Some had even reentered the legal labor market and became reconciled with their families prior to discovering cocaine in its smokable form.

The transmission of HIV to the fetus is one of the most tragic dimensions of the sex-for-crack dynamics that we documented. One of the six pregnant women in our sample of forty was HIV positive. She was not receiving prenatal care and was unaware of her status. Given the crack addict's overwhelming craving for the drug, it is only logical that crack prostitutes should become pregnant more frequently than other prostitutes on the street and that they should engage in riskier behavior. Because of the physical disruption caused by regular crack binges, many women are not even aware that they are pregnant until after their first trimester.

Our statistics on HIV and syphilis infection rates are worrisome. Eighteen of forty prostitutes registered positive on the syphilis test. Seven of the forty women who were tested for HIV infection were positive. Only one of these seven HIV-positive women admitted to a previous history of intravenous drug use. If we disqualify the other three self-identified former intravenous drug users from our sample of forty, we find that 16.6 percent of the prostitutes (six of thirty-six) contracted the AIDS virus exclusively through sexual transmission.

On a more positive note, some of the dynamics of crack use diminish the risk of HIV infection. Most notably, the inability of many crack-using men to reach orgasm may reduce the transmission of potentially infected body fluids. Further, many women and men are weaned from needle use by smoking crack. This is probably the biggest "AIDS prevention" component to the crack scene. The general pattern is for the intraveous-drug-using women—who tend to be over age 30—to cease injecting heroin and/or cocaine when they begin smoking crack. Significantly, crack is found in great abundance at shooting galleries. We confirmed this in interviews and through participant-observation (see also Bourgois 1992b):

> Jo Ann learned about crack in a shooting gallery. She had heard about it before, but it was in the shooting gallery that she first tried it. She had to smoke it a couple of times to understand the high. It eventually became the only drug she used. She has been in and out of various programs and was on methadone but was also shooting cocaine when she learned to smoke crack. Crack was a big hit with her because she did not have to look for a vein. It was much easier to get high smoking .
>
> After smoking crack for about seven months she stayed so high that she kicked the methadone/heroin habit. She became very sick, however, and was told by the doctor that her body had become confused by the combination of her constant crack high and her body's craving for methadone/heroin. (Dunlap field notes)

I finally made it to a shooting gallery last night, but it looked more like a crack house. People would only shoot heroin once upon first arriving and then smoke crack the rest of the night pursuing the speedball high. (Bourgois field notes)

## Conclusion

Taken out of context, our ethnographic data might confirm any slew of sensationalist demonizations of crack. The levels of sexual degradation, violence, and aggression that accompany sex-for-crack exchanges are extreme by any measurement. Our most important conclusion, however, is that the social relations around the sex-for-crack phenomenon are not an aberration for America. They are merely a contemporary public idiom for poverty, ethnic segregation, and polarized gender relations.

The media and popular consciousness have seized on the "fact" that crack is an aphrodisiac. Throughout American history, most new drugs have been associated with uncontrolled sexual impulse (cf. Morgan 1981). Although we were repeatedly told stories of female crack users who craved sex—for example, "It's all about women who come out of their clothes when they smoke"—in fact, our observations reveal that only a relatively small minority of crack users, male or female, become sexually aroused by smoking crack.

Regardless of how small a proportion these sexually aroused crack addicts actually represent, popular consciousness has seized upon them as the explanation for the existence of the new cohort of women milling through Harlem's streets desperately selling their bodies for a three-dollar high. Ideologically, this is a convenient way to dismiss the crisis in gender relations that is so blatantly visible on inner-city streets. It is also part of an overall demonization of the pharmacological properties of crack. The alleged omnipotence of crack allows society to absolve itself of any real responsibility for the inner city. It also allows the addicts themselves to continue pursuing their self-destruction.

We have tried to set the degradation associated with the sex-for-crack scene in an ethnographic perspective that analyzes the larger reign of terror governing inner-city street life. This emphasis on the details of daily horror in Harlem risks confirming stereotypes against the poor and the nonwhite. At the same time, by neglecting or whitewashing a mode of survival pursued by too many Americans, we would be ignoring a reality that has been politely denied for too long. Women and their children—the most vulnerable sectors of American society—suffer the most. Crack has brought their suffering out of the closet and onto the streets. By the same token, the growing heterosexual AIDS rate is obliging the medical establishment to pay long-overdue attention to the plight of inner-city mothers and children who are dying in municipal hospitals. We have to confront and recognize the crisis of public sector breakdown and extreme urban poverty head on. The experience of racism and social marginalization in the United States is overwhelmingly painful and destructive. The ultimate proof is that no other wealthy industrialized country in the world is capable of spawning the sociopathology that is rampant in American cities.

# References

Althaus, F. 1991. "As Incidence of Syphilis Rises Sharply in the U.S., Racial Differentials Grow." *Family Planning Perspectives* 32 (1):43–44.

Baca Zinn, Maxine. 1989. "Family, Race, and Poverty in the Eighties." *Signs* 14(4):856–874.

Biernacki, Patrick. 1979. "Junkie Work, Hustles, and Social Status Among Heroin Addicts." *Journal of Drug Issues* (Fall):535–551.

Bourgois, Phillipe. 1989. "In Search of Horatio Alger: Culture and Ideology in the Crack Economy." *Contemporary Drug Problems* 16(4):619–649.

———. 1991. "Everyday Life in Two High-Risk Neighborhoods: Growing Up." *The American Enterprise* 2(3):30–33.

———. 1992a. "From Jibaro to Crack Dealer: Confronting the Restructuring of Capitalism in Spanish Harlem." In *Articulating Hidden Histories: Festschrift for Eric Wolf*. Edited by Rayna Rapp and Jane Schneider. Berkeley: University of California Press.

———. 1992b. "Enquête sur le terrain de la drogue." *Actes de la recherche en sciences sociales*, Septembre–Octobre.

———. Forthcoming. *In Search of Respect: Selling Crack in El Barrio*. New York: Cambridge University Press.

*Contemporary Drug Problems*. 1989 and 1990. "Research on Crack." Volumes 16 (4) and 17 (1). Special issues.

Deschenes, Elizabeth Piper. 1988. "Cocaine Use and Pregnancy." Drug Abuse Series Paper of the Drug Abuse Information and Monitoring Project, California Department of Alcohol and Drug Programs, Health and Welfare Agency.

Dunlap, Eloise. 1991. "Crack Sub-Cultural Norms and Sexual Behavior: Male and Female Behaviors and Interaction Patterns." Paper presented at the fiftieth annual meeting of the American Society of Criminology. San Francisco, November.

———. 1992a. "Inner City Crisis and Drug Dealing: Portrait of a Drug Dealer and His Household." In *Crisis and Resistance: Social Relations and Economic Restructuring in the City*. Edited by Suzanne MacGregor. Minneapolis and Edinburgh: University of Minnesota and University of Edinburgh Presses.

———. 1992b. "Impact of Drugs on Family Life and Kin Networks in the Inner City African-American Single-Parent Household." In *Drugs, Crime, and Inner City Isolation, Barriers to Opportunity*. Edited by Adair Harrell and George E. Petersen. Washington, D.C.: Urban Institute Press.

*Editor and Publisher*. 1989. "Crack Project Goes Awry." Vol. 2 (December).

Feldman, Harvey W., M. H. Agar, and G. M. Beschner. 1979. *Angel Dust: An Ethnographic Study of PCP Users*. New York: Lexington Books.

Finestone, Harold. 1957. "Cats, Kicks, and Color." *Society for the Study of Social Problems* 5(1):3–13.

Greenleaf, V. D. 1989. *Women and Cocaine: Personal Stories of Addiction and Recovery.* Los Angeles: Lowell House.

Haller, D. L. 1991. "Recovery for Two: Pregnancy and Addiction." *Addiction and Recovery* 11(4):14–18.

Johnson, B., T. Williams, K. Dei, and H. Sanabria. 1989. "Drug Abuse in the Inner City: Impact on Hard-Drug Users and the Community." In *Drugs and Crime.* Edited by Michael Tonry and James Q. Wilson. Chicago: University of Chicago Press.

Massing, Michael. 1989. "Crack's Destructive Sprint Across America." *New York Times Magazine,* October 1, pp. 38–41, 58–62

Morgan, H. Wayne. 1981. *Drugs in America: A Social History, 1800–1980.* Syracuse: Syracuse University Press.

Musto, David F. 1987. *The American Disease: Origins of Narcotic Control.* New York: Oxford University Press.

New York Department of City Planning. 1984. *Community District Statistics: A Portrait of New York City.* Special Report from the Neighborhood Statistics Program of the U.S. Bureau of the Census.

*New York Post.* 1989. "Babies Who Spend Their First Year in Jail." April 11, pp. 5, 30–31.

*New York Times.* 1987. "Crack Addiction: The Tragic Toll on Women and Their Children." February 9.

———. 1989a. "Crack: A Disaster of Historic Dimensions, Still Growing." March 28, p. E14.

———. 1989b. "Crack, Bane of Inner City Is Now Gripping Suburbs." October 1, p. A1.

———. 1989c. "Number of Mothers in Jail Surges with Drug Arrests." April 17, pp. A1, A16.

———. 1992. "The 1980's: A Very Good Time for the Very Rich." March 5, pp. A1, C13.

*Newsday.* 1990. "Pregnant Addicts, Aborted Funds." October 29, pp. 8, 30.

*Newsweek.* 1988. "Crack: The Drug Crisis." November 28.

———. 1991. "Innocent Victims." May 13, pp. 56–60.

Phillips, Kevin. 1990. *Wealth and the American Electorate in the Reagan Aftermath.* New York: Random House.

Reinarman, Craig, and Harry L. Levine. 1989. "Crack in Context: Politics and Media in the Making of a Drug Scare." *Contemporary Drug Problems* 14(4):535–577.

Rosenbaum, Marsha. 1981. *Women on Heroin.* New Brunswick: Rutgers University Press.

Sanchez-Jankowski, Martin. 1991. *Islands in the Street: Gangs in Urban America.* Berkeley: University of California Press.

Scheper-Hughes, Nancy. 1985. "Culture, Scarcity, and Material Thinking: Maternal Detachment and Infant Survival in a Brazilian Shantytown." *Ethos* 13(4):291–317.

*Signs.* 1989. *"Common Grounds and Crossroads: Race, Ethnicity, and Class in Women's Lives"* 14(4). Special issue.

Sutter, A. G. 1966. "The World of the Righteous Dope Fiend." *Issues in Criminology* 2(2):177–222.

Taylor, Carl S. 1990. *Dangerous Society*. East Lansing: Michigan State University Press.

*U.S. News and World Report*. 1991. "The Men Who Created Crack." August 19, pp. 44–53.

Vigil, Diego. 1988. *Barrio Gangs: Street Life and Identity in Southern California*. Austin: University of Texas Press.

Wilson, William Julius. 1987. *The Truly Disadvantaged: The Inner City, the Underclass, and Public Policy*. Chicago: University of Chicago Press.

Worth, Dooley. 1989. "Sexual Decision-Making and AIDS: Why Condom Promotion Among Vulnerable Women Is Likely to Fail." *Studies in Family Planning* 20(6) (November–December): 297–307.

# 5

# Street Status and the Sex-for-Crack Scene in San Francisco

*Harvey W. Feldman*
*Frank Espada*
*Sharon Penn*
*Sharon Byrd*

Cocaine has a rich and florid history. In the past, its enticing effects captured the imaginations of world-famous leaders and thinkers: Sigmund Freud, Robert Louis Stevenson, Thomas Edison, Sarah Bernhardt, Queen Victoria of England, Pope Leo XIII, and even the fictional character of Sherlock Holmes (Horowitz 1974). Prior to the invention of crack, cocaine enjoyed a reputation in the United States as an elite, if dangerous, drug because of its expense and its association with the jet set, highly paid athletes, and popular entertainers. In San Francisco, the crack cocaine scene has tended not to be associated with the intellectual elite or with prominent figures in literary or professional circles. Rather, it became a preferred drug of the underclass in inner-city neighborhoods.

The word *crack* as it relates to cocaine first appeard in the *New York Times* on November 17, 1985. Michael Aldrich (1986), an ardent bibliophile, reported since that first article that thousands of press stories appeared in the years following. The reports have emphasized the negative aspects of crack: the violence connected to trafficking, the damage to careers of athletes when they test positive for drugs, and the painful physical symptoms of newborns attributed to crack-using mothers. In short, the public media has portrayed crack as the monster drug of the late 1980s and early 1990s. More significantly, the crack fad has coincided with a legitimate HIV/AIDS epidemic and has raised serious questions about its potential for increasing the rate of HIV infction because of the reputed connection between its alleged aphrodisiacal effects and risky sexual activities. In San Francisco, where the AIDS epidemic had hit with full force, this concern elevated the importance of crack, not simply as a drug that caused physical harm but one that had the potential of disaster on a par with Armageddon.

## San Francisco Research Respondents

Respondents for the study in San Francisco were recruited by Community Health Outreach Workers (CHOWs) who, under the direction of the Youth Environment Study (YES), were assigned to provide HIV/AIDS education to out-of-treatment injection drug users, their sexual partners, prostitutes, runaway youth, and, in recent years, crack smokers. The YES CHOWs were asked to select known crack users in their respective communities and to refer them to the study. Forty respondents were selected: thirty-four females, five males, and one transsexual. Respondents came from four communities and populations: the Western Addition, a predominantly African-American community; the Mission District, where Latinos were the majority population; the Tenderloin, a transition zone and sex trade area; and the Polk Gulch, one of the major gathering areas in San Francisco for homeless and runaway youth.

In selecting respondents for the study, we did not state specifically that they must have histories of trading sex for crack, only that they should acknowledge their own extensive crack use and have street reputations as crack users, which CHOWs could confirm. Later respondents were selected on the basis of their use of crack as well as their known participation in the sex trades as street prostitutes. The respondents were typically poor people from poor neighborhoods with high unemployment rates. Interviews were carried out in the natural environments of the respondents. The preferred setting was a respondent's home; when this arrangement was not possible, interviews took place in restaurants, in interviewers' cars, or on park benches, usually close to the action of the street. Forty interviews were carried out, tape-recorded, and then transcribed into typescript. The senior author read and analyzed the interviews with the aim of developing appropriate conceptual categories that captured the various aspects of both individual crack smokers and the social context of crack use. The major emphasis of data collection was on the exploratory interview with limited participant observation.

### General Characteristics of the Population

Most respondents were people of color, with African-Americans and Latinos predominating. Respondents recruited from the homeless/runaway youth populations were, for the most part, Caucasian. In the beginning phases of the study, we emphasized recruiting female respondents because it was believed that females rather than males would be the individuals offering sex and receiving crack and that they more than males would be vulnerable to HIV infection and other sexually transmitted diseases. Later, we attempted to balance this recruitment strategy and interviewed males who had purchased sex in exchange for crack in order to gain some understanding of the interaction between these consenting parties. In addition, one transsexual participated who was both a street prostitute and a heavy crack smoker.

## Families

Respondents in this study generally came from what could be termed dysfunctional families. In almost all cases, the parents had separated, and as children, respondents were sent to live with relatives or placed in foster homes. The family life that existed was often complicated by parental drug or alcohol use and frequently accompanied by violence. When asked about her early childhood, for example, Lynn, one of the few women in our study who traded sex directly for crack, provided a vivid description of violence in her family of origin:

> Like I said, my father was an alcoholic and he used to get drunk a lot of times and gamble and come home and ask my mother for money and she would tell him she wouldn't have it. And he beat her. One time he pulled a shotgun on my sister because she tried to pull him off my mother. But that happened all the time. They were always fighting. All the time. One time she had a busted lip and I went for him and I tried to hurt him because he hurt her. And it just got bad.

In less dramatic description, Caroline, a crack smoker and heroin injector, described her family as scattered and criminal: "I'm my mother's only daughter. She has another son but she don't see him. My father has about twelve kids. He's passed away now. All my brothers and sisters use [take drugs] and are in and out of the penitentiaries except my mother's son. He's in the air force."

In all cases, respondents either grew up in or moved to neighborhoods in San Francisco where drug use was prevalent and where crack cocaine became a popular street drug. Even where families were intact, the social or neighborhood environments typically contained street scenes in which respondents participated in gang activities that included stealing, fighting, and early drug consumption. In rarer cases, respondents reported growing up in families that were highly religious, overprotective, and restrictive. In these cases, families were usually ignorant of the individual's secret sexual or drug indiscretions.

The overriding feature of respondents' view of their families was parental inability to be loving and nurturing because of the parents' own personal needs and difficulties, some of which included problematic involvement with alcohol and drugs. It was surprising to discover how many of our respondents were exposed as children to their parents' drug use in the home. In one case, a young woman reported that her mother sold "crank" (methamphetamine), and access to it led to her first drug experience. The shift in initiation to drug use from the peer group to parents among a minority of respondents was a surprising finding and clearly different from earlier studies that pictured parents as both ignorant of illicit drug use and disapproving.

In some cases, female respondents reported being either sexually molested or raped as children by male members of the family, especially by stepfathers. Almost without exception, respondents described being abandoned, turned over to grandparents or stepfathers, or placed in foster homes. Despite these early experiences of neglect and, in some cases, of sexual abuse, many of the respondents reported consistent efforts to maintain contact with their parents and sought whenever possible to present to them a conventional image of themselves.

Given their early experiences, it was not unexpected that few respondents established stable families of their own. They frequently selected unreliable partners, some of whom exploited them or provided their initiation into drug use and encouraged or approved of their selection of prostitution as an occupation. One woman described her three consecutive male partners whom she either married or with whom she lived as (1) a con man in and out of jail and a "junkie," (2) a husband who died of alcoholism, and (3) her current boyfriend, who uses crack heavily.

Many of the respondents reported having children. Only a few of them were able to care for the children in a consistent fashion. Some of the children had been removed by the courts; others were living with relatives or in foster homes. Those who were active in drug dealing or had other steady but illegitimate hustles were proud of the fact that they provided regularly for their children. Most respondents expressed a general dissatisfaction with their current lives and looked to their children as a source of motivation to make what they described as a change for the better: stopping drug use and adopting an orthodox life-style. Sadly, their children's lives appeared in many cases to be a repetition of their own family experiences. And even if our respondents did not have an immediate plan to alter their present situation, they projected a wistful desire to modify their lives and at some future, undefined time raise their children in a conventional fashion.

## Education and Employment Histories

Most respondents implied that education and attendance at school was not a significant part of their growing up. While they did not report great difficulty with school, the majority of our respondents dropped out before high school graduation. The topic of school and education was not of great importance in their lives, and it appeared unconnected to either their current life situation or future plans.

Almost all of the respondents readily stated that the major portion of their incomes came from illegitimate pursuits, most commonly prostitution. We believe that this finding, however, is an artiifact of our own respondent selection since the majority of them were recruited at sites known as prostitution strolls. With few exceptions, respondents were economically marginal—even those prostitutes and shoplifters who claimed to earn substantial amounts of money. One crack dealer who operated a crack house stated that much of his money supported a heroin habit and the sixteen children he had fathered by several different women. In maintaining his heroin use and valiantly striving to remain a responsible father, he was not the picture of the successful ghetto crack dealer portrayed in the media (*Time*, May 9, 1988). According to Larry, his expenses greatly outweighed his profits: "In cash I use about five hundred dollars' worth of dope between crack and heroin. Cash money from my pocket after I drop twenty dollars toward this child and ten dollars to this child and this woman get ten dollars because of this baby, I come up with a hundred dollars a day if I'm lucky." The few who held legitimate jobs did so for only short periods of time in low-paying menial labor or dead-end jobs such as fast food operations. A small minority received welfare or disability benefits. Respondents were noticeably outside the conventional economic system of the city, and income from legitimate sources was negligible.

Some of the respondents had rather sophisticated approaches to shoplifting, prostitution, or drug dealing. Carmen, a particularly energetic illegitimate businesswoman, stated pride in her ability to "boost," claiming great skill in each step of the necessary operations from the actual stealing to the way she selected customers. Usually shoplifters would steal from department stores and then search out customer or known "fences." In contrast, Carmen was pleased with her skill in stealing and was especially proud of her ability to organize purchasers and the respectful way they treat her:

> Oh, yeah, I got my clients. I got clients I call up and tell me to get in a cab and come over. I get in a cab, they pay for the cab. There's a joint [marijuana] waiting for me or a hit [crack] . . . you know. And I throw everything on the bed, and they say, "I want this and that, and that, and that, and that." And I say, "Give me two or three hundred." And they say, "Here." And they pay for my cab back, and I'm gone. I have very good clients. Because they know I'm the best.

For most respondents, however, illegitimate activities were more opportunistic. The women were generally street prostitutes who "picked up tricks" in specified "cruising" areas. Some had steady clients and could depend on them for a regular income. Occasionally prostitutes would steal from clients, but this occurred only rarely, not with regular "dates," and only when the opportunity was presented.

Overall, we would describe the economic condition of our respondents as "getting by." Even for respondents with regular illegitimate schemes, their inability to budget their money or to control their drug and alcohol consumption, in conjunction with their periodic attempts to meet family responsibilities, combined to limit their ability to accumulate savings. As a result, their general outlook reflected their economic situation: planning was on a day-to-day basis with only sketchy visions for some distant future, most of which entailed a more conventional life and escape from their present environment. Almost without exception, they attributed their failure to escape their environment and their inability to implement plans for conventional living to personal defects of character, exemplified for them by their involvement with crack and other substances.

## Drug Histories

Although the study focused primarily on crack smoking, the respondents' drug histories illustrated that crack was not their only drug selection. Almost without exception, respondents reported having used a wide variety of drugs. Most of them had begun their drug-using careers very early with alcohol. One woman claimed that when she was 3 years old she drank with her alcoholic father and was similarly introduced to marijuana when she was 6 years old. Although all respondents stated that they smoked crack on a regular basis, there were often parallel patterns of heavy use of other drugs, most often alcohol or, in a minority of cases, heroin. In some instances, respondents reported alcohol or heroin as their primary preference. It was common for respondents to admit that they were phsyically dependent on alcohol or heroin but not physically dependent on crack, even if they experienced what they described as a periodic and uncontrolled desire for it. A substantial portion of the respondents claimed that alcohol was a pleasant companion to crack, a cooling and balancing counterpoint to the jangled effects crack often produced. Moreover, while crack was a drug they used on periodic binges, alcohol was often consumed daily. In the words of one female respondent, "I drink like a sailor."

The most distinguishing feature that appeared to accoount for simple or complex drug histories was *age*. Older respondents had typically experimented with dozens of different substances and tended to report using drugs as they appeared as fads during a past era. For younger respondents, their move into crack smoking did not entail wide experimentation with gateway drugs. They generally had experience with one or two introductory drugs and then moved quickly from alcohol or marijuana use directly into crack and/or speed, which were often interchangeable or progressive.[1]

Although our study singled out crack for special attention, respondents in our study considered three other drugs equally compelling, with similar or more serious consequences: alcohol, heroin, and speed. Unlike heroin, which developed identifiable physical symptoms of tolerance, respondents understood that crack did not produce physical dependence and that they would *not* experience extreme discomfort if they suddenly stopped using crack.

## Learning About Crack

At the time of the study, crack had become a major drug selection for all our respondents, even for individuals for whom other drugs and narcotics competed for priority. Respondents typically reported that their introduction to crack was through a friend or a close associate. Surprisingly, respondents in San Francisco stated that they had first heard about crack not through the street grapevine but through the mass media, particularly television. In the past, Brecher (1972) noted how the media, under the guise of reporting news, served to advertise new drugs and thereby "create" an interest and curiosity about them. This media phenomenon appeared to be the way interest in crack developed in San Francisco: widespread media reporting of it on the East Coast served to generate interest among members of the San Francisco street scenes who had already made commitments to drug careers; and once crack was introduced into the street systems, experimenters gravitated to it. The respondents selected for this study became devotees.

Another feature of crack that accounted for its instant popularity was the general reputation that powdered cocaine traditionally held among street system participants. Prior to the introduction of crack, drug users in the street scenes of San Francisco considered cocaine an *elite* drug, if not *the* elite drug, not only for its high cost but for its association with successful public figures in the worlds of entertainment and athletics. With snorting, the effects were usually quite subtle, mildly pleasurable, and cleary expensive (Waldorf et al. 1977). When freebasing developed, the notion, if not the exact chemistry, of preparing cocaine for smoking became common knowledge on the street. It was unusual, however, for the average street person to possess the necessary materials, the know-how to prepare them, or the money to purchase the drug and its paraphernalia to carry out freebasing.

The introduction of preparing cocaine for smoking by cooking it with baking soda offered a number of advantages over former ways of ingesting it. First, and most important, it lowered the cost dramatically and made "rocks" or "hubbas"—the street name in San Francisco for small amounts of crack cocaine—available to even the poorest street participants. Rather than being merchandised in bulk, small rocks could be sold for five or ten dollars, thus making one or two "hits" financially accessible.

Second, cocaine's reputation as a high-status drug made it a product of special importance to a ready market of users who were eager, even enthusiastic, about experimenting with a drug that was symbolically associated with success in life. What had been embellished by myth and the popular media allowed the common man and woman in the absence of legitimate

career accomplishments to enjoy vicarious association with the rich and famous.

Finally, the initial physical effects smokers experienced—a "head rush"
and a sudden exhilaration—were initially so pleasurable that users, delighted
with the immediate and powerful lift in spirits, found themselves with an
overwhelming desire to repeat the experience.

These three features—cocaine's elite reputation, its marketing convenience and low cost, and its gratifying effects—accounted for the quickness
and persistence of the crack phenomenon among the populations we studied
in San Francisco.

Because of crack's relative cheapness and popularity, combined with
widespread unemployment, the role of street dealer became an available and
valued occupation in low-income neighborhoods (Williams 1989). Rather than
the notion of cocaine's being available from only jet set distributors, almost
any poor man or woman (or daring adolescent) willing to chance arrest and
assault from competitors could enter the crack business and enjoy an income
that was superior to whatever legitimate opportunities were available for
persons with limited work experience or little formal education. With the
proliferation of small-time street dealers, crack became ubiquitous on the
streets of inner-city neighborhoods so that persons eager to experiment with
it could buy it cheaply from street mechants they knew and trusted.

## The Attraction of Crack: The Setting and the Drug

Much has been written of the importance of the social context of drug use
and of the necessity of understanding the influence of these contexts in
shaping drug selection, drug experiences, and drug careers (Zinberg 1984).
Street drug ethnographers over the past twenty-five years have noted that
the adventure associated with the action of urban street scenes has been a
significant motivating factor for both inducing individuals to experiment with
illicit drugs and then to continue using them (Sutter 1966; Feldman 1968;
Preble and Casey 1969). Participating in the street scenes of San Francisco
was part of the attraction of crack use. Shanine, a young prostitute whose
considerable earnings went largely to crack use (and to clothes), explained
this feeling-state in the following interview:

> *Interviewer:* The feeling I'm getting from you is that you have been giving
> a lot more thought than you said as far as quitting crack and getting
> out for awhile.
> *Shanine:* I mean I want to, but it's like this place is so. . . . Sometimes
> I have so much fun that I don't want to leave. Because, I don't trust
> too many people. . . . But my associates—I'm not going to call them

my friends because you have no friends out here. . . . You know, I just get out of there and get to talking and bullshitting. . . . You know, I just like to go out a lot. I don't know, I just have fun.

Shanine went on to explain that when she left the area—in this case, the Tenderloin—she was drawn back to the neighborhood, not necessarily to the use of drugs but to the excitement and pace of living there. Another respondent in response to being asked what caused her relapse to crack put her answer in the context of the neighborhood: "The environment. Being out there. It's like a trap, you can't get out of there."

Our emphasis here is to underscore the importance of the social context and the way use of crack (and other drugs) facilitated participation in these action scenes. From a street perspective in which a fast-paced life required alertness and energy, crack had a distinct beneficial function.

## Routes into Crack Smoking

When crack appeared in the marketplace, recruits came from three sources: old-time heroin users (some in methadone programs), persons with histories of extensive drug experimentation, and young street participants who were attracted to new adventures associated with "partying."

### Heroin Users

Use of cocaine in conjunction with heroin dates back to the 1880s (Feldman and Beschner 1988). Traditionally, users have reported that the interaction of the two drugs—often called "speedballs"—enhanced both drug effects. For heroin users with either steady habits or currently stabilized in methadone maintenance programs, smoking crack allowed them to regain the valued sensation of the "rush"—that sudden, intense pleasure when a narcotic is injected. Experienced heroin users compared the rush from smoking crack with its counterpart of injecting heroin. For them, the new phenomenon of crack smoking was a rediscovery of a lost but prized sensation. Pat, one of the old-time heroin users in our study, explained the practicality of crack smoking for him: "I got into this smoking of crack because I can't feel dope [heroin] over the methadone and I can't get a hit [injection] anyway; I don't have any veins." Caroline, an experienced heroin user prior to her experimentation with crack, reported how the mixture affected her and prompted her to continue mixing the two drugs:

> *Interviewer*: What's the difference [between crack and heroin]? How does crack make you feel differently from heroin?
> *Caroline*: Well, one's a downer and the other one's an upper. So it's like

when you're loaded on the heroin, you're down and you're nodding. And you take a hit of crack. It's kind of like it kicks the heroin and it kicks the crack. And it gives you one big giant feeling.

For the heroin users in our study, crack became an important supplement to their regular use of heroin (or methadone). Even for individuals heavily addicted to heroin and with a clear preference for it, like Caroline, the lure of crack remained a mysterious and powerful attraction: "It's just something about it when you take that hit and feeling good; it just makes you feel like you just want more and more and more."

## Drug Experimenters

Other drug users with less inclination for drug preferences usually experimented with crack as it became popular among their street acquaintances. Crack became simply another one of the many drugs they tested. In comparing crack to previous drug experiences, it most often ranked high in preference and sometimes became the fatal attraction other confirmed crack smokers reported.

## Party Types

Partying was a route into crack smoking taken by young women who were usually curious conventional types from middle-class or religious families. They usually defined themselves as "good girls" who were attracted to life in the fast lane. Although they admitted to minor transgressions in their adolescent years, such as smoking marijuana or having premarital sex, they were unconnected to street action scenes, which both horrified and fascinated them. They viewed their own move into regular crack use as a descent into wicked activities that contrasted sharply with their earlier depictions of themselves. They were usually introduced to crack use by a close friend who was similarly oriented toward partying. Shay, who came from a conventional family and spent a year and a half in college, described how her initiation to crack smoking was the outgrowth of friendship and her twenty-seventh birthday:

I was with some friends. Some friends turned me onto this shit. They bought the powder, and the rock already, a case of wine—red and white mix. Beer, champagne. We went to my house and they pulled out their pipes and all that. I never had experience with that before. He told me they wanted me to try some. So the guy put a little piece of rock in a pipe, and he told me he'd give me experience in how to hit it. Act like you're smoking weed [marijuana] but just don't suck hard. Just pull it in nice and easy. When you see the smoke coming, then let it cloud up real white and then start pulling it in. And then you hold it a little bit. You hold your nose and go [respondent sucks in air]. And a little bit more out your nose and a little bit out your mouth. Then let it all out your mouth and nose and just totally exhale until you let it all out of your system. Let all the smoke out. And I got one hell of a hit which I'll never forget. I heard bells for three or four minutes. . . . I can't explain it. It's a feeling like, "Ooooh, I want to do this again. Give me some more of that." I like the way—you can't compare it to alcohol. You can't compare it with weed. It's a kind of feeling that you feel like you're on clouds. You feel like you're in heaven.

## The Lure of Crack: More and More and More . . .

Almost without exception, respondents expressed a paradoxical attraction and antipathy for crack. They seemed to cling more to the promise of its first pleasures than to any enduring satisfaction it brought. A common theme underscored the intense enjoyment of the initial experience followed by a losing struggle to have that intense feeling repeated. Respondents were often unable to find appropriate imagery to describe what was obviously a different kind of sensation from other drug adventures, and users expressed both a desire for its repetition and a disappointment about failing to achieve it. As one respondent claimed, "The only time you get high is the first hit of a binge."

Perhaps the single feature about crack that was reported most consistently was the way it captivated the user and evoked an overpowering desire to repeat the experience. Despite what respondents implied was a feeling state that was indescribably delicious, they unanimously found fault with the inexplicable search of trying to regain the sensation. Each respondent tried in his or her own way to capture in words the appeal found in crack. The following excerpts are three examples of the many verbal attempts of respondents to express their powerlessness to control their desire for the effects of crack:

It's just that it comes to a point when you take that first hit. After you do that, it's like you feel like you've got to get some more. It's telling you need some more. . . . Sometimes I can [control the urge] and sometimes I don't know. I'll get on the phone or I'll walk around or something. But it all depends on what type of mood I'm in. Sometimes I can take a hit and just say, "Well, that's cool." But then sometimes it's just like this urge that I just got to have it. [Lisa]

The methadone is worse than heroin will ever be—to get off of it. When you go to jail, they detox you awfully quick. Some people been on the program for a long time—thirteen, twenty years. But this crack. I got into this and figured I could handle it. If it don't make me physically sick, I figured I could say no, but it's not that way. . . . I spend every dime I get on it with the exception of a pack of cigarettes. . . . But any money I make I'll spend on it. Any kind of money at all. What am I going to do when there's no money and stuff? I guess I could go without dinner. That's when I'm hungry and I wish I had bought something. I've never, even on heroin, I always made sure that I had groceries. I've always took care of that. But this stuff, you really convince yourself that you don't care what you do. You get hungry. It has that much control over you. It's hard for me to deal with something like that. It's hard for me to deal with it because I'm not strong enough. And I'm too old to be doing this shit. I'll be 49 next week, on the sixteenth. [Pat]

It [crack] makes me feel good but then it also depresses you, too, when you smoke a lot of it. I have this feeling like, "God, why am I doing this . . . ?" And you want more. Sometimes it's no good. You don't get satisfied. Then it depresses you. And you're just running around. You're a crazed person. Always wanting more. It's mainly feeling that you just want more. And it just more or less runs your life, really, is what it does. [Caroline]

## Crack Binges

All respondents reported going on crack binges that lasted anywhere from two or three days to a week or more. These experiences were both exhilarating and exhausting, where a kind of inner struggle went on to keep from yielding to the temptation of "more" and satisfying the urge for continuance. The theme that permeated respondents' descriptions of these binges was the struggle against the drug itself. Anita, one of the few respondents who traded sex directly for crack, admitted that she stepped knowingly into this aspect of dependence:

*Anita*: When I first smoked it, I knew it was a . . . controlling drug.
*Interviewer*: It would *control* you?
*Anita*: Yeh, controlling, where it seemed to control everybody that uses it.

Some users found that crack cocaine was a useful corollary to their other activities. Kim, a transsexual prostitute, found that crack kept her alert. After experimenting with heroin and other drugs, she made a conscious choice for crack because it aided her performance as a prostitute: "It's very rushy. . . . It keeps you up and alert. I got tired of nodding all the time on heroin and going to sleep on weed [marijuana]. . . . It helps me make more money."

The actual binge itself had many variations. The essential element was a compelling desire to continue smoking crack in a relatively uninterrupted pattern. Some respondents mixed business with the binge, especially prostitutes who, like Kim, found that it kept them alert. Shanine wrote letters and made entries into her diary.

None of the respondents looked on these crack binges in a totally favorable light. The most common complaint was that the initial pleasure, which was the only one they sought, did not last long, and the pursuit of recapturing it was elusive, time-consuming, and expensive. April's description was typical:

> It kind of levels out and then goes so that you can't feel it hardly. It's like you want to keep smoking to get the rush and the five-minute high, but if you keep smoking it for a long time, like I did, it's like when you go to quit, you can just drop it because it doesn't give you the same high that it did at first.

Still, all the respondents stated that they were caught up in wanting more. This pursuit was the most frustrating part of the total drug experience because it did not deliver what it had originally promised. This dissatisfaction was increased by smokers' powerlessness to stop the pursuit, with the result that it drained them of energy, money, and eventually of the self-respect that goes with controlling one's fate. In several instances, respondents described the drug as having a command over them and of their being helpless once they were in its power. In fact, three respondents compared crack to a pimp, implying that they were in an undesirable subordinate relationship with the drug.

By the end of the crack binge, users reported a depletion of money and energy. The physical conditions they described were often a series of unpleasant bodily symptoms and an odd state of disquiet and regret. For the period of time they submitted to the temptation and remained under the drug's influence, there was, at least in the beginning, a sense of exhilaration, a "head rush" that came on suddenly and gloriously and then drifted quickly away. Although successive "hits" did not produce the same intense exhilaration, smokers remained committed to pursuing that elusive sensation they found so gratifying.

At the end of the binge, the most common complaints were related to the physical wear and tear that came from fatigue and lack of sleep. Each user reported negatively on this condition, one claiming that "it ties up your legs and muscles"; another said that it "makes me look tired, worn out." At the end of the binge, users more or less caved in and slept from exhaustion. Many crack smokers were keenly aware of the drain on their health and took special care to eat regularly and dress neatly when they were not on binges.

## Controlling Binges And Quitting

While there was unanimity on the pleasures and pains of crack use, there was divergence of opinion on quitting and seeking drug treatment. Most of our respondents had at one time voluntarily attempted to stop smoking crack. During their initial period of abstinence, they reported a physical state of chronic irritability. One respondent's attempt to quit produced a condition that was decidedly unpleasant:

> *Interviewer*: Tell me how you felt the two days that you were off.
> *Shanine*: Like a bitch. I was crabby at everybody. I tried to sleep. Matter of fact, I did sleep. I slept most of the time. . . . But I kept waking up. . . . I'd sleep for an hour and then wake up.
> *Interviewer*: And then what?
> *Shanine*: I'd want a hit. Try to eat and go back to sleep. Try and fill myself up so I'd go back to sleep.
> *Interviewer*: So that went on for how long?
> *Shanine*: For like a day and a half. Probably not even a day and a half. . . . I couldn't go out there and be around everybody and tolerate all that bullshit. Sometimes I just have to be high, you know, to tolerate everything. To tolerate those tricks [prostitute customers]. Everything. I can't stand some of them.

Other respondents stated a desire to break out of the pattern of chronic use but expressed a personal helplessness in managing the task alone. Kim, the sexually active transsexual who found crack functional to her prostitution, typified the sense of mystification in coming to grips with the compelling nature of her desire for the crack high: "To tell the truth, I wanted to get off it, but I just couldn't get off. . . . I tried to stop on my own, but I couldn't do it." For some respondents, the lack of an immediate support system to pave the way for drug treatment provided the explanation for their limited motivation: "[There's] a long way to go," one woman said with sad resignation, "and nobody there to help me."

## Drug Treatment

Only a minority of respondents had ever entered drug treatment programs or even considered it. For those who had, the problem drug that motivated them to treatment tended to be heroin rather than crack. For individuals who had voluntarily entered drug treatment programs, the experience was either unsuccessful or unsatisfying. After enjoying the freedom of street life, they found that residential programs were too regimented. For heroin users who had recently taken up crack use, methadone maintenance was an option. Once they entered treatment, however, their pattern was to supplement methadone with street drugs, which for our population was primarily crack. It was the exceptionally motivated client who cooperated with treatment regimes and reduced the use of street drugs.

The major tension between crack-smoking clients and drug treatment programs was the discrepancy between the treatment program's demands for conventional behavior and the nature of street life, whose excitement and adventures were intertwined with drug consumption. The crack smokers we selected were geared to perform in the street systems of their choice, and they viewed the options for treatment as having to give up valued activities, even those they often defined as dissatisfying or harmful. As a result, drug treatment was not a significant part of their world, and it rarely entered into their conversations.

## Sex Histories and Crack Use

Almost without exception, respondents reported having early sexual experiences. For the women, the most common age for their first experience was 13 years old, but a number of them claimed to have been sexually molested or abused when they were younger. Remembrances of these instances of sexual abuse were always described with bitterness and resentment toward the offender, who frequently was a stepfather. Others claimed to have had sexual encounters with other family members (e.g., brothers and/or cousins).

All of the respondents had been sexually active prior to their use of crack. In most cases, they were introduced to sex in some mutually determined act with an intimate for whom they claimed either affection or love. In some cases, alcohol eased the introduction, but none of the respondents believed that drugs or alcohol was the "cause" of their sexual motivation or the source of their desire. The prostitutes in our study did, however, associate their entry into street prostitution with the use of crack or, in a few cases, heroin.

Few respondents claimed to be sexually excited by crack. In fact, the opposite reaction was the more common description. Rather than crack's acting as an aphrodisiac, women often stated that it reduced their interest in sex. One woman when asked whether crack excited her sexually claimed flatly, "You don't be in the mood at all." Berta, a prostitute and sexually active woman throughout her life, explained how crack made sex repellent:

> He'd [a date] always said, "Come and smoke some." So, one day I smoked some. Ain't no such thing as having sex after that shit. You talk about some pussy, I'll kill you. It takes away my sex drive. It just, I have no emotions whatsoever. Okay, I'm froze to death. Even when I was shooting cocaine, same thing.

For men, the sexual response to crack was more ambiguous. While they associated crack with sexual activities, they found that it tended to undermine their ability to maintain erections and to ejaculate. These sexual encounters, usually fellatio, were seldom totally satisfying for either the man or woman since the woman's aim was to complete the act as soon as possible and acquire the crack and the man's desire was to sustain the sex act indefinitely. Under these circumstances, sexual encounters often veered off into power plays rather than sessions of erotic sexuality.

Most sexual encounters were carried out in the privacy of apartments, hotel rooms, or automobiles. When these encounters took place in crack houses, they were often performed where others could observe. Women who participated were quickly identified as "toss-ups" or "crack whores." Some of the men who used crack as a lure for quick and dirty sex also recognized its theatrical value, one stating: "For a little crack, you can make them act like circus animals." The consequence for the women was assignment to such low status that local descriptions of them were in dehumanized terms, and the stigma they felt was bitter and burning.

Stories of "crack whores" and "toss-ups" abounded even though other sexual encounters that involved crack were far more frequent. These stories were used principally as anticrack propaganda to illustrate crack's evil powers. Although they were atypical situations, they were used as dramatic evidence of the destructive nature of crack smoking. Most sexual encounters involving crack, however, entailed a business component that consisted of mutual agreements between consenting partners. These encounters generally took three forms: opportunistic situations, sale of sex for money, and sexual favors for crack.

## Opportunistic Situations

Opportunistic situations to exchange sex for crack presented themselves spontaneously and depended on the willingness of the individual to capitalize on their availability. A male prostitute in our study, for example, came across two gay men in one of San Francisco's gay neighborhoods. Having known the men from previous experiences, he was invited to participate in a group sex arrangement where crack was an inducement. According to his report, they said, "You come over and spend the night and party, and you can get as high as you want." The respondent, trying to clarify the distinction between this arrangement and being a "toss-up," stated, "Look at it logically. . . . I'm not a toss-up and was going to buy it anyway. And if it's there . . ."

## Sex for Crack

Although respondents referred to sex-for-crack exchanges throughout the study, they tended to be more common in discussion than in practice. Furthermore, the exchange of sex for crack for many of our San Francisco respondents did not always have overtones of degradation in which the woman was a demeaned and subordinate participant but more closely resembled a bartering situation. Anita explained how she negotiated sex for crack, not as a way of begging or losing control but as a way of eliminating an unnecessary and intrusive financial proceeding:

> *Anita*: I only come out at night. You know, a lot of times I don't get paid. I exchange. It's understood from the get-go.
> *Interviewer*: Exchange for what?
> *Anita*: Exchange for crack. It's like, I've got so much amount of this and I want you to do this. Although sometimes they don't tell me right off. But it's understood.
> *Interviewer*: If you understand it, how do you understand it?
> *Anita*: Oh, just because they say something like, "You want to smoke?" You know, so right there it's not for free.
> *Interviewer*: It's an exchange for sex.
> *Anita*: And sometimes they have a quarter-ounce. You know, they have to have big dope because I'm not a twenty-dollar [prostitute] . . . you know, wrong person.

When the exchange of sex for crack was made in lieu of currency and the price in crack was carefully calculated, the encounter was called "working a twist." In this circumstance, crack was a substitute for money. And the woman involved maintained control over the exchange unlike the "toss-up" when her negotiating power was absent. Rather than viewing the activity as a severe loss of status and self respect, "working a twist" was a convenient but not degrading way to satisfy the desire for the crack high. Caroline, a heroin addict primarily, explained the circumstances in which "working a twist" fit in with her prostitution:

> *Interviewer*: When did you first exchange sex for crack?
> *Caroline*: I'd say within the last three years on and off.
> *Interviewer*: About how many times during a thirty-day period do you do that?
> *Caroline*: Maybe three times . . . because it's really not that necessary. I mean I can keep track and I always have money because I do date. So I can always buy my own crack. But there is sometimes when I get down and out, and I want some crack and somebody will come along and say, "Hey, let's work this twist" or whatever. Then, yeh, I'd get crack in exchange instead of money.

Other times, exchanges of sex for crack were expedient and convenient methods to continue a binge. Rather than being sought after, they were frequently the result of partying, which was not associated with being demeaned. Lynn, whose social life frequently centered on partying, explained how she had her first "twist":

> *Lynn*: The first time I did it, I was high. I was really tweaking. I mean I had my high beams on. I was really mellow. I was real high. But we didn't have no more drugs. It was like three in the morning. And we still wanted to get high.
>
> *Interviewer*: Who's we?
>
> *Lynn*: Me and my two friends. . . . And we were over my friend's house. And the dope man came and he had bags of rocks. Bags of rocks. We was like trying to get credit from him, and he knew we was high. He wasn't going to give it to us. And he was like, "Well, suck my dick and I'll give you all a rock." That's how I first started.

In these situations, the exchange of sex for crack was not necessarily a humiliating experience, and several of the women remembered them in highly favorable ways. Shay recalled that her first experience in exchanging sex for crack was a mutually satisfying sexual encounter that developed when she worked the stroll as a prostitute:

> This was the first time it happened. And he asked me if I wanted to have sex. I said, "Sure." [He said,] "I got some rocks." I said, "I beg your pardon?" "I got some rocks but I'm going to pay you up front for your services before we even get into anything because I don't have no money." So, he had a hundred dollars of dope. "I'm going to give you [an inaudible amount]. You can take that with you and we can smoke what we have left." He gave me three rocks and we smoked the rest. I gave him head. . . . He gave me some head. And we really had a nice time.

Other women, particularly young ones new to the drug scene, found that more streetwise crack users and dealers readily exploited them. Michele, a young prostitute, explained how she participated in sex for crack in the beginning stages of her crack career and then rejected the practice, preferring the independence and finances of prostitution for money: "I was getting cheated on the deal. That's why I started coming out here [on the stroll]. I used to go over there a couple of times a week. And he wanted me to do his cousin and his friends. Most of it was oral sex. . . . He was a dealer."

When young women discovered that their youth had market value in the sex trade, they frequently stopped performing sexual acts for crack. Instead they entered prostitution as beginning professionals. This choice gave them control of their finances and prevented their developing reputations as toss-ups and crack whores.

## Sex for Money for Crack

Most of the respondents we selected insisted that they never traded sex directly for crack, although they acknowledged entering and remaining in prostitution as a primary means for earning money, much of which was spent on crack. The intermediate step of working for money—prostituting or "boosting"—was to them an important distinction, one they saw as distinguishing them from "toss-ups." The women had little hesitation in describing their work as prostitutes and were candid about the sexual favors they provided and the cost of each activity; but most of them were adamant about preserving a self-image that was not totally driven by a passion for drugs. The issues of pride and self-esteem appeared to allow them to define their financial exchanges as business rather than an obsession for drugs or loss of inner control. By receiving money rather than drugs, they were able to avoid the kind of dependency relationship with males that they perceived as subordinate and degraded. In managing their own finances, they were able to have options for other purchases, such as buying food, clothes, toys for their children, and the like.

The most important feature in exchanging sex for money was their achievement of independence. Although they admitted that much—in some cases, most—of their income was spent on crack, they were able to maintain their individual autonomy. As young businesswomen, they controlled their money, and that aspect of financial independence preserved their self-esteem. This does not mean that during encounters with "dates" they did not smoke crack. They would share crack with customers or accept it in amounts that were equal to their standard prices. In some cases, if a crack smoker was on a binge of crack, she might drop her price to induce a customer. As Anita stated, "On hubbas, it [the price] used to go down to forty bucks for half-and-half [part vaginal sex, part fellatio]." But even on crack binges, the majority of respondents maintained the principle of a monied transaction. Several of the women voluntarily underscored the importance of money transactions and spoke of them with a sense of high moral integrity.

## Standards of Behavior: Family and Personal Responsibilities

Similar to the rules that governed the exchange of sex for crack, respondents determined spcific standards of behavior in other spheres of their lives that they tried to keep crack use from corrupting. They placed rather strict moral values on behavior associated with family responsibilities. Many of the women had children and tried within their means to be caring parents. Anita, for example, set limits around where her prostitution activities would take place. Since her daughter lived with her, she would not bring "dates" to the house. This decision set an ethical boundary for her—a kind of bottom line below which she would not fall. By retaining a private resolve, she was able to preserve the sanctity of the dwelling she shared with her daughter and a view of herself as a caring mother who had not been totally degraded by crack use. "No," she insisted. "That's family. That's out."

Perhaps the most important measure of maintaining respectability even during crack binges was preserving a good appearance. For the prostitutes in the study, a good appearance was necessary for business reasons since it was crucial that they project an image of sexual appeal. It was, however, the audience of friends and peers that influenced whether crack binges and sustained drug use had taken its toll on an individual. Respondents were sensitive to negative comments about the physical effects of crack binges, and women especially went to great lengths to look fresh and healthy. During those periods when crack binges drained them of energy, women would frequently withdraw from circulation until they recovered sufficiently to rid themselves of telltale signs of weariness and exhaustion. As one respondent claimed, "I stop calling people and would stay away. I don't want people to see me like that." When women in the midst of fatigue would appear dirty or disheveled on the street, it was a signal that they had surrendered a valued principle, and it marked a descent in their local status.

## Social Types and Hierarchical Order

There appeared to be a hierarchy of local social types in the crack scenes of San Francisco. Its underpinnings were determined in at least two ways: by control over the direction of one's life and by the degree of participation in the monied economy. At the high end of the hierarchy were individuals who controlled their crack consumption and earned top dollar in whatever field of legitimate or illegitimate pursuits was valued in the study communities. At the bottom of the hierarchy were those who had lost control of their crack use and exhibited to a highly competitive street system personal weakness that allowed others to exploit them. If a person were sexually exploited and humiliated, their sexual services as well as their personal worth within the neighborhood system were devalued. As persons at the bottom of the prestige scale, they became subject to ridicule and scorn. In essence, they were the failures of the street system with little to offer except quick and dirty sex, performed more for the amusement of onlookers than for any sexual excitement of the encounter.

In between, there existed a complicated set of measures that each individual employed to determine whether he or she rose or fell within the local status scheme. The place where a prostitute performed her sexual favors, for example, provided one measure. Lower status was accorded prostitutes who accepted "car dates" and carried out their sexual activities in the darkness of an automobile. Higher status was conferred on those whose sexual encounters took place in hotel rooms or private apartments.

Of greatest importance in determining an individual's local status was management of immediate family. Individuals who had the wherewithal to support themselves and their children were generally looked upon with a measure of respect. This achievement need not, however, be visible financial support. Sending children to live with relatives indicated that a level of responsibility had been accomplished; placing them in foster homes denoted inadequacy or failure as a parent.

Too often crack use and crack binges provided respondents with evidence of their inability to manage the expected roles of parent or spouse, particularly during and after episodes when crack smoking overrode all other priorities. Such failures in the performance of these valued family roles induced self-loathing and depression. Many of them expressed feelings similar to Diane's, who stated bleakly, "I hate myself sometimes. . . . It's just me in this world, all by myself. . . . I feel that way with or without crack." Her sense of chronic melancholy and loneliness was not uncommon. Like others in the study who expressed disappointment with their general condition, with crack she could periodically lift her mood, if only momentarily. For a few sweet moments, a "head rush" replaced her depression, and the potency of crack revitalized her. And the sudden surge in energy became a soothing counterbalance to a life that moved alternately between anguish and danger.

## AIDS Knowledge, Risk of HIV, and Serology

San Francisco's model for managing the HIV/AIDS epidemic has become world famous. As the HIV epidemic moved from the gay community to injection drug users, sexual partners, and people of color, strategies for prevention and education took new shapes. In 1985, when San Francisco public officials first addressed the probable movement of the epidemic into the drug-injecting networks, the drug treatment establishment and the San Francisco Department of Public Health proposed that the only approach to preventing the spread of HIV among intravenous drug users was to recruit them into drug treatment programs, where they would presumably abstain from injecting drugs and thereby be protected from infection. Under the leadership of the YES project, a San Francisco agency that specialized in applied ethnographic research, the Mid-City Consortium to Combat AIDS pioneered an effective street-based strategy. It consisted of utilizing ethnographic findings as the basis for sending outreach workers into the natural hangouts of drug users, where they provided AIDS education and distributed condoms and one-ounce bottles of bleach to disinfect needles. During the time data for this study were being collected, the YES project deployed some thirty outreach workers and field supervisors and passed out bottles of bleach with such regularity and consistency that on the street bleach may have been better known for its capabilities of disinfecting potentially contaminated needles than it was for doing laundry. Other agencies added to the prevention effort and provided posters, pamphlets, comic books, billboards, and video-tapes addressing the connection between sharing contaminated hypodermic needles and HIV infection. In San Francisco, the term CHOW—the acronym for "community health outreach worker"—had worked its way into the street idiom and become as well entrenched as the slang for crack. AIDS workers gave away thousands of condoms every day. During the heyday of this outreach effort, there was hardly a hidden population of injection drug users in the city of San Francisco that had not been targeted for street-based intervention.

With such a concerted, if politically jumbled, AIDS prevention program, it came as no surprise to discover that the respondents selected for this study, particularly the prostitutes, were AIDS aware. As a result of intensive health outreach strategies, respondents had acquired a working knowledge of the HIV epidemic and generally put into practice those measures that would protect them against infection. One of the significant findings of our research in San Francisco is that where AIDS educators penetrate drug-using networks and establish positive, helping relationships, members of the target groups will practice risk-reduction methods. This appears to be especially applicable with street prostitutes when they have the wherewithal to negotiate transactions on an equal basis with customers. These women reported consistent use of condoms in those business transactions, and the results of their serological testing provided some evidence of their truthfulness.

As we examined the street systems in San Francisco and the drug scenes found in them—both in this study and over the past four years—it became apparent even under the best of prevention circumstances which social types were more vulnerable to HIV infection. In San Francisco, it was clear that the AIDS message had reached those drug-using networks and those individuals who had been targeted by the outreach effort. What this study specifies is that a wide variety of social types exist in low-income, urban communities, most of whom can be reached with the street-based intervention methods we have developed. Crack smokers were neither unresponsive nor uncooperative with these public health measures. In fact, the existence of injection drug users, who had adopted crack smoking and had been the primary target of the original street-based outreach, were the focal points of AIDS education within their respective communities. In their way, these injection drug users as they mingled with crack smokers became ad hoc AIDS educators within those networks that were not primary targets. As a result, crack smokers profited from the prevention effort even when they themselves had never met or talked with an outreach worker. While their use of crack may have been problematic to society for reasons of morality or good taste, it did not appear that crack smoking automatically put them at risk for AIDS.

There were, however, among those populations who lived on the margin or outside the law social types whose self-esteem and local status were so low that infection with a deadly, incurable disease was of little, if any, concern. As we looked at the various crack-smoking social networks and their hierarchies of local social types, it was readily identifiable that among our target group, as street status diminished, activities that could lead to HIV infection increased. In San Francisco, one of these social types was the crack toss-up and those with social standing only slightly above them. These individuals, both male and female, periodically slipped into unsafe sexual practices, not simply because they were intoxicated at the moment or driven by their desire to seek another hit on a crack pipe. They were at risk because in assessing their present reality, they did not in the silence of their hearts believe that their lives were worth preserving. And while San Francisco may have produced a world-renowned AIDS model, it had not even in its best, most financially secure days found an intervention strategy to address this class of at-risk person.

During the latter part of this study, forty crack smokers (thirty-five females and five males, one of whom was a transsexual) were recruited to be tested for HIV and other sexually transmitted diseases, principally syphilis. Of the thirty-nine confirmed results—one lost due to a missing consent form—there were four individuals who tested seropositive for HIV. Of the four seropositives, three of them were injection drug users, all of them males. The other person who tested positive for HIV infection was a young African-American female who had never injected drugs and had only limited drug experience other than crack.

While the numbers in the serological study were far too small to draw definitive conclusions, the fact remains, no matter how slim the data, that 30 percent of the males—who were also drug injectors—tested positive for HIV antibodies while only one female (less than 4 percent) was HIV infected. If we were to employ these data as a measure of tracking the HIV epidemic in our target communities, then we would have to conclude that in San Francisco the HIV epidemic outside the gay community remains with the injection drug users. The future direction the HIV epidemic takes regarding new infections in low-income communities, we believe, will depend largely on how well our health agencies can access or continue to access injection drug users and keep their infection rate low. Because of his role in exchanging sex for crack, the injection drug user has great potential to spread HIV to female sexual partners, particularly individuals at the lower end of the status hierarchy. Given the limited data, however, we should not assume anything more than noting the potential of this possibility. As long as the seroprevalence rate among the injection drug users remains low, as it has with an aggressive outreach program, this potential can be contained.

## Predicting the Path of the Epidemic

At this juncture, it is fair to ask, based on this study, what role, if any, crack would play in the spread of HIV/AIDS in San Francisco. The answer seems to depend on three factors: identifying as precisely as possible where the present infections are located, identifying those behaviors and activities that would predictably transmit the virus, and assessing the education and prevention methods that would interrupt what would otherwise be the natural path of the epidemic.

In San Francisco, the overwhelming percentage of HIV infections remains among gay males. If San Francisco does, in fact, have a model system of intervention, it tends to be in the treatment of HIV/AIDS and not necessarily in preventing its spread. Most services for HIV/AIDS have been directed primarily to the gay community. Just how crack smoking would extend the epidemic within the gay community has, to the best of our knowledge, not been researched, and our study would not contribute any information to that aspect of the potential spread of HIV. Several ongoing intervention programs address the issue of sexual disinhibition attributed to drug and alcohol consumption among gay men. To the degree that the annual seroconversion among gay men in San Francisco in recent years has dropped to under 1 percent, it can be assumed that crack smoking has not become a major variable in HIV transmission within the gay community.

Among out-of-treatment injection drug users, seroprevalence stabilized at approximately 15 percent during the four-year period that the CHOW program was in operation. What had not been identified until this study was the potential role crack-using, injection-drug users might play in transmitting HIV to females who may or may not be their permanent or regular sex partners. If crack smoking is an activity that has potential for spreading HIV infection in San Francisco, then injection-drug users must be considered central figures in the equation. Our study indicates that injection-drug users are not simply sexually involved with steady partners but appear to play a significant role in the exploitation of toss-ups, although this phenomenon needs further ethnographic exploration. To the degree that the infection rate among injection drug users rises, then the potential spread of HIV increases. In San Francisco, as long as the seroprevalence rate remains low, the possibility of sudden increases of HIV among crack-smoking females is not likely, although this may not be true for other sexually transmitted diseases (or in other cities).

To assess the possibility of a surge in seroconversion, it would be necessary to examine the methods for addressing prevention of HIV infection among injection drug users and their female sexual partners. As we noted, as long as an intervention structure existed that penetrated these hidden populations in San Francisco and provided consistent education and prevention to injection drug users and their partners, the seroprevalence rate remained steady, with only slight annual increases between 1 percent and 3 percent (Moss 1989). Since December 31, 1990, however, the YES/CHOW program has been shut down. To the best of our knowledge, there has been no alternative plan in San Francisco to replace it with a comparable street-based intervention strategy. Given the absence of the consistent distribution of condoms and the discontinuance of the daily distribution of bleach at the street level and the way those activities served as reminders to populations that had been originally described as hard to reach and difficult to serve, it is not unrealistic to speculate that the incidence of high-risk behavior, such as sharing contaminated needles without disinfecting them, will rise. Whether Prevention Point, the bootleg volunteer needle exchange program in San Francisco, which reaches approximately 6 percent of the estimated 16,000 injection users (Rubens 1990), can substitute for the missing outreach effort remains to be determined. What was once a highly optimistic outlook for managing the HIV epidemic among injection drug users in San Francisco has taken a frightening turn, and crack smoking, which did not appear to have a significant future in accelerating the spread of HIV, may now have an unanticipated opportunity.

## Note

1. Brecher, in his classic report for the Consumers Union, discussed and classified methamphetamine (speed) and cocaine in the same category, most notably because of the similarity of their pharmacological effects—the elevation of mood, the decrease in hunger, indifference to pain, and the antifatigue properties. In fact, Brecher attributed the boom in cocaine smuggling during the late 1960s to the successful banning of the precursor chemicals for the manufacture of speed (Brecher 1972:302).

## References

Aldrich, M. R. 1986. "Crack (Garbage Freebase)." In *Cocaine Handbook: An Essential Reference*. San Francisco: And/Or Press. Second Edition.

Brecher, E. M. 1972. *Licit and Illicit Drugs*. Mount Vernon, N.Y.: Consumers Union.

Feldman, H. W. 1968. "Ideological Supports to Becoming and Remaining a Heroin Addict." *Journal of Health and Social Behavior* 9(2) (May–June).

Feldman, H. W. and Beschner, G. 1988. "Ten-City Report on 'Speedballing.' " Prepared for the National Institute on Drug Abuse. Unpublished.

Horowitz, M. 1974. Editor's Preface to *History of Coca: The Divine Plant of the Incas*. By W. G. Mortimer. San Francisco: And/Or Press.

Lamar, J. V. 1988. "Kids Who Sell Crack." *Time*, May 9.

Moss, A. R., P. Bacchetti, and D. Osmond. 1989. "Seroconversion for HIV in

IVDUs in San Francisco." Abstract number T.A.O. 11, Fifth International Conference on AIDS, Montreal, Canada, June.

Preble, E., and Casey, J. H., Jr. 1969. "Taking Care of Business—The Heroin User's Life on the Street." *International Journal of the Addictions* 4(1).

Rubens, N. 1990. "A Needle a Day . . ." *San Francisco Bay Guardian*, November 21.

Sutter, A. G. 1966. "The World of the Righteous Dope Fiend." *Issues in Criminology* 2.

Waldorf, D., S. Murphy, C. Reinarman, and S. Malone. 1977. *Doing Coke: an Ethnography of Cocaine Users and Sellers*. Washington, D.C.: Drug Abuse Council.

Williams, T. 1989. *The Cocaine Kids: The Inside Story of a Teenage Drug Ring*. Reading, Mass.: Addison-Wesley.

Zinberg, N. E. 1984. *Drugs, Set and Setting: The Basis for Controlled Intoxicant Use*. New Haven, Conn.: Yale University Press.

# 6

# "To the Curb": Sex Bartering and Drug Use Among Homeless Crack Users in Los Angeles

*Kathleen Boyle*
*M. Douglas Anglin*

Los Angeles is so vast and the crack cocaine scene so widespread that any decisions about when and where to learn about the sex-for-crack phenomenon are really decisions about what not to study. The word *decision* implies that our selection process was logical and guided, but, in reality, chance and opportunity had a large role in determining the sample to be studied. What looked to be a study of prostitution connected with crack cocaine use became also a study of homelessness among crack cocaine users.

At the outset of the study, repeated attempts were made to access the crack-using locations and sex-for-crack barterers who had become infamous in Los Angeles through media reports. This area is characterized by a very poor, predominantly African-American population (though recent Central American immigrants are moving into the area), an overloaded or nonexistent social service delivery system, high crime, heavy gang activity, and increasing numbers of drive-by shootings. By summer of 1989, the beginning of the sex-for-crack study, the Los Angeles (City) Police Department (LAPD) was heavily involved in "cracking down" on drugs and crime. Use of a fortified vehicle with a battering ram to knock down the fronts of the crack houses (themselves heavily fortified) had been suspended in the face of vehement community protest, but the police were very active in closing down crack houses as soon as they sprang up. Contacts in this community were reluctant to have interviewers around, stating that it was too dangerous, that the community was volatile, that situations were very fluid, changing rapidly from day to day, and that an outsider, especially a white outsider, would be the target of verbal, or even physical, abuse.

We decided to begin interviewing among the homeless on Skid Row in downtown Los Angeles, since we knew from other studies that homeless people are often crack users. In addition to homeless people who used crack recreationally, there were many heavy crack abusers who had become homeless and spilled over into the downtown area almost as refugees. As a result there were areas of Skid Row that were dense pockets of homeless crack users whose use was so extreme that they had "burned out" their resources and connections in other neighborhoods. They were living on the streets, in shelters, or in single room occupancy (SRO) hotels downtown where there were more services for the homeless and a concentrated market for crack and sex.

We later began studying the crack-using homeless who live in MacArthur Park, located in an area, once elegant but now poor and run-down, that has been most recently populated by recent Central American and other Latino immigrants. The park has been inhabited by economic-refugee homeless, both Anglo and Latino, for several years. Later crack users took over large areas of the park.

In addition, some observation was conducted in crack-using neighborhoods in the San Fernando Valley, the San Gabriel Valley, and, later, South Central Los Angeles. Some time was spent in the three juvenile halls of Los Angeles County, but we found a low level of crack use and almost no sex-for-crack exchange among the juvenile population. The interviews used for analysis were conducted in homeless shelters, in jails, and (one) in MacArthur Park.

The report includes a description of the main areas of observation, the downtown Skid Row area and MacArthur Park, characteristics of the study sample, and epidemiology of crack use in Los Angeles. The words of the subjects themselves, taken from the transcripts, amplify depictions of prior drug use, initiation of crack use, heavy crack use, depletion of resources, sexual activities related to crack use, HIV-related issues, and cessation of crack use.

## Areas of Observation

### Skid Row

The Skid Row area of downtown Los Angeles has grown quickly in the last decade and has spread from the traditional Bowery-style neighborhood inhabited by chronic alcoholics and served by rescue missions to an area about seven blocks wide and fifteen blocks long. The newer areas inhabited by the homeless are, or were, commercial districts, consisting of warehouses, distribution operations, and light industry. The homeless in the Skid Row area have segregated themselves by type: intravenous drug users, crack users, alcoholics, and economic refugees. The homeless mentally ill are scattered throughout the downtown area. For some of the larger groupings, such as the crack users, there is self-segregation by language. Spanish-speaking crack users, including some Cubans, are found apart from English speakers. The English speakers are predominantly African-American.

When observation began downtown in the early fall of 1989, the crack users were concentrated in the central part of the Skid Row area. On one corner alone, Fifth Street and Crocker, hundreds of crack users congregated day and night to buy, sell, and smoke. Men and women milled around three and four deep on the corner and leaned against the walls of the buildings on Crocker from Fifth Street to Sixth Street. Sleeping took place on some of the surrounding streets, especially Towne, the street directly east of Crocker, which at that time, day and night, was a solid line of "curb creatures" (people living on the streets) in sleeping bags on both sides of the street. At that time the police seemed to follow a hands-off policy as long as the users did not move into other areas.

The daily activity of crack abusers in the Skid Row area revolves completely around crack. Upon awakening from a "cocaine coma" (after not sleeping for several days in a row, crack users sleep for many hours or even days), users start the hustle to get the drug. The first act is usually to panhandle or to sell sex to get the money for the first rock. Many people use this initial money to score a rock, sell it for double the price, and then buy more with the money. The rocks are smoked right on the street; there is not much attempt made to hide the smoking.

In the crack-using area of Skid Row, sex (in exchange for money or directly for crack) is engaged in behind dumpsters, in cars, or in alleys. Often, with money in hand from a drug deal, people rent hotel rooms in the area and continue drug use and sex in the room. Many sell or barter hotel vouchers that are given out by General Relief, a county-administered program of assistance to the indigent.

In spite of the many services available for the homeless in the downtown area, life is harsh. Food and clothing are fairly easy to come by once a person learns the ropes, but the physical environment is barren, and the users view each other with distrust and suspicion. Street dwellers complain about the living conditions at the accommodations provided by the mission, shelters, and SRO hotels and agencies.

The missions, like most of the shelters, did not permit residents access during the daytime, allowing them in only at night for sleeping and, in some cases, meals. Mission staff usually expect residents to take part in prayer services and Bible readings, and, although the informants in our sample unanimously told us that they believed in God and prayed themselves, they did not want to be forced into these activities.

The shelters are often very run down and vary in what they offer residents. The first shelter that we accessed, Transition House, is a large, mixed-sex housing unit providing residents a place to live until they can establish themselves. Meals are served; there are full bath facilities; Alcoholics Anonymous and Narcotics Anonymous groups meet on a regular basis; an all-house meeting takes place after dinner every night. Other amenities include a TV room, a "library," a basketball court, and staff social workers to help with referrals to job opportunities and social services. Residents who come in under the influence have to leave the facility, and the staff was fairly diligent in monitoring behavior. There is a waiting list to get into Transition House. At the other end of the range, and more typical of downtown shelters, was a single-sex (in this case, women-only) facility that consisted of two open areas that became wall-to-wall cots at night. Only women with children were allowed to remain on the premises during the day, and there were no amenities for residents. Baths had to be taken at other facilities, and two Porta-Potties outside were the only toilets available to residents. Those who were more independent and more resistant to rules and regulations, especially those still using crack, preferred the looser atmosphere of these smaller shelters to Transition House.

The SRO hotels were universally condemned as being vermin infested, unsafe, with poor plumbing and little personal privacy. According to our subjects, hotel staff routinely entered rooms with a pass key and looked for drugs in residents' possessions. Many said that they preferred to live on the street where they had freedom and were not subjected to the rules of others. Others left the downtown area and moved to MacArthur Park, which was considered friendlier and more comfortable.

The Crocker Street area has changed considerably since it was first observed in 1989. During 1991 police crackdowns hit Skid Row. The line of smokers that stretched down Crocker Street is gone, as is the concentrated knot of hundreds of people on the corner of Fifth and Crocker. Because the police are quick to break up a gathering, smokers prefer to spread out and not concentrate in any one area. They can be seen in several of the streets in the area in much smaller grops.

## MacArthur Park

MacArthur Park (until 1945 Westlake Park) was once the center of the elegant Westlake neighborhood, one of the first new neighborhoods created when Los Angeles began leaving the central city and moving west. Built in the 1920s, the neighborhood contained beautiful hotels, apartment houses with ornate lobbies, and movie palaces in the grand tradition. The park was the heart of this and until recently had maintained its role as the place for Sunday strolls, paddles across the lake in rented boats, chess and checker marathon tournaments, and concerts in the bandshell on summer evenings. Even with the influx of homeless, the beauty of the park is still evident, with its grassy slopes, palm trees, and lake.

In the summer of 1989, the park, which is about four blocks square in size, operated under an unwritten agreement between the crack users, other park inhabitants, and the police. One side of the park served as a recreation area, characterized by Hispanic families on outings; another side was for the non-drug-using homeless; and one large area was occupied by crack users— both the homeless who lived in the park and others who came to the park to buy and sell. Crack users and police told us that the crack use was being tolerated within a certain area on the southwest corner of the park. To stray into other areas was to risk a stop and search by the police. From observation and informal interviewing in the park, we found that many of the crack users, most of them African-American, were also often from South Central and had become homeless as a result of crack addiction. Some had been living downtown on Skid Row and came to the park for a break from the barren life there. The park was seen as friendlier and not as cutthroat as downtown. Because there were very few social services or facilities in the immediate area, park residents had to depend on each other for food and for other help in survival. During the winter months, tents and other makeshift shelters built by the crack users dotted the area.

Some Hispanics from the neighborhood, and some of those who were already living in the park, tried crack, and some became addicted and stayed on the scene. While there were some whites among the crack-using inhabitants of the park, most of the whites who were observed cruised by in cars looking for crack to buy on the park's western edge. They would typically stop very briefly when a source was seen and throw money out of the car. The seller would throw the crack in the car window, and the car would speed off. Others came by in cars looking to buy sex. Again, the trade would happen quickly. The car would pull up, a woman, usually, would speak to the driver, and then she would jump in the car. Within a few minutes, the car would be back and woman would hop out and disappear into the throng of the crack market.

Daily life in the park was in many ways similar to downtown: a constant scrambling for money to buy crack, buying crack, smoking crack for days on end, and then eating and crashing. A common hustle was to hang out on the perimeter of the park and assist those who drove by looking to buy crack. Most of those on the park perimeter were go-betweens who would steer customers to dealers and often collect drug "bonuses" at both ends. Women would also hang out in a special area of the perimeter waiting for "car dates." Other sexual activity took place in the park itself, at night, almost anywhere, and by day, behind bushes or in the public bathrooms of the park.

The park residents seemed to maintain a certain solidarity among themselves, very different from the feeling of crack users in the downtown community. During the winter months, different people would keep bonfires going, and crowds would huddle around each fire, to cook and to keep warm. Since there are no missions around that serve food, park residents scavenged the local markets for surplus produce at no or very low cost. We saw some communal stew pots being cooked over fires in metal trash cans that seemed reminiscent of hobo camps of the 1930s. We heard of people giving hits of crack or even rocks to someone who was without resources, which we were told would not often happen downtown, where even a light from a lighter would cost a hit. Yet the park was also dangerous. Several murders and numerous assaults had taken place during the year.

The biggest changes happening in the park were the result of increased police presence, marked by both more patrol cars and more police walking the beat within the park. Crack users who moved from the formerly "safe" area into other areas of the park were stopped more frequently. At the same time, given the greater visibility of crack users throughout Los Angeles, various well-coordinated, repeated enforcement "sweeps" hit key areas, typically on weekends. MacArthur Park was on the list, and the crack users there were periodically rounded up, searched, and booked if evidence was found of illegal activity. The tent city was dismantled. As the former "safe" area in the southwest corner became too "hot," some people moved to the northwest corner of the park, formerly "reserved" for recent Latino immigrants.

In the spring of 1990, a fence went up around the park, and some areas were closed off for the renovation of the park as part of the Alvarado Street station of the new Los Angeles subway system. However, crack users and others were still allowed to mingle in the park until around 10:30 P.M. when police in cars ordered everyone to leave. The crack users then spilled out of the park and into the surrounding streets, especially a private parking lot about a block away, where they spent the night dealing and smoking. The same selling, using, and sexual activities by crack users appear to be taking place on the neighborhood streets but in a less concentrated, less overt way.

## Characteristics of the Sample

Potential respondents were approached in jail booking facilities, in homeless shelters, on the streets of Skid Row, and in MacArthur Park. Detained respondents were given a cigarette and a candy bar for their interview since the police had requested that we not pay them in the jail setting. All others were paid for the interview. Once the voluntary nature of the study was explained and confidentiality and anonymity assured, there were no refusals to participate, although many of the respondents could have made more money with their own hustles during the time of the interview than the interview paid. Most made the comment that they found the interview process enjoyable and that talking about their lives had helped them.

Sixty-one taped interviews were conducted. Of these, forty-two were current users of crack who had exchanged sex for crack (or money to buy crack) or who had exchanged crack for sex in the month prior to the interview.

The other nineteen interviewed did not meet the strict exchange criteria but contributed to our understanding of the sex-for-crack phenomenon. All of those interviewed were heavy crack users who often spent hundreds of dollars per day on the drug. The great majority of the respondents used crack daily, or almost daily, except for a few days off every so often to "crash."

The sample included four lesbians who had sex with men for money or for crack. Two of them were in long-term relationship with each other. Of the nine male prostitutes in the sample (who were paid to have sex with men), one said he was gay, one said he was bisexual, and one said he was heterosexual. The other six male prostitutes were transsexual; they claimed that they felt they were a "woman trapped in a man's body," and all had had the hormone series that suppressed facial hair, raised voice tones, and promoted breast growth. None had had a gender-changing operation. The transsexuals were all interviewed in men's jails and so were counted in the sample as males. The number of Latinos in the sample is low, yet surpassed our expectations of being able to find any Latino heavy crack users.[1] Characteristics of the sample are contained in table 6–1.

## Interview Topics

The recorded interviews were transcribed and analyzed for content. Many of the interviews contained repeated themes of childhood abuse, substance abuse in the family of origin, and other heavy drug use prior to crack. The topic of HIV risk and transmission was not often brought up by the respondents; it was apparently not high on their list of priority interests. Other conceptual categories emerged from the data. Religion, for example, was mentioned by every one of the respondents, both in the context of hoping that God would help them resist the temptation of crack and in the context that crack was an instrument of the devil (if not the devil himself).

**Table 6–1**
**Characteristics of the Los Angeles Sample**

| | African-American | | White | | Latino | | Other[a] | |
|---|---|---|---|---|---|---|---|---|
| | *Male* | *Female* | *Male* | *Female* | *Male* | *Female* | *Male* | *Female* |
| Homeless shelters | 1 | 11 | 1 | 1 | 0 | 0 | 0 | 0 |
| Jails | 14 | 5 | 3 | 12 | 8 | 3 | 0 | 1 |
| MacArthur Park | 0 | 0 | 1 | 0 | 0 | 0 | 0 | 0 |

[a]A young native American woman.

## Family of Origin and Early Childhood

Respondents typically reported dysfunctional childhood relationships with parents and other primary caretakers. As reported, family life seemed chaotic and often violent. Substance abuse, especially alcoholism, was a common denominator in these families. Early memories most often revolve around being beaten by one or both parents or of a father's beating the mother. The African-American and Latino respondents seemed to have a few more options: they could go to extended family members' homes and stay there. Many of the whites, who more often were living in nuclear families, ran away from home because they had nowhere else to go.

A picture emerges of a culture of powerlessness. Although many of the respondents did not come from families that could be characterized as being poor or underclass, even their parents were unable to get what they wanted from the world at large in terms of services, education, and recognition. The women in these households were often powerless to defend themselves from the physical attacks of their husbands and boyfriends or to protect their children (who were the respondents) from physical and sexual abuse. The children were without power to stop the abuse; indeed, they were often not able to convince adults that the abuse was taking place.

Many subjects reported substance abuse in their family histories.

He [subject's father] used to come home drunk from the bars. I used to go to the bars with him. Sit there and watch him play pool and get drunk.

My dad was an alcoholic. . . . I left home when I was 13. Came out to California to be a movie star.

My father used to drink and beat my mother up. . . . I started smoking crack at nine because I was in a foster home. . . . My mom couldn't take care of us. We were incorrigible. Out of control.

My uncle brought some cocaine into the house and I saw him using so I tried it.

Others encountered other types of abuse while growing up:

I had a rough life growing up. . . . I have a mentally retarded [older] brother and he used to whip my ass.

I was child abused when I was 8, from a man. I liked the man . . . when I was real young, because I needed some kind of affection, so he was giving me that affection. When I ran away from home, he pushed me aside. He said he didn't want anything to do with me.

Many of the subjects complained of being raised by a single parent or other single caretaker:

> A male takes it kind of hard being raised by a female. . . . Made me learn from trial and error rather than upbringing.

In addition to problems with the family, many subjects reported problems in school, where attendance was not a positive experience for many of the subjects in the sample:

> I had an identity problem. An inferiority problem. I was denied a lot of credit that was due to me [in school] and it made me feel uneasy a lot.

> I would withdraw from everybody else . . . I was a loner. I did it [use drugs] to kind of mingle, to fit in with everybody else, to acquire friends, relationships.

## Prior Drug Use

With very few exceptions, crack users interviewed had been users, most often heavy users, of other drugs before initiating crack use. We had thought that many crack users would be people who had a previous addiction or heavy use pattern with powder cocaine, but this was not the case. Previous drugs of choice were most likely to be PCP, marijuana (smoked in large amounts), and "downers," such as barbiturates.

> I always liked valiums . . . and . . . I always liked them strong ones [pills], like muscle relaxants.

> It [PCP] was more of an escape [than marijuana]. . . . There were times when I'd hallucinate; after smoking it, it took me to LaLa Land.

One subject said she knew a "lot" of "hope-to-die dope fiends" [heroin addicts] who had "changed over to crack," but of the sample interviewed, only one person reported having directly transformed a heroin habit into a crack habit. Others had previously stopped heroin use prior to introduction to crack or maintained a heroin habit along with crack use:

> It [crack] just dominates your whole being. It's worse than heroin. . . . It's scary.

For some, the previous drug of choice had been alcohol:

I started having problems with alcohol. . . . Just bored. Didn't have anything else better to do.

After my mother died, that's when I started drinking heavy. By the time I was 19, I was an alcoholic.

One respondent compared the effects of "sherm" (PCP) and crack:

It [crack] brought something different out in me, took me away from the feeling I was getting from the sherm. The sherm had me slow, dragging, and I'm very hyperactive as it is, and so that's the kind of feeling that I wanted. And I enjoyed the high; it was a real pleasure you know.

Some were previous users of amphetamine, uppers, and diet pills:

It [amphetamine] keeps you moving, speeds you up . . . give you energy. That's what I liked.

## Initiation of Crack Use

Most subjects were initiated into use by a person close to them. Experimentation happened in social settings, with friends or family members with whom the subject had typically used other drugs previously.

The way I got introduced to cocaine was that I was using sherm, and someone came and said, "Why aren't you smoking cocaine," and so I said OK. And so when I tried it, I liked it. I liked the high.

It [first use] was at a friend's; we were having a party. And it [crack] was going around.

A cousin [gave it to me the first time]. He was just trying it, too. . . . [I had heard] when you first hit it, you get this big rush out of it.

There did not seem to be a time period in which these neophyte users "learned" to like the drug, unlike with many other drugs. The only thing that new users needed to learn was how to manage getting strong "hits" from the crack pipe. For the heavy users, the single most salient attribute of crack was its strong and immediate effect: the rush.

It was a different high, I guess. It was like a higher high.

It's the best high in the world.

It was like right away, after that first time you do it, you want more and more, and never really satisfied.

They were talking about how good the high was. I put this big boulder on there, man, and you should have seen me, Scotty [crack] was calling me!

So I went into this house and I smoked it [the first time] and I couldn't leave.

Felt like I was happy, felt like doing all kinds of stuff. It felt fun doing it for a while. But then I found out that that's not true. It's not fun. It might be a good feeling for a while, but afterwards it's all misery.

I like to get high. . . . It's just more fun. I talk more when I'm high . . . [I don't think about] the reality of things, the reality of this world and the shape it's in.

The subjects interviewed seemed to have had few negative expectations of crack prior to first use. However, since these subjects had all been using for years, it might be that crack's reputation as being dependency producing was not as well known at the time of their initiation. They also had few positive expectations; nobody told us that they had heard how great crack was and could not wait to try it. Most stated simply that a friend, relative, or drug buddy had given them their first hit saying, "Try this."

It's [crack] there. Everybody else did it; why not me?

Most crack users were using other drugs or alcohol concurrently with crack:

[I drink] a twelve pack [every day]. I just keep drinking until I either pass out or run out of money.

I hit the pipe all day, all night, I don't sleep for two, three days. Finally, I try to get some weed, marijuana, smoke it so I can go home and eat, sleep; rest up for a couple nights then I go and do the same thing all over.

Some subjects were using heroin and crack concurrently; these are all people who were previously shooting heroin and cocaine together (speedball). Now with the ready availability of crack, they were smoking it rather than looking for powder cocaine to shoot. Nobody in the sample had turned to heroin as a means of coming down from crack, as has been reported in other sites.

## Heavy Crack Use Stage

The great majority of subjects claimed that they progressed from their first hit to regular use immediately:

> I . . . started [crack use] in September. By November I started neglecting my responsibilities, as a mother, and quit paying my rent.

> I started smoking with friends and [three months later] things just got out of hand.

Subjects were unanimous in their appraisal of crack as a drug that gives a smoker the "somemores." Users of crack do not reach a point of feeling satiated; there is always the urge to have another hit. It is not uncommon for these heavy users to stay up for several days in a row smoking. The term "24/7" refers to those who stay up twenty-four hours a day for a week; recently we heard the term updated to "24/8," reflecting those whose use had surpassed all limits:

> They gave him a hit, he gave me a hit, and the party was on again.

> That blast is going to lead to another blast, and another blast, and lead to another blast, and you going to be all fucked up, you going to be kicked out on the streets again.

> If I woke up in the morning and started smoking, I'd be sort of hooked for the whole day until I went to sleep again. Every day I woke up, it was like I quit, but once I'd always take that first hit again, so the rest of the day I'd be wanting to smoke, trying to get money to smoke.

> You want more, you're gonna go get another hit, . . . you get out and look for some more.

> Two days without stop. . . . No sleeping, no eating. Just time out to go to the bathroom.

> Just wake up, eat, get high, go to sleep, wake up, eat, get high.

> Even when that's happening [the rush from a hit], I start this craving, put my hand in my pocket to get more. It's no satisfaction anymore.

> [In answer to a question about what she thought about when she was using heavily] Nothing. I was gone. I thought about a rock and where I'd get the next man. . . . When this rock ran out, go to the next rock. . . . That's all I did for years.

Subjects unanimously stated that they felt that their crack use was out of their control:

It's a very jealous thing. It doesn't let you think about anything else or want anything else. It just devours your whole existence. Everything you do is for it.

The binge users in this sample found it difficult to estimate how many times per day they get high, saying that they got high "all day." The daily ritual of these users revolved around crack: getting the money to buy it, purchasing, and using. After several days of this routine, most would use a "downer" of some sort, most often alcohol or marijuana, to come down, eat something, and then fall into a "cocaine coma." Many of those interviewed in jail said they were glad to have been arrested because they could give their bodies a rest.

Several subjects stated that in addition to the desire for more crack, there was a perception that no hit was as good as the first hit of the day (and no hit was *ever* as good as the first one). Binges were a vain attempt to recapture the pleasure of the first hit. One subject, however, said that such compulsive use was the very reason that users did not feel the high. She recommended waiting an hour between hits to be able to feel the intense effects each time.

While most subjects claimed that they became addicted to crack solely because "crack is so addicting," a few offered other reasons for their heavy use:

> Getting high. That's how I deal with pretty much of everything. Getting high.

> I was killing myself because a man didn't love me; society didn't want me; my family rejected me, so I said, "Fuck it, you know? Why not hit the pipe?"

> When I first did crack, it was like this fabulous rush. I was capable of doing everything. I suddenly became Mr. Intellect. . . . I had the gift of gab . . . suddenly I knew everything.

> It [crack] tells you that you that you're going to rectify all the mistakes that you've made, and that's the big lie. You constantly use it to make everything all right, but everything never gets all right.

Several respondents reported that they became suspicious and distrustful—paranoid—when smoking crack:

> I don't like it when it gets you nervous, gets you panicked. You think, "Oh, I don't feel good here, I think the cops are gonna come. I got to go somewhere else."

> Now . . . it's [crack] more of a paranoia trip. I take one hit, I feel this slight rush. . . . I swear up and down everyone is looking at me.

When I go get a rock and smoke it, I'm by myself. I used to be a very sociable person, but now I'm so withdrawn. It does that to me.

## Depletion of Resources

One of the most surprising findings of this study was the overwhelming power of crack cocaine to disrupt the lives of these users. Many of our subjects, though heavy users of other drugs, had fairly stable lives before heavy crack use. Some of the sample, especially the white women, had chaotic lives prior to crack use and crack added to their instability. For all, the quick escalation of their need for the drug seemed to catch them by surprise. Given the binge quality of crack use, chronic users in this sample exhausted available resources and eventually became homeless.

The time interval between first use and "going to the curb" (becoming homeless) varied for the users and depended on the person's resources and family solidarity. Those who had been heavy users of other drugs previous to crack were often already close to financial instability. Others had jobs, homes, and material possessions that cushioned the fall for a time. A 22-year-old computer programmer (one of the few subjects with very little previous drug use) kept going to the automated teller of her bank until she was surprised to find out that she had gone through her family's savings. One MacArthur Park resident, son of a West African industrialist, claims he managed to siphon off close to $100,000 from his father's New York account before he was discovered.

> One night he got so, so, so fucked up, he sold me his truck for two G-rocks [gram rocks].

> I could buy automobiles . . . with rocks! People started off with a twenty-dollar rock, after they got through spending all their money, give me the pink slip to their cars. Rocks!

> Shit [crack] takes your money quick. All of it. If you've got fifty dollars, it will take fifty. If you've got three hundred, you'll spend three hundred.

> It's all misery . . . when you want to get some, but you don't have enough money. You try to work, or you try to steal, or some other people deal . . . then you end up in jail like I am now.

> I was into Perry Ellis, Calvin, the designers, and I ended up being in the streets. Sleeping in the alleys. Looking like a monster.

## Homelessness and Identity

Many of the subjects were from Los Angeles and had families nearby but were reluctant to call them. In some cases the family had asked them to stay away; in other instances, the users themselves did not want family to see them in their current condition.

> Since I didn't want the responsibility of having nothing, he [subject's father] was going to make sure I didn't have nothing. So he just took it [a house] and sold it and they put me out.

> It used to torture me to the point where I was embarrassing my people. . . . So that's why I'm really out here, because all I have to do is get on the phone, call my people and tell them I'm ready to straighten out. And evidently, I'm not ready to straighten up, to strengthen up my way. Because I wouldn't want to go back to them and hurt them.

> When your family leaves you, that's bad. Rock bottom. I had hit rock bottom.

> So the last time I left it was on my birthday and I knew I could not come back in the house. . . . I figure as long as I'm using this drug, I'm not going back to disgrace my father.

> I don't write to them now because the only thing I have is something bad to tell them and I can't.

> My parents own several houses in Los Angeles. They offer me . . . anything to get me home. . . . I'm sleeping in the park in a sleeping bag when I have somewhere to go and people who love me and care about me and come to the park three and four times a month looking for me. I just choose to be there because I can identify with people there that are having the same problems I'm having.

There are many different social hierarchies operating around street crack scenes, with different rules of behavior. People vary widely in where they draw the line or establish rules for their behavior and what they consider acceptable in the behavior of others:

> No matter what the drug, I don't want them to tear me down to the point on that side of this wall. This is the respect that I have in myself because I know what they can do to you, these drugs. I know because I have seen it done to some of my best friends.

> I know I'm an addict and I know addict ways. I know things that I went through to get this [crack] when I didn't have it. Sex, hey. But when I go sex, I'm not no two dollar nothing. I go all the way—you've got to give me some money. Not no dollar.

> They [other women] . . . sleep on the street with you all night long because you got rock. No, I'm not ready. I've never been ready for nothing like this. But you know it's not very healthy to go out with women that do sex for crack, 'cause they're all sluts, really.

> I won't sell my body for drugs. I won't get to the point where I don't have any clothes on my back or I won't starve. . . . I know when to say no.

> The ones that's on the street they call raspberries or strawberries, has-beens . . . the ones that let themselves really go. That are not clean, and nasty.

The notion of "rock bottom" or of having gone "too far" varies greatly. For many, resorting to prostitution or property crime was a boundary they did not cross. For others being homeless was a significant marker:

> I got tired of . . . wondering where my next meal was coming from. You can't help feel that's rock bottom. I used to pay rent, look after myself. When your family leaves you, that's bad. I had hit rock bottom.

> I got tired of—the ceiling broke [at the shelter] and came falling down . . . and the drops be coming down on the floor and the cockroaches coming round. And I said, "No, I can't cope with that." I said, "This is rock bottom."

Some claim to have no rules:

> There is no such thing as rules when you're smoking. . . . You just smoke . . . for three or four days until it knocks you out.

Other subjects had multiple stigma to manage. In some ways the transsexuals seemed to be one of the most stigmatized groups.

> Society is willing to accept gay men, but not willing to accept transsexuals. . . . They [gays] don't want you around.

## Sexual Activity Related to Crack Use

For almost every woman, there was a lack of interest in sex when high on crack. Sex was merely a way to obtain the drug:

> I don't want sex at all. As a matter of fact, when I take a hit, I want to be over here, and I want you over there.

One woman, a prostitute, reported that she never liked sex. Some drugs made sex easier for her because she did not have to think about it as much. Cocaine, however, was worse for her sexuality because she did not like to be touched when under its influence; she called herself "too paranoid."

The men had differing responses to crack. About one-quarter of the sample fit the media stereotype of crack users as hypersexual studs: they became sexually stimulated when high on crack and would want a woman or women around for sexual activities:

> A couple of ladies would be there seven, eight, nine, ten hours, and if I made love to both of them, . . . I would go get somebody else and would be even more excited.

> I get freaky and I would want somebody extra, extra freaky to turn me inside out as well. Two or three times with the same lady, then I would change up.

About three-fourths of the men beca ne impotent or became unable to climax. For some this came with prolonged use, but usually impotence occurred soon after entering a heavy use stage. For a few, this condition resulted in a loss of interest in sex.

> Like when you think about it you want to, but for me, each time there's nothing you can do.

> It doesn't turn me on when I'm using crack, because I don't have time for sex. I just wanted to smoke, smoke, smoke, smoke.

The impotent men typically wanted sexual services (usually oral sex) performed anyway, claiming that it was still pleasurable, especially when performed in conjunction with smoking crack. Nevertheless, their physical capacity for sex fell:

> They [the male customers] can't get it up at all regardless of how long you suck them.

> They [men] have the mental drive but not the capacity [to have sex]. . . . Cocaine draws their nature all the way up to their necks.

Frequently the men would demand that the women "freak" for them to receive crack. Freaking was loosely defined as any sexual activity that was beyond the person's norm. For some, oral sex fit in this category. Although we heard non-eyewitness stories of women being made to have sex with dogs, the most common freaking activities were having women perform sex on each other and having women perform sex with all the men present.

> Girls, that's how I got into it [using crack], freak girls. We'd be sitting up there and the girls would walk around naked. They'd just be smoking. . . . So I said what the hell, I'd start taking a hit every now and then, and I got addicted to the fun, I think.

> There was this girl on a bed, and there were these three guys. . . . One of them was having sex with her while the other two were waiting their turn, and while the one was having sex with her she was jacking the other one off.

## Prostitution

The women in the sample seemed to fall into two categories: those who were prostituting prior to crack dependence and those who were not. In almost every case, this distinction also reflected racial differences between the white and African-American women. (There were too few Latina women in the sample for patterns to emerge.) The white women were much more likely to have been professional prostitutes prior to crack dependence. The majority had dropped out of school and run away from home at an early age and started selling sex to support prior drug habits. Most were taught the ropes by older prostitutes. Since these women were accustomed to working as professional prostitutes, they were less likely to be willing to exchange sex directly for crack. They insisted on receiving payment in the form of money from a "date" or customer, who was typically an outsider on the crack scene. They were more likely to use condoms than the women who were not prostitutes prior to crack use, more likely to care for their appearance and health, and also more successful at keeping a roof over their heads, even if it was a cheap motel room paid for by the date.

The African-American women were more likely to have stayed in the extended family environment for a longer period of time and to have progressed further with their education. In most cases, they had jobs or other means of support, such as husbands or family prior to crack dependence. With their dependence came the depletion of resources and the break with family and friends. They turned to prostitution as a last resort and saw it as a sign of how far crack had brought them down. They tended to trade sex for crack directly with men who were also involved in the crack scene. With little or no initiation into professional prostitution, they were less likely even to think of using condoms, and, given their less powerful position of trading sex for the drug directly, they were less able to negotiate such use. They tended to neglect their appearance more than the professional prostitutes did and to sleep in the streets or in homeless shelters.

Then it came down to where I sold myself for three dollars because I might already had two dollars. . . . Hey, that's a nickel piece [five-dollars' worth] right there.

The majority of them [men] it's like, "Suck this pipe, suck my dick."

We smoked some, and he said he had more, but he wanted to have sex with me. That was the only way I could have more. . . . That was my first engagement in homosexual activity.

The computer programmer mentioned previously finally left her husband because he tried to limit her access to crack, and she turned to prostitution. Other women were quicker to see prostitution as a way to cope with the financial demands of a crack habit, though many were surprised and dismayed at the degradation of their lives:

We didn't have any more money [to buy crack], and she said, "Hey, the pussy works. . . . We can go out there and get us a date. . . . Men be paying."

Women who exchange sex for crack are called "strawberries" and are treated with scorn, especially by the "professional" prostitutes in this sample—those who exchange sex for money to buy crack. These prostitutes think that the strawberries are devaluing the profession and make it hard to get good money for services. The strawberries (and their male counterparts, called raspberries) often are among the most addicted users and can be identified by their deteriorated physical condition and lack of hygiene:

A strawberry is somebody that will do anything, any sexual thing, anything to get that hit.

You can get anything you've ever wanted from a woman if you show her this little white rock.

The thing with the strawberry, she's just a prostitute, but the pimp is that rock. The rock is pimping her.

There were times where men . . . would feel like . . . "she's just a strawberry . . . I'll take her anyway." And when I tell them pay me, "Pay you? Who the fuck you think you are?"

I wasn't keeping myself clean. . . . I was dirty, nasty . . . seemed like my pubic hairs were beginning to fall off, I was so nasty.

There were too few male prostitutes in the sample for strong patterns to emerge. Most of the sex they engaged in was oral sex, although a few reported unprotected anal sex. The gay, the bisexual, and the heterosexual male hustlers all reported prostitution after their crack use was established. They did not use condoms regularly, although they said they would use them if the customer wanted. The transsexual prostitutes had been involved in the sex industry prior to crack dependence and were more likely to use condoms with customers (but not within a primary relationship).

## HIV-Related Issues

The majority of crack users in this sample were not concerned with AIDS or HIV transmission. The topic had to be brought up by the interviewer. Their lives were almost completely taken over with far more compelling issues. For most, getting money and getting crack was a scenario played out a dozen or more times a day, each time requiring care not to be cheated by other buyers and sellers and vigilance in avoiding arrest. When they decided to sleep, they needed to find a safe place. They needed food. Clothing must be replaced regularly; homeless people do not go to the laundromat to do laundry. The possibility of acquiring an invisible virus that would take years to manifest itself was too remote for this here-and-now mentality.

When asked to comment on AIDS, most were quite fatalistic about their own chances.

I figure we're all going to die of something.

You're either going to get it or you're not, you know?

Those in the sample felt as powerless over their health as they did about other aspects of their lives.

Information about HIV and routes of transmission is being disseminated differentially to the crack-using community. Professional prostitutes, especially male prostitutes, and IV drug users, the targets of street outreach teams, seemed most aware of HIV transmission and how to minimize their risk. Crack users who were also IV drug users seemed open to the idea of using bleach to clean needles and were making an effort to do so, although most were not able to "not share" or "bleach needles" consistently.

Professional prostitutes who are convinced that condom use can protect them seem to be able to negotiate condom use with their customers, typically from outside the crack world. Their only power over the prostitute is within the sex exchange, and there seems to be no shortage of customers. Some women refuse the "date" if a man does not want to use a condom. Other prostitutes claim to be able to put a condom on a man without his knowing it. One woman demonstrated her technique for hiding a condom in each cheek; she routinely "double bags" her clients before oral or vaginal sex.

Unfortunately, both male and female prostitutes have unsafe sex with primary sex partners, even knowing that the partner may have other sex partners. For this group, not using condoms is a sign that the relationship is special and "long term." "We've been together a real long time," said one woman commenting on her relationship. "It's been almost three months now." Perhaps because they have heard so much about the dangers of "casual" sex, they assume noncasual sex to be risk free. There is a feeling that the mere fact of caring for a partner offers protection against the virus.

Those who are new to prostitution and are exchanging sex directly for crack have the lowest rate of condom use. They have the least information about HIV transmission, and are more inclined to be fatalistic about their personal risk factors. Most important, they have the least power in negotiating for condom use since they are the lowest status group within the crack scene. A man who wants to trade crack for sex can pick from among the willing sex providers. The potential sex provider who insists on using a condom will miss out on getting crack and may receive verbal or physical abuse.

Many subjects used their own methods to determine if a potential sex partner was safe:

If I do [have sex] I use my judgment. I look for lumps and scars.

[In answer to a question about condom use] No, [she didn't use condoms], because I've always been clean and I never fooled with no one that wasn't. I never thought they could give you something.

I never did [use a condom]. I would always check [for an odor], and I've been safe. I never use a condom.

It [AIDS] come to mind, but it wasn't top priority because the ladies weren't trampy type ladies.

I usually don't fool with them [condoms].

Some were more cautious:

That man might look clean, but I know that if he's been here a while then he's dealt with everything.

The transsexuals have seen more of the effects of AIDS and are consequently more aware of the issues, but even this knowledge does not always translate to safe behavior:

I've seen people pass away from it. And a lot of my girlfriends, old girlfriends, are dying from it, too. . . . I don't have anal sex with anybody.

Not unless I really liked the person and that's gonna be with me for awhile. The time I had this guy, it was for three months, and he was having anal sex, and I'm scared to go check myself because of him. (from a transsexual)

The sample included two people, a bisexual man and a woman prostitute, who knew they were HIV positive. Neither was using condoms when interviewed, and both displayed a fatalistic attitude about the consequences of their behavior: the man noted,

If I tell them [potential partners, that he is HIV positive], then I might get beat up. It's just not something you tell someone. I myself, I really didn't care. (Q: Do you think of what the consequences might be of having sex without a condom?) I think they're probably already sick themselves. . . . I have . . . like forty-five [partners] a month. Mostly people from Mexico. . . . They just don't . . . seem to be aware of the AIDS epidemic. . . .
I'm just going to assume I don't have AIDS and go on and live a normal life.

The HIV-positive woman prostitute, in answer to a question about why she did not use condoms or tell customers that she was HIV positive, said, "I look at it this way, somebody gave it to me."

## Cessation of Crack Use

Many of the crack users in this sample were getting burned out on their drug use. The years of addiction had caused physical and emotional deterioration. After "coming down," the user would often decide that he or she would stop using but would then give in to a hit, which would start things going again, establishing a pattern of daily defeat.

Every day I woke up, it was like I quit, but once I'd always take that first hit again, so the rest of the day I'd be wanting to smoke, trying to get money to smoke.

I was supposed to have been coming home again. And that same urge hit me again and I was gone again.

After that, something happened and I got depressed or something. Next thing I knew I just went and bought me some coke. I bought a couple of healthy rounds . . . and smoked it, got through smoking it, go on and buy some more. Bought some more, smoked and smoked.

Some had been in treatment but had gone back to using crack. Many felt that a long-term residential treatment was the only modality that could help them get off crack. There were too many lures on the streets for those in the early stages of cessation.

Many of the women had had their children taken from their custody. The drug was seen as all that was keeping them from getting their children back and resuming a "normal" life. For some women, motherhood seemed to represent a healthy and normal life. Some did not try to prevent conception: getting pregnant was symbolic of life and health, and they did not think of the consequences of crack use for the fetus or for themselves. For those whose menstrual cycles had stopped due to poor nutrition, getting pregnant was a sign of hope.

> They [her sons] don't need a mother that they have to worry about using drugs. . . . Drugs is not a mother's love. . . . I want this for them. I don't want me to be an addict, running around trying to sneak around trying to find drugs. I want them to feel that they've got a mother that's a friend.

> I'm tired of drugs. I've been on drugs too long. I want to get myself on the right track. I want to see my children and my granddaughter.

> That's when I said no; it's too much, because I had two children to raise. That was too much money taken from them.

> I want to get myself on the right track. I want to see my children, and my granddaughter.

This was true for men as well as women:

> I want to get myself together before she goes to school. I want to be able to be there, to pick her up from school, just be there for her.

For many addicts, the hope of rejoining their families was also a motivation to leave the drug scene:

> I just wish I could quit going to jail, get away from drugs. My main problem is my family. I would like to be around them, 'cause you know, my family— they don't want me around.

Most users in the sample were isolated from sources of social support. For most, seeing family members and other friends from the past was not a positive experience because the users were ashamed of their condition and because they would inevitably be lectured on their drug use. Although users have large networks of "dates," drug customers and fellow users, there is little trust or exchange of personal information.

## Religion

The overwhelming majority of the respondents spontaneously mentioned God and the power of faith as one of the few things that they thought could help them get off drugs and off the streets. Most had been brought up in homes that were at least nominally Christian but felt that their faith intensified as a result of feeling that they had "hit bottom." Respondents reported feeling too embarrassed at their situation and appearance to go to church but said they would go to church when they got out of their current situation.

> I've always grown up believing in an ultimate being . . . It [crack] doesn't fit it. It can't. It says in the Bible that homosexuality is an abomination in the eyes of God and I know that it is. (from a male hustler)

> So I keep on being strong, keep on trusting in myself, trusting in God. This is my man [God]. I have tried to turn myself to the point that he could help me.

> We're here for a reason. I don't know what mine is but I think more people should take interest in God and what he is all about. . . . When I tried to take my life, I feel that I met him. I don't go to church but I'm religious.

Many subjects expressed the belief that crack represented the devil:

> It's [crack] the devil, playing with your mind. Trying to kill you. But there is a God . . . even if you're gay. . . . That high. I wanted to get that high, 'cause you want to change, but your body still wants that old part of you. The devil is grabbing you.

Only one person viewed crack differently:

> I think God put drugs on this earth for a good purpose. Cocaine is a form of medicine. I think what's happened is that everybody's abused everything on this world and you'll pretty much die from anything that's abused.

## Desires for Conventionality

Respondents in the sample included both those who had run away from home at an early age and had never had a conventional adult life-style and those who had led more conventional lives as adults prior to crack dependence. In both cases, the desire for a normal life was a pervasive theme. Sometimes the expressed desire reflected a single aspect of life on the streets that seemed to sum up for the respondent the current misery: "I just want to cook my own food in a kitchen with pots and pans" or "I want to take a hot bubble bath." Others wanted back what they had before crack—families, homes, jobs, cars.

In some of the interviews, there emerged a picture of a life that was difficult in many aspects but that contained elements of excitement. The constant challenge of living by your wits, the wheeling and dealing, and the extensive interactions with others hinted at a certain "fast-lane" atmosphere, although certainly not a glamorous fast lane for those in this study. However, when asked if the excitement of the life-style was keeping them in the crack scene or if they would miss the excitement when they left the scene, all respondents denied it vigorously:

> I wish I just can move out of the neighborhood that I live in [Skid Row]. Move out to the Santa Monica area. Help the seniors or something. Take them out to lunch, push them around in the wheelchairs or something. Get away from the environment I'm living in.

> Lately my life hasn't had no meaning to it. . . . I just don't enjoy things like I used to do, like going to the beach or a painting, pretty plants.

> The good thing to think about it would be try to be an honest person, not doing drugs, having a family. . . . [I need] to stop smoking crack. To get my weight back. Get married.

> [*Q*: What do you want out of life?] Family.

## Conclusion

Unlike the heroin epidemic of the 1960s and 1970s, crack's impact on users has been more degrading and destructive for personal behavior, especially for the extreme users represented in this study. Conditions contributing to crack's impact have included changes in the social structure, urban blight, the collapse of the public sector, and the economic recession. The psycho-pharmacological effect of the drug itself is also a contributing factor. Although it is the minority of users who become dysfunctional, the craving and binge patterns of crack use are an important consideration in explaining these consequences. This, combined with a low dose cost, results in dysfunctional use for many people.

The people in our sample experienced chaos in their lives before and after their introduction to crack cocaine. As children they were abused by substance-abusing parents and family. They often had difficulties at school because they felt different from the other students. They began rebelling and soon found themselves in with the wrong crowd; they then started using drugs and alcohol themselves. Some ran away. Some were sent to the juvenile justice system and came out tougher. They went from being victims to being perpetrators very quickly; they had their own children and often neglected or abused them. Some have had their children taken from them, often at birth. Some have left children with other family members so as not to expose them to the drug world. Their lives have been disrupted and their social networks splintered as a result of their crack use. Becoming homeless and selling sex makes them feel degraded. Being unable to say no to the first hit of the day and knowing they are entering the downward spiral again makes them feel hopeless and helpless to change.

Although all users in the sample expressed a desire to get off crack, they typically did not have any concrete plans or ideas on how they were going to do this. The seemingly minor (to an outsider) detail of needing identification (in California a driver's license or official identification card) to receive medical treatment or social services becomes insurmountable to one who is already feeling helpless. Many respondents do not know what drug abuse treatment is or where to seek it. They equate it with medical treatment that involves getting some *thing* (a pill, a potion) from a medical practitioner and then being "cured": "I wanted treatment and they just wanted to sit in a room and talk," said one young woman who had dropped out of treatment.

Most homeless crack users, especially the prostitutes, are arrested frequently and use the time in jail to recuperate. In jail, they are reflective about their lives and the future and are probably open to the idea of treatment, but they have no access to information on treatment and other services. When they leave jail, they usually have nowhere to go but back to the same streets they came from, so the cycle continues.

The existing social service and drug treatment programs are fractured and woefully insufficient. Drug treatment focused solely on the drug usually does not work because drug use is only one aspect of the users' lives. Health services for crack-dependent women seem focused not on them but on their biological roles: as sex partners they are possible vectors for HIV and other STDs; as child bearers they are potentially harming their children. Outreach programs target prostitutes for condom education campaigns while ignoring those who have the money, the power, and the penis to use a condom: their customers.

For homeless crack abusers, integrated treatment programs are needed that address their myriad needs. Residential programs could help the users learn new coping strategies while removed from the temptations of the streets or the old neighborhoods. Homeless users also need medical care for the many health problems they incur while sleeping and eating in unsanitary conditions. Programs that work with the whole family could build on the fact that children and other family members are most often a strong motivation to stop using drugs. Such programs help to foster a social context for staying drug free. Job training and job placement assistance are especially necessary for those who have been prostituting; it is difficult to break the habit of getting "easy money" when you are broke. Many of the crack users have criminal records, which makes job finding even more difficult.

HIV prevention and education efforts have not yet been targeted specifically to crack users. Given the unsafe sex practices among homeless crack users, it is vital that they receive information about the transmission of HIV. They often feel that as non-IV drug users, they need not worry about AIDS. Myths abound about how to prevent getting the disease and how to protect yourself: "don't share food," "don't share cigarettes," "check out the person [a potential sex partner] to see if he looks clean," and even, "I don't attract that kind of energy." Many do not consider oral sex to be "sex" and so feel safe not using a condom.

Most important, safe-sex messages should be aimed at those who pay for sex with money and with crack. Providers of sexual services may sometimes be able to negotiate condom use successfully, but often there is physical or verbal harassment when the subject is raised, especially with a primary partner.

Treatment programs and medical and social services required to address the problems associated with crack cocaine use would cost money that is said to be unavailable. However, considering the compound cost of crime, incarceration, disease, and child placement, we must realize that we also cannot afford the cost of not providing treatment and services.

# Note

1. In Los Angeles, the Hispanic population is sharply divided into Chicanos—persons of Latino descent who were born (or grew up) in the United States and who are usually bilingual—and recent immigrants, who are often monolingual. These groups have distinct cultural and behavioral differences, including drug use. Historically, drug-abusing Chicanos typically have used heroin as their drug of choice. The recent immigrants, most of whom come from rural areas of El Salvador, Guatemala, or Mexico, typically have been nondrug users. A few had used marijuana, but for the great majority, the only substance of use or abuse was alcohol. As we interviewed for the sex-for-crack study, we were surprised to find that this pattern is changing for both groups. We now see Chicano and recent immigrant men (not women) using and even abusing crack. The Chicanos fit into the pattern of having been users of other drugs before first use of crack. The recent immigrants present a different picture. They generally have no regular job and hang out in parks or on certain street corners that are known as places that day labor can be recruited. One corner of MacArthur Park serves this function, as does a corner of Sepulveda Boulevard in the San Fernando Valley. Both locations are adjacent to areas where prostitution and crack use take place. The immigrants' first crack use came about through curiosity as they observed others using it. Most whom we interviewed stopped use when they realized there was the danger of becoming addicted, but some did become addicted.

# 7

# Crack, Gangs, Sex, and Powerlessness: A View from Denver

*Stephen Koester*
*Judith Schwartz*

> They call the pipe the devil's dick. Sucking the devil's dick. Chasing
> that ghost. When the pipe fills up with smoke—that's the initial hit.
> And why they call it chasing? Because that initial hit is the main one
> off it. You can never get that hit back. You can't.

While freebasing cocaine hydrochloride was a common form of cocaine ingestion in the 1970s, smoking crack cocaine did not become
a significant part of Denver's drug scene until the early 1980s. It
has since emerged as the drug of choice for a significant proportion of the
city's illegal drug users.

Crack use in Denver is most visible on the city's northeast side, and it
appears most intense within the black community. Neighborhoods with
highly visible crack scenes include Five Points, Park Hill, Capitol Hill, Curtis
Park, Montbello, and Aurora, an adjacent eastern suburb. One reason for
the drug's preponderance in the black community is that its sale is a primary
business endeavor of two largely black gangs, the Crips and the Bloods.
Along with freelance entrepreneurs, they process cocaine into crack and
market it in these neighborhoods.

In Capitol Hill, a near eastside community, crack networks include both
white and black users. On the city's predominantly Hispanic north and west
sides, inhaling or injecting cocaine hydrochloride seem to be more common
methods of ingesting cocaine than smoking crack. Recent reports from users
suggest, however, that crack has become popular among Hispanic users. In
this part of the city, it is not sold as "ready rock"; instead, these users more
frequently buy powder cocaine and "rock it up" into crack themselves. The
failure of "ready rock" to penetrate this seemingly lucrative northside and
westside market may be due in part to the reticence of Hispanic users about
buying from black youth gangs. A common perception among Denver users

in general is that black dealers often sell overadulterated cocaine. They do not use the term "crack"; instead, they refer to this as "smoking cocaine" or "basing." This chapter is based almost entirely on interviews with users and street-level dealers on Denver's northeast side.

A total of forty-four taped interviews were completed—thirty-one with active crack users and the rest with dealers associated with the crack scene who did not use crack themselves. Of the crack users, twenty-four were female, and seven were male. All of the individuals interviewed were black, with the exception of two crack-using females who were white and a crack-using man who was Hispanic. The ages of the women ranged from 20 to 43; the average age was 30. The men ranged in age from 22 to 45 and averaged 32 years. Additional data were collected through participant-observation, through interviews with intravenous polydrug users conducted as part of another NIDA-funded project, and through discussions with Colorado state health infectious disease outreach workers.

## The Socioeconomic Context of Subjects' Lives

The rapid increase in crack use since the mid-1980s has been described as a symptom of the ongoing social disintegration of America's inner cities, a problem that has accelerated with the restructuring of the American economy (Bourgois 1989; Fagan and Chin 1989). In Denver, this link between growing social problems and economic transformation is less apparent than in midwestern and northeastern cities. Between 1970 and 1984, when these cities were losing industrial jobs, Denver showed a minor increase in industrial employment (Kasarda 1986). Nonetheless, problems associated with the social isolation of the inner city—drugs, gangs, and violence (Wilson 1987)— are all present in Denver. This combination of social pathology is most intense on the city's northeast side, which includes some well-established middle-class neighborhoods, as well as some of the poorest neighborhoods in the city. Single-family homes on quiet tree-lined streets are the most common type of housing. Duplexes, small two- or three-story apartment buildings, and an occasional public housing project are also present. Even in the northeast neighborhoods that were the focus of this study (Five Points, Capitol Hill, and Park Hill), there is not an overwhelming sense of poverty or social pathology. Poverty's most visible manifestations are tempered by the small scale of these neighborhoods and by their proximity to more economically stable areas. Substandard, dilapidated housing often shares the same block with the homes of working-class families. The public sector has not broken down; whole neighborhoods are not without basic public services.

Census statistics gathered for Five Points and parts of Park Hill and Capitol Hill indicate that although not always nakedly apparent, poverty persists among a substantial minority of the area's households. A quarter of the households had incomes placing them below the federal government's poverty line, unemployment for men and women over 16 years of age was among the highest of any part of the city, and only 50 percent of residents over 25 years of age had completed high school (U.S. Census 1980).

The individuals who participated in this study were among the poorest members of these communities. Some were homeless or had only temporary living arrangements when interviewed, and few had marketable job skills or significant work experience.

## The Crack Scene: Social Organization and Economics

Crack use became common among drug users in some Denver neighborhoods in the mid-1980s. The drug's increasing popularity seems to have coincided with the arrival of organized groups prepared to sell it. Jamaican gangs as well as the Bloods and the Crips from Los Angeles were all mentioned as playing an important role in the introduction and spread of crack cocaine among northeast side drug users. Prior to the arrival of these organized operations, local dealers sold cocaine powder and left its manufacture into crack up to users. With the advent of gangs, crack shifted from simply being a method of ingesting cocaine to a separate commodity.

Currently, Crips, Bloods, and freelancers are competing for market shares as they attempt to build an oligopolistic crack business on the east side. Gangs are attempting to introduce an organized distribution system backed up by a shrewd marketing strategy. Street-level gang-affiliated sellers (servers) compete for franchise rights to specific intersections or blocks by introducing high-quality crack cocaine at a favorable price. They temporarily offer "double-ups" or two-for-one deals; instead of getting a twenty-dollar piece for twenty dollars, the buyer will get a forty-dollar piece of crack. Such marketing techniques help create a demand and short-lived buyer loyalty. Independent dealers have difficulty competing. Violence or its threat is also used to define and maintain a sales territory. Graffiti proclaims the gangs and their territories.

Within a gang there are a number of separate sets. A set is a more closely aligned group than an entire gang, and it is the level within which most day-to-day activities take place, including drug dealing. A member's primary allegiance is to his set. Each set has its territory, and it is within this territory that members sell crack. Most individual street dealers sell less than five days a week and usually not for more than a few hours in a single day. They limit their time on the street in order to minimize their visibility, and thus their chances of identification by the police. This limitation provides an opportunity for multiple sellers in a single territory. It also acts to extend the economic benefits of selling to a large number of young men. Because they sell crack part-time, gang members who deal may often be in school or hold legitimate employment. Restricting the amount of time one sells seems to be a common characteristic of the crack business (Reuter, MacCoun, and Murphy 1990). Several users interviewed for this study estimated that the gangs now control approximately 80 percent of the east side crack trade.

We have observed the introduction of crack and gangs into the traditional and highly visible heroin and cocaine copping area of east Denver. Intravenous heroin and cocaine addicts who frequent this scene sound almost like conservative members of the middle class when they describe the changes in their social setting since the introduction of crack. These IV heroin and cocaine addicts feel harassed and threatened by the younger generation of crack dealers and users. They complain of the violence that has accompanied it and the increase in police activity that has resulted.

A standard crack operation centers around a distributor and his servers or runners. The distributor usually operates his sales from a house. His street)level dealers (servers or runners) come to the house to "re-up," or replenish their supply, which they take to the streets and sell. Normally, the distributor employs managers to run the operation. Distributors also operate from cars and resupply their servers when they call. Servers or runners take care of street-level sales; they may or may not use crack themselves. Distributors are frequently not gang members; some sell to both Crips and Bloods. Although most active gang members operate as servers, some occupy more senior positions, including distributing. One server explained how he got started:

> So once they [the Crips] know you're a server, that you will sell, they'll give you a good deal. Like say once I come get a dime piece, sometimes you have to start that low, I come back an hour later and I got thirty dollars. Then for thirty dollars they give you a half, fifty dollars' worth. I turn around go get 50 and get 16, which is a gram and a half. As long as I keep spending and showing them that I'm twisting and wheeling and dealing I can get more dope. Which means I make it better for me because I can get more for myself too and I can still twist and take care of my habit. Twisting is hustling, selling.

Longevity in the crack business seems to be directly related to one's abstinence from the product. This reality is manifested in a value structure that assigns higher status to nonusing distributors and servers than to those who "tweek." The term "tweeking" describes a kind of nervousness or paranoia that comes from repeatedly doing crack; it is applied as a derogatory term to anyone who uses. The high and accompanying craving that comes from smoking crack is called being "sprung"; it also connotes the loss of control ascribed to users. Thus, a server who gets "sprung" or "tweeks" would be a poor risk, since servers are almost always given crack on consignment.

The term "crack house" covers a wide range of places where people go to buy and/or use crack. A crack house may be someone's residence or it may be as temporary as a motel room. Some crack houses are simply places where distributors package and sell crack to their servers, or street-level dealers. Traffic in and out of these houses is limited to the individuals working for the distributor and possibly to a handful of well-known customers. Most often, the distributor has a manager who operates the house. As a black female manager of this type of "buy and fly" house explained: "You must call before you come and I don't serve anything under fifty dollars. That keeps down traffic. . . . No one sits here and smokes, you get your shit and you leave." This crack house was busted by the police when the manager began using, and thus failed to maintain this rule. She began selling twenty-five-dollar pieces and taking stolen merchandise in exchange for crack. As this case illustrates, the life of a crack house is generally short; the steady traffic draws attention and eventually the police. Dealers may use another person's residence for dealing; in exchange the owner receives money or crack.

A crack house can also be a place where users go to buy crack and/or use it. Users must pay to stay and smoke or to rent a pipe. If the individual running the house smokes, payment is usually in the form of a hit. In many cities this kind of crack house is called a smoke house. A black male manager of this kind of crack house described how it operates:

> Say you come in with a quarter [of a gram], you know a twenty-five-cent sting, I'll say give me a hit. Every quarter you smoke you got to give me a hit. . . . What we do is we let a person smoke a quarter, then you got to buy from the house. . . . You don't go out somewhere and bring it back and smoke it. . . . I got it in my house for sale, so I'll let you come in with it the first time when you start, but after that you got to pay me.

This type of house serves the same purpose as formal shooting galleries among drug injectors by providing a degree of privacy and security for street-based users. It also provides a place for those without money to negotiate other kinds of exchanges.

Most of the women interviewed for this study preferred not to frequent crack houses regularly. Instead, they liked to buy the drug and go some place they considered safer or more private to smoke. Fear of police raids was often mentioned; one user explained, "I would rather wait until I get home. It is a long wait sometimes for the anticipation, but I feel safer." They also complained that in crack houses, other users would often beg for a hit of their crack.

## Sex for Crack

The exchange of sex for crack cocaine seems to have less to do with any possible aphrodisiacal qualities of the drug and more to do with its addictive nature and the poverty of the people who use it. Poor women with limited marketable skills trade sex for crack because they are addicted and because they have no other means of supporting their habit. Their powerlessness and marginality fuel the sex-for-crack phenomenon. The position of women in the underground or illegal economy mirrors their location in the mainstream economy. For the most part, they suffer the effects of social isolation; they occupy low-level and low-status positions, and their opportunities for advancement are restricted. The most unrestricted and economically rewarding avenue open to them is to sell their bodies. A male crack user who gives women crack for sex summarized the position of many crack-addicted women:

> When they smoke some dope . . . and they are poor and they just want some more—that is what I mean by getting sprung. . . . Once a person gets broke, especially a woman, if she ain't stealing or hustling any kind of way she is going to give up her body.

Drug-using male members of the underclass have a greater variety of possible economic strategies than women. Potentially violent criminal activity and all but the lowest levels of drug dealing are dominated by men. Men, even those with limited educational skills, can more readily find jobs as manual laborers through temporary labor pools. The crack-using men interviewed in this study dealt drugs, pimped, worked as janitors, did landscaping, or scrapped junk cars. Only one of the women interviewed had a legal job at the time of the interview. While several of the others had service-sector employment in the past, they were now dependent upon a combination of family or friends, prostitution, and public assistance, although few reported receiving welfare.

Of twenty-four women interviewed, only four had sold crack; two of these had managed crack houses. All four of them worked for boyfriends who were distributors or crack house managers. These women lost their jobs in the crack business when their relationships ended, when their boyfriends went to prison, or when they were unable to control their addiction. Even these positions reflected their powerlessness; the crack house manager and server mentioned above was pistol whipped by her distributor for suggesting that he should pay his street-level servers more.

Exchanging sex for crack appeared to be the most reliable means available to the women we interviewed. Most exchanged sex for both money and drugs. However, there was a continuum from those who identified primarily as prostitutes selling sex to those who simply bartered directly for crack.

Among this latter category there was a distinction based on the frequency and degree of anonymity involved in the exchange.

Prostituting for money gave women greater control over the sexual exchange. They were frequently able to negotiate both price and the sex act to be performed. This implies a business arrangement rather than an act of desperation and loss of control. Having the power to buy the drug meant not being at the mercy of someone who would cheat them or demand sexual services they did not want to perform. In addition, it enabled them to have extra cash to take care of other needs, especially the care of children. It was also more likely that condoms would be used when women sold sex than when they traded it directly for crack. On some occasions, they were able to manipulate their tricks into letting them buy crack. In these instances, the woman would pinch a piece to be used later. The women explained that if they could get the trick sprung, they could keep buying crack for him and probably not even have to have sex since he would probably be too high to perform. As one black prostitute explained:

> Yeah, I will take them sometimes and buy the dope, go back to the hotel and by the time we get in there and get situated he started smoking so he can't do nothing. I be sitting there twenty minutes and he ain't getting hard and I will tell him I have to go.

Generally, Denver subjects who exchanged sex directly for crack had fewer partners than reported by women in the other cities included in this study. A few of the women interviewed in Denver exchanged sex for crack on a regular basis only with one or two partners. One woman who lived with a female lover and her daughter regularly exchanged sex with four men, all of whom she described as friends. She explained the exchange not as a blatant transaction but as more of an unspoken understanding.

Several subjects who exchanged sex directly for crack exhibited similar behavior to their counterparts in the other cities. These are the "strawberries," "rockstitutes," "skeezers," or "crack whores"—street terms for women who exchange sex directly for crack and who, in our experience, number among the most marginal and vulnerable members of the crack scene. Their low street status is a reflection of their powerlessness, and it seems to come from the combined effects of their addiction and the hopelessness that pervades their lives. They do not possess the degree of control over the sexual exchange that prostitutes are usually able to exercise. Instead, they are often ripped off when giving sex directly for crack. The man may demand sex first and then give the woman bunk (fake) crack, or, as is often the case, he may only give her a hit for a sexual favor worth far more on the street. This degree of vulnerability may make these women more susceptible to situations involving high-risk behavior. A black male user and petty seller described the plight of these women: "They beg for it. These guys treat them like shit. . . . They might give them a hit before they start and then when they get through they kick their ass out of the house. I have seen people begging, banging on the door."

We asked these women why they would exchange sex directly for crack when it seemed that they could do better by going out on the street and exchanging sex for money, which could then be used to buy crack. They agreed that this might make more sense economically, but they explained that once they were in the crack house smoking, it was easier to stay there to be close to the drug. One black female stressed this point:

> Nope. No. You're taking a chance out there in the street with the police . . . you're probably going to get busted. Especially if you're already sprung. You go lay in the dope house with the dope man and you take off your clothes, you can get anything you want.
>
> I know some girls who do that. They just work the street, make their money and then go to a rock house and get high. It is gone so quick. We could sit down and I could have a gram of rock . . . and within thirty minutes I'm not going to have anything left. . . . The whole thing is just the rush and then the craving starts. You want to feel that again because it only lasts a couple of minutes.

They expressed similar misgivings about boosting (shoplifting), a common strategy among female opiate users. Only four of the women we interviewed reported boosting as part of their hustle.

Several factors may account for their unwillingness to partake in illegal endeavors like theft. Stealing requires a degree of planning and skill, and there is a delay between the time the act is committed and the time the desired end is achieved. Experienced shoplifters often take orders from customers or spend time selling their merchandise. Since most Denver heroin users inject no more than two or three times a day, it is possible for them to "work" for long periods between ingestion. This is not the case with crack; its effects are short-lived, and the desire for more is immediate. Once a user is "sprung" the compulsion to continue using is overpowering. One female crack user explained, "Sex is easier to deal than trying to go boost." Stealing is perceived as more dangerous and difficult, and the time lag is incompatible with the pharmacological properties of crack.

The almost instantaneous desire for more crack combined with the unique way in which it is marketed encourage frequent sexual exchanges.

> If you shoot some heroin you are high, and you just kind of sit down and mind your own business. If you shoot some cocaine, you shoot it, and you have a desire for more but it's basically something that will pass. But with rock, the craving, that craving for more, that is unbelievable.

Crack is compatible with sexual bartering because it can be broken down into small, inexpensive units. The quantity required to give a user a brief but intense high may be as little as a five-dollar piece in Denver. For women who are addicted and without other sources of income, this amount may translate into the standard rate of exchange for a sexual act. One male street-level dealer explained:

> If she wants it real bad you could probably get away selling her a nickel head [five dollars]. Give her a nickel hit. Once she gets the hit she is cool for a minute, and then she will be willing to do something else for another hit. I don't care if you give her crumbs. I just tell her, "I will give you this," and she sees the bag is loaded with dope. She knows if she keeps on sooner or later she'll get a fat rock.

At such an inexpensive price per hit, even low-level street servers can afford to barter their product for sex. Heroin and cocaine powder cannot be broken down into such small quantities. As a result, a dealer or user of these drugs might think twice about trading as freely for sex.

Sex for crack most often occurs while the woman is craving the drug and in a situation where she has little, if any, control. The crack house can provide an environment that is conducive to the exchange of sex for crack. One woman described her experience:

> I was sitting around smoking and I had my money when I came in. . . . Another girl and then a couple of other women came in and they get high, and you could pretty much tell they were getting ready to ask the dealer for a favor because they ask him if they could talk to him in the other room private. Sometimes they don't even do that. Sometimes they will try and ask him in private but the dealer will front them off and make it where everybody can hear and say something to the effect about, "Yeah I will give you something if you do this. Take off your clothes and freak off." That is what they usually say and the next thing you know somebody is going to do it. Maybe two or three women or maybe more sitting there and then the dealer is going to ask the other ones, "Do you want to get in on it or something?" And it always usually ends up that everybody gets in on it. . . . They end up doing it for the sexual favor because they don't have no more money.

The most common form of sexual activity for both prostitutes and "rock-stitutes" is oral sex, performed alone or as a preliminary to intercourse. Most women prefer it because it is comparatively easy: "It was faster. I didn't have to get undressed, I didn't have to get dirty—no touching. It was just easier." Women and men both reported that oral sex is what men seem to ask for most as well:

> I think it's oral because, like I said, the man has the desire but they can't get hard and they know they can't get hard. Plus in their mind they know

that these girls are running around here in and out of dope houses and committing these sexual acts with any and everybody for some rock. I think men have it in their mind that if I just let her have oral sex with me she can't give me anything.

Some male and female subjects shared the view that oral sex is not "real" sex and that it is therefore not as risky as other sexual activities. Women also reported that men liked to give them oral sex, particularly while the woman is hitting the pipe.

## Sexual Degradation

One of the most disturbing and recurring themes that surfaced in our interviews was the degree of degradation surrounding the exchange of sex for crack. The following quotations by two women describe this debasement and demonstrate how an individual who will do anything to get crack becomes an object under the total control, sexual or otherwise, of another person or group of people. These complicated behavioral issues cannot be explained in only sexual or erotic terms.

It is degrading to think about some of the things I have done for drugs and that I wouldn't even do with my man, but I did them with the dealer because that is what he wanted and that was the only way I was going to get it, if I did the sex his way. It might have been painful like anal sex they call it, but I did them and it is degrading because it just is.

They are taking their clothes off, doing whatever is necessary to get the money. I am talking any kind of sexual activity. You know, not just straight screwing, it can be oral, it can be in the behind, just something humiliating, just something degrading. It is degrading just doing it period, but taking the one step. . . . Even what's worse then that they will ask you to do things that you normally wouldn't probably do it. They just seem like they just be using people and dogging them because they know they can because they are high and they want some more and they are not thinking clear. All they can think of is another hit would get them together instead of just coming down and leaving.

Performing sexual acts that they do not perceive as normal or something they would willingly do is called "freaking." For some women, anything other than vaginal intercourse was considered freaking. Their characterization of what constitutes freaking appeared rather conservative. Many of the women considered oral sex to be freaking, and practically all considered anal sex to be freaking: "Putting it in your booty hole is freaking to me." They wanted no part of group sex and were disturbed at two women being asked to perform together when they did not consider themselves lesbians. A typical example of freaking would be two women having oral sex with one another while the dealer and his friends watched, often followed by oral sex or intercourse with the men. Having sex with several men was also considered freaking.

Freaking often involves more than simply doing something one considers a bit out of the ordinary. Women and men both described instances where the act was not only psychologically abusive but physically hurtful as well. A 25-year-old gang server explained what he might insist a woman do for crack:

> I might do like I did in Kansas City. . . . This chick wanted a hundred dollars' worth of dope. I had her fuck everybody in the house. There were about eight drunk motherfuckers. They tore her ass up. Then I turned around and didn't give her exactly what I told her I was going to give her.

Two informants claimed to have witnessed sexual episodes between women and dogs. Even if these stories are crack folklore, they are significant as indicators of the level to which this humiliation might be taken, and they illustrate the issue of power that seems to pervade the sex-for-crack phenomenon. Implicit in freaking is domination. Getting someone to freak is to be in control and to exhibit power. A quotation by another female subject underlines this theme:

> They wanted me to be with another woman and it was like I needed it so bad and I was doing more drugs and I would do whatever you want. . . . You get to a point where it doesn't matter.
> . . . You would think when a man come over to your house and want to be with you—but all he want is your ass. They tell me I look good. It's not because I look good but because I'm skinny. I look good because they think I have some good booty. . . . Yeah, for twenty dollars . . . for a twenty-dollar rock you got to be in the time of sodomy.

When asked why men ask women to do such submissive and personally humiliating acts, a male crack user and occasional small-level dealer replied:

> Power. I think it's this feeling that you can dominate somebody. You know, cause here you know they beg for it. It just turns some guys on. Like, gimme that and I'll do this for you. Most guys if they've got cocaine they think they have power cause cocaine bring them money. It make you think power, I don't know, that you can dominate.
> Yeah I don't know, I like power. I'm just dying sort of like. But then every once in a while I like to feel like I'm important and all that, like I got something, you know?

It is imperative that this phenomenon be viewed within a larger social context. Forcing women to degrade themselves may very well be a way for essentially powerless males to increase their self-esteem. In the process, they reproduce the powerlessness that accompanies their own social isolation. This sexual debasement of women may also be part of the internalized self-destruction that Bourgois (1989) has identified in the regular displays of violence and dominance that are characteristic of the underground drug economy. Such displays promote a man's image and affirm his credibility on the street.

## Sexual Arousal and Sexual Dysfunction

Women explained that, on occasion, smoking crack was a sexual stimulant for them; a few stated that the first two or three times they hit the pipe, they had orgasms. Nonetheless, our research seems to refute the notion that crack possesses some innate quality as an aphrodisiac. In working with intravenous drug-using women, we have heard similar claims made for cocaine, methamphetamine, heroin, and alcohol. More often and more consistently, however, users reported that smoking crack cocaine lessened their sexual desire and their physical ability to perform. When sexual arousal did occur with crack, it was almost always during the initial stages of use. Daily users who had been doing the drug for any length of time more commonly described sexual dysfunction. As one woman explained:

> We feel like we really want each other. . . . But when it comes right down to it I'm dry as the Safari Desert and he doesn't have an erection and it's damn frustrating. I keep telling him it's the crack, it's this shit. . . . We can go two or three days and not use and then it's normal. I respond like I'm supposed to respond physically and he responds the same way. As long as we're doing that shit, I mean even if he gets hard, it takes so long, I mean hours. You're tired. It takes both of us a long time just to climax.

Women also stated that when smoking crack they often wanted to be left alone:

> Crack makes me kind of tense up and I can't socialize too much. I am just in my own world and I don't want to be bothered. I don't want to be touched.
>
> Well you know, I didn't like sex because when I get high—don't touch me—you know the feelings in your body, someone touching your body, it's like OH! Don't touch me because I'm going to continue to get high. I'm going to chase this ghost, that's all I want. But mostly men . . . take off their clothes and want to fuck. But they can't do anything . . . the thing will get hard but that's all its gonna do—stay hard.

Consistently, interviews with both women and men indicated that when men are smoking crack, they may mentally desire to have sex but are often unable to perform physically. Both male and female subjects stated that some men have difficulty getting an erection and that most have difficulty reaching a climax. When they do achieve orgasm, it is usually after a prolonged period of intercourse or oral sex. A black male explained his response to this dilemma:

> I won't sit and smoke with a woman. Say if I have a fifty-dollar rock and I want to use this rock to get me some pussy . . . I will take a portion of it and spring a broad, whoever, and I will put me some back for later on, but I wouldn't smoke none right then because it fucks up my nature. I don't do nothing.
>
> It take me so long sometimes that I just get frustrated. Like I had this one broad I was telling you about. I was smoking with her and I thought in my mind that I wanted to get down, I wanted some pussy. I told her, "I will give you some to turn you on but I want some." So she starts sucking on my dick and shit and it took me about two hours before I could cum.

A woman who exchanges sex for both money and crack complained:

> They can get it up, but they just can't get off for a long time. So it seems like you have to work forever. . . . Sometimes they don't get off. They just tell you to go. Sometimes I think they know they are not going to, the way they tell you. . . . They will say something like, "Well you can go now, that is enough." But you would have been there for an hour or something trying to get them off. They make you want to stop prostituting.

Others stated that men do have difficulty getting hard, and one woman summarized her experience exchanging sex for crack as "chewing on limp dicks." Another female informant explained that those men who do achieve orgasm are either nonusing dealers or users with enough crack to keep both himself and her satisfied while she works at bringing him to a climax.

## Sexually Transmitted Diseases

The exchange of sex for crack places men and women at high risk for contracting HIV. Thirteen of fourteen women reported having had sexually transmitted diseases (STDs); nine of them reported having had two or more different STDs. Three of five men also reported having had STDs.

Our subjects' personal experience with STDs was evident by their awareness of these various diseases and their use of medical jargon to describe them. There was no need to use slang or to simplify the medical terms:

*syphilis, gonorrhea,* and even *trichomoniasis* were words used by the women themselves. All subjects knew that condom use could reduce their risk of these infections. The fact that they did not normally use them illustrates their subordinate position to the men with whom they have sex.

## Safer Sex

Condom use varied from never to always among our subjects. The most steady users were professional prostitutes; the least likely to use condoms seemed to be women who regularly found themselves bargaining for crack without the money to pay for it. The women who exchange sex directly for money were particularly well versed in safer sex. Two street outreach projects and state health department STD specialists have been carrying the message to this population since 1988.

Crack-addicted women who are not seen by these projects or do not arrive at the city's STD clinics or jail may not have received the safer sex message, and they do not have the same access to the free condoms distributed by these projects. These women all had regular unprotected sexual encounters. Even women who said they always used condoms differentiated between tricks and their lovers or friends. Women often expressed the notion that they felt secure with men who were familiar to them. There was also some confusion expressed by both men and women about the need to use condoms for oral sex. Women did seem to think that men are using condoms more now than they did in the past. One woman recited a popular street rap to indicate the change among men, especially young men: "Skeezers, snatchers, big disease catchers." It seems to be a cruel irony that their utter contempt for these women may actually provide their motivation for practicing safer sex.

Condom use was greatest among prostitutes, who often reported using condoms 100 percent of the time. While this seems exaggerated, we do have reason to be optimistic with regard to sex industry professionals. Street outreach programs have been reinforcing a safer sex message and handing out condoms to these women for over three years.

Condom use was also reported for crack dealers and others frequenting crack houses. While condoms were said to be used with customers, dealers reported that in personal relationships, that was not the case; dealers reported that they wanted a closeness and trust with their partners that they felt would not be there if they used condoms. This is a common problem with STDs in general.

Many men also questioned the need to use condoms when receiving oral sex. One reason for their resistance may be that they often have difficulty ejaculating if they are smoking crack, and condom use may exacerbate this problem. While the risk of HIV infection and drug addiction may, from our perspective, be the most pressing problems confronting women exchanging sex for crack, they may disagree with this assessment. Many report a multitude of serious problems that they regard as more immediate than the risks of HIV infection. As Mays and Cochran (1988) have stated: "Most women, particularly when their life reality is that of being poor, black, Latina, or outside the law through drug abuse or street prostitution, have always lived with risks of some kind. AIDS is simply one more risk with which to be concerned."

Our interviews with these women confirmed this reality. They were consumed by issues about money, relationships, shelter, and, perhaps most important, the care of their children and the fear of losing them because of their drug use. These women's own concerns must guide the development of programs aimed at helping them. It is unlikely that efforts focusing exclusively on their drug use or HIV risk will be effective.

## Crack and Intravenous Drug Use

Among those we interviewed, past and/or present experience with intravenous (IV) drug use was common. Six of the women interviewed reported that they were current IV drug users. This may be partly due to the fact that our cohort averaged approximately 30 years of age; none of our subjects was under age 20. It is likely that members of our cohort entered the drug world before crack was common. The intersection of crack- and IV-using social networks was made clear while observing the operations of a dealer-operated shooting gallery. During the course of the day, the dealer traded hits of heroin for crack, and a few minutes after injecting heroin, he and his assistant smoked a piece of crack. This combination of injecting heroin and smoking crack has become a new form of speedballing. In part, this seems due to the increased availability of crack and scarcity of powdered cocaine, the result of the greater profits to be had by converting powder into crack. This direct connection between crack and intravenous drug use increases the likelihood that crack users may be the sexual partners of IV drug users.

## Summary

The exchange of sex for crack is widespread and a common means used by poor women to obtain the drug. Women prostitute themselves for both money to buy the drug and the drug itself. The most frequently performed sex act is fellatio. Other sex acts engaged in include vaginal intercourse with one or more partners, anal sex, group sex, homosexual sex, and diverse other sexual acts considered aberrant by the respondents. The sexual exchange often occurs when the woman, and possibly her partner, are high on crack. These sexual encounters frequently are described as degrading or humiliating.

The exchange of sex for crack appears to be high-risk behavior for HIV transmission. Sexual encounters are frequent and with multiple partners, and condom use is haphazard and situational. The direct link between IV drug use and crack is also cause for concern; many of those interviewed had a history of IV drug use or mentioned that they had sexual partners who had one. Finally, two subjects in our sample were seropositive, and the majority of those interviewed had a history of other sexually transmitted diseases.

## Recommendations

The most obvious recommendation that follows from an ethnographic description and analysis of the crack scene is the need to view crack users within a holistic framework. Educational efforts and treatment approaches must understand the material circumstances of crack users' lives, and they must be cognizant of other serious problems confronting users on a daily basis. The danger of contracting HIV may not be the chief worry of these women; poverty, addiction, abusive relationships, the risk of incarceration, and the loss of their children may be of more immediate concern.

Research and prevention efforts need to address the involvement of gangs in the crack scene. Our work on this aspect of the crack world is far from complete. Nonetheless, it seems clear that women frequently exchange sex for crack with gang members. Subjects interviewed for this study also indicated that sex is an important aspect of gang initiation. The involvement of gangs in the crack world and the relationship of crack-addicted women to gangs may have important implications for HIV transmission. We need to learn about this relationship, and we need to develop AIDS educational strategies aimed at gang members.

The themes of humiliation and abuse that appear so often in exchanges of sex for crack make it unlikely that prevention efforts that simply tell women to negotiate safer sex with their partners will be successful. It is likely that women involved in sex-for-crack exchanges would reject this suggestion. Attempting to get a male unconcerned with HIV infection to use a condom under the circumstances described in this chapter might encourage an abusive or violent reaction or may result in the man's changing his mind about the transaction. The power imbalance that exists between the sexes suggests that an educational effort directed at males as well as females is needed. Prevention efforts would do well if they could convince the men who dominate the exchange of their own vulnerability and of the destructive potential of their risky behavior.

# References

Bourgois, Philippe. 1989. "In Search of Horatio Alger: Culture and Ideology in the Crack Economy." *Contemporary Drug Problems* 16(4):619–651.

Fagan, Jeffrey, and Ko-lin Chin. 1989. "Initiation into Crack and Cocaine: A Tale of Two Epidemics." *Contemporary Drug Problems* 16(4):579–618.

Kasarda, J. D. 1986. "Urbanization, Community, and the Metropolitan Problems." In *Handbook of Contemporary Life.* Edited by D. Street et al. San Francisco: Jossey-Bass.

Mays, Vickie M., and Susan Cochran. 1988. "Issues in the Perception of AIDS Risk Reduction Activities by Black and Hispanic/Latina Women." *American Psychologist* 43(11):949–957.

Rueter, Peter, Robert MacCoun, and Patrick Murphy. 1990. *Money from Crime: A Study of the Economics of Drug Dealing in Washington, D.C.* Washington, D.C.: Rand Corporation Drug Policy Research Center.

Wilson, William J. 1987. *The Truly Disadvantaged.* Chicago: University of Chicago Press.

# 8

# Pipe Dreams: Crack and the Life in Philadelphia and Newark

*John F. French*

> Do your crying for the living, hustling their butter
> and lard
> 'Cause dying comes easy, but it's the living
> that's hard.
> —Jailhouse poem

## The Life

The world of drug dealing, prostitution, gambling, and confidence games among inner-city residents has traditionally been called "the Life." It is distinct because it thrives primarily on the business of pleasure, the kinds of pleasures that have been defined as illegal. The crimes are most often petty and victimless (Wepman, Newman, and Binderman 1976). The people who commit the crimes and devise the hustles are called "players." The Life and its players were first popularized for the public more than half a century ago in George Gershwin's *Porgy and Bess*. The antagonist of this folk opera was named, appropriately enough, Sportin' Life; he was a gambler, pimp, and cocaine dealer who lured women into the Life by addicting them to cocaine.

The key element in the Life, the "game" or the "hustle," is the foundation of the economy in the Life. Often the hustle is simply an illegal business that supplies goods or services that cannot be bought on the legitimate market. Frequently, the players manipulate an outsider, or "mark," to get money. Games include such activities as pool hustling, prostitution, and drug dealing (Wepman, Newman, and Binderman 1976). Many games involve isolated events in which the victim is hustled infrequently or only once. Once the

This chapter was significantly improved by the editorial assistance of Harvey Feldman. Atiba Akili-Obika conducted interviews for the study. Through his insight into the Life and its players, he added much to the richness of the chapter.

205

"mark" has been "taken"—separated from his money—he may realize that the hustler has deceived him. Good hustlers are able to convince the victim that the outcome was a fluke or that the service received was worth the payment. Most hustles, however, are made between consenting parties who most often are all in the Life. They occur smoothly and without trickery. When one of the participants is cheated—called "a beat"—the victim cannot take his complaint to legal authorities for redress, and the result is often the violent retribution of street justice. Violence in these instances is purposive. It clarifies the rules of conduct for illegitimate transactions and the consequences to persons who violate them.

Within the street life of the inner-city ghetto, there exists a status system (Feldman 1973). The highest status goes to those who deal—but do not use— illicit drugs such as cocaine or heroin. Criminals who practice confidence games are also assigned high status, along with successful thieves and robbers. The status of prostitutes varies according to the amount of money they earn. And low status is assigned to drug addicts of all persuasions who have lost control of their drug consumption and whose activities bring financial loss rather than profit. The lowest status of all belongs to the females who trade sex for drugs because along with their compulsive use of drugs they allow themselves to be humiliated in public scenes where they become the object of mean-spirited ridicule.

## Prostitution

The hustle, whether it is prostitution, robbery, or begging coins from passing motorists in exchange for wiping their windshield, is intended to separate victims, or "vics," from their money. It is an essential ingredient in the economy of inner-city neighborhoods, especially when legitimate jobs are unavailable.

Through the years prostitution has been one of the traditional hustles for women in the Life. With the advent of crack cocaine, prostitution has become a significant feature of the economic life for low-income women who become involved in crack smoking. For almost all of the women in our study in Newark and Philadelphia, prostitution is their chief means of income. For that reason, I shall describe it in greater detail than the other hustles.

Women in the ghetto are often offered money in exchange for sex, usually in a joking manner. When they accept the money, it can quickly become a business, the detailed rules of which inner-city women learn from their peers. Most street prostitutes conduct business on the "stroll" where they can solicit a "date" from passing motorists or pedestrians.

Prostitute strolls are so named because the women walk slowly in restricted areas that are generally known to prospective customers. The areas are often found on a side street, usually one block away from and parallel to a major thoroughfare. In Philadelphia, the stroll extends for three blocks on the first street parallel to Main Street. Most of the activity takes place on the corner nearest the Plaza Hotel, a block away from Cross Street. In Newark, it is on an angled street at a corner that forms the apex of a triangle with the main street as the base. At night, the prostitutes move to Main Street itself.

At the far end of the Philadelphia stroll, a few homosexual males occasionally solicit customers. Unlike the female prostitutes, they remain isolated and do not associate with local women. Many other strolls, including two that we visited in Newark, integrate male homosexual prostitutes who as cross-dressers or transvestites are able to pass as females with their customers. Their female fellow workers know that they are men, accept them as part of the local scene, and may even pair up with them when an opportunity for mutual profit arises.

Among prostitutes there also exists a status hierarchy. Expensive street prostitutes, those who consistently earn twenty dollars or more for a standard "date," are assigned high status. Although there are prostitutes who use drugs of different sorts, few of them will accept drugs in lieu of money. For the most part, their drug use does not extend beyond occasional snorting of cocaine, although a minority may be regular heroin users. The advent of crack cocaine has changed this scene; a number of unsophisticated, inexperienced women, addicted to smoking crack, have invaded the strolls and undercut the prices of the more experienced professionals.

## The Date

Prostitutes usually refer to their customers as "dates," "tricks," or "johns." They sometimes refer to the transaction itself as "having a party" or "turning a trick," but "having a date" is the most common euphemism. Often dates are made with men in passing cars. As cars drive down the street, the woman attempts to make eye contact with the driver. If he returns her glance and maintains eye contact with her, she may call to him as though she knows him. If he stops, she comes to the car window and asks an introductory question. The question is usually sexually based but not incriminating—for example, "Are you looking for a good time?" or the more direct, "Do you like blow jobs?" An incriminating question, which directly solicits money in exchange for sex, is earnestly avoided in case the prospective customer is in reality a plainclothesman with the local vice squad. A poetic statement we heard one time once the customer's veracity was established was, "For twenty dollars I'll give you hips, lips, and fingertips." The driver is expected to make a direct offer of money before a deal can be made. If he does not, the woman will ask a self-protective question, such as whether he is a police officer, under the misapprehension that he cannot arrest her if he lies about being an officer.

If the potential "trick" passes the woman's scrutiny, the solicitation begins. Most dates are for the act of fellatio—commonly called "beejays," an abbreviation for "blow jobs." The price of ten to twenty dollars is standard in today's market and is determined by several factors: the lateness of the evening, the weather, the physical condition of the prostitute—if her feet hurt and it is raining, she might accept a five-dollar date just to get off the street—and the extent of her drug involvement.

Sex tends to be a quick episode that takes place in the customer's car, on a back street, in an abandoned building, at the local hotel, or—if the prostitute is a cocaine smoker—perhaps at one of the many nearby crack houses where cocaine smokers congregate.

Rita, a prostitute since she was 17 years old, now lives with her mother. She is an active young woman of 22, a "mud kicker"—one who is on the stroll in good weather or bad. She explained how easy her introduction to prostitution was. It is also noteworthy to point out her clear distinction between marijuana and what she perceived as "harmful" drugs:

*Interviewer:* Tell me about your first date.
*Rita:* There used to be a bar over here called the Franklin and I wanted to know what went on there 'cause my mom used to always tell me, "Don't go in that bar there" when we used to ride downtown. "Don't go in that bar there 'cause they hurt people, kill people, and rape people" and stuff like that, so I said I wanna go in there, I wanna see what she be talking about. So I went in there. Back then money used to be so good down here 'til you really didn't have to do nothing. Person walk up and give you money. This white man came to me said, "I'll give you thirty dollars for some sex." So I looked at him like he was crazy, 'cause you know by that being my first time down there and never doin' that type of stuff, I didn't know how to take it. So I went along with him anyway. We went around to the hotel, and that's how it all began.
*Interviewer:* Did you buy drugs with the money?
*Rita:* No, I wasn't using drugs yet—I bought reefer [marijuana].

## Dangers of Prostitution

Prostitution has occupational hazards. Because the women eventually find themselves alone with customers, they must make quick character analyses to avoid dangerous or assaultive situations. Rita provided us with insight into her work, including the dangers prostitutes must face in the course of their work and distinctions regarding attire for prostitutes:

*Interviewer:* Is the average date white or black?
*Rita:* Black. I run into some nice white guys but you don't never see 'em

again. You know, that's life. It's luck, as far as I'm concerned. I don't wear high heel shoes, I don't put no wig on, I don't wear skirts up to my ass, so if I happen to get a white guy gonna give me a little money, I'm lucky. I call that luck.

*Interviewer:* What's the worst date you ever had?

*Rita:* One time I had a gun stuck to me right here in the neighborhood. I was in this car with the trick. He paid me. I call it rape because I gave him his blow job, then he stuck a gun in my head, took his money back, and told me to get out his car, so I call that rape. I don't know how you may see it, but I felt as though it was rape.

*Interviewer:* Were there any other times you were raped?

*Rita:* Yeah, I was 19 and it was during the Christmas time and I was trying to get some money to pay my rent. This guy was always asking me for a date. This particular time I needed the money, and he seemed as though he was for real, so I went with him and we was walking past these abandoned houses [pointing]. It was dark. We got near the abandoned house and he pulled me in there. I didn't have no knife or nothin' with me that day and he had a knife stuck to my neck. He said, "You better not scream or I cut your throat." So by me not thinking I had to go along with it. I didn't know if that man was going to kill me or not. Took me into the house, made me stay there, made me give him blow jobs you know. He bit my chest all up, bit my ass all up and stuff like that. He held me for four or five hours before he let me go.

Rita shows us that she has rules of conduct and expectations of how her customers should act but that she has no control over what happens when they get violent. She attempts to gain control sometimes by carrying a knife; but like most other women on the streets, she seldom uses it for fear of retaliation.

Prostitution is the most common hustle in the Life. The compelling nature of sex as a drive and its perceived scarcity as a commodity make it a staple of the Life when other opportunities are shut off.

# Methods

Over the course of a year, we interviewed one hundred crack cocaine smokers in Newark and Philadelphia. Most interviews were conducted by me and Atiba Akili-Obika, a street-smart interviewer who had previously worked with me. Our first subjects were contacted by going to known drug-dealing areas and talking to those we believed were drug users or dealers. Access to subjects was considerably aided by my almost forty-year involvement with inner-city drug-using communities.

After our initial contacts, more subjects were recruited using snowball sampling. We were introduced to subjects on the street and during about fifty visits to crack houses. Several were recruited in a welfare hotel. After finding no juvenile crack smokers in any of these locations in either city, we attempted to recruit from new admissions to two drug treatment programs in Newark. Again, we were unsuccessful, although we did interview several teenaged cocaine dealers who occasionally smoke "koolies," cigarettes with a small amount of powdered cocaine inserted in the end, and "woolies," marijuana cigarettes with a small amount of powdered cocaine.

Subjects were paid between five and twenty dollars per interview, depending on the length of the interview and whether a tape recorder was used. Many subjects were interviewed more than once, allowing us to verify responses. Several subjects assisted us in gaining entry to crack houses and helped establish our credibility with new subjects. For example, when the 250-pound, 16-year-old bodyguard of a cocaine dealer asked emphatically who I was, Charlie D., my "guide," assured him he need not worry, that I was "stand up." This assurance protected me from what might have been the serious consequence of being in the wrong place.

## Respondents

We completed formal interviews on eighty-six subjects: forty-seven in Newark and thirty-nine in Philadelphia. The median age of our subjects was 28 years. Somewhat more than half were females. All but two were black.

We made a special effort to ensure that some homosexual and bisexual subjects were interviewed. Of the thirty-eight males, two reported having had sex only with males in the last thirty days. Another five reported sex with both males and females. Of the forty-eight women, five had sex only with other women, and another eleven had sex with both men and women in the last thirty days.

More than half of the subjects reported living with one or two other adults. One-fifth reported that they live alone. Only six said they were homeless, but the living arrangements of many were tenuous. For example, one subject told us there were five to ten adults living with her at any one time. She was living in a crack house.

Over half of our sample left school before completing the twelfth grade. Only eight of those who left early went on to get a general equivalency diploma. Seven subjects were attending school at the time of the study. These were the younger, nonaddicted subjects who smoked koolies or were nonusing cocaine dealers.

One-tenth of the women and one-fifth of the men were legally employed at the time we interviewed them. Ten subjects never held a legal job. Thirty-one subjects reported that they received some form of public assistance.

# Site Descriptions

## *Philadelphia*

The intersection of Main and Cross streets is a major transportation hub in North Philadelphia. During the day subways, buses, and trolley cars move workers to and from the center city. Unmarked, unlicensed taxis sit on the corner. The owners solicit business from passersby, calling out "taxi, cab" in anonymous voices. They serve the poor in an area where legitimate cabs seldom venture.

Within a few blocks of the corner are two fast food restaurants, a hotel, a shelter for the homeless, and three drug treatment programs. Only one bar serves the neighborhood, although there is a carry-out store that sells beer by the case. There are several general stores and a food market, all owned by Koreans, most of whom came into the neighborhood in the early 1980s.

At sunset, store owners draw steel curtains down over store windows and doors, and the owners leave the neighborhood. The fast food places stay open until 10:00 P.M., but they have armed uniformed guards on duty at all times.

Because it is convenient to outsiders, the area around Main and Cross streets is a fruitful ground for prostitutes, drug dealers, and other street hustlers. In the street life of today cocaine is by far the most available drug in the neighborhood. There are a dozen crack houses within two blocks of the intersection.

## *Newark*

The downtown area around the Shamrock Hotel is a stopping-off place for many of Newark's poor. In bad times, they might end up in one of its welfare rooms. In good times, they might visit the popular disco across the street. Good times or bad, they buy their cocaine from the teenage dealers bedecked in their gold chains and fashionable sneakers who stand in front of the disco. In spite of the guard in the lobby of the hotel who screens all entrants, the rooms often serve as crack houses for hotel residents and others.

Our study was concentrated in the hotel and in two residential neighborhoods a short distance from downtown Newark. In one, a block-long ten-story apartment building with a guard at the only entrance had four inner stairwells and elevators, each leading to forty apartments. The lower floors are more desirable since the elevators usually do not work.

In the second neighborhood was the Father Martin Project, one of Newark's oldest low-income public housing projects. There are no guards here. The project consists of six buildings, each ten stories high with ten apartments per floor. Two buildings were sealed, but the seals had been broken. Another was mostly unoccupied, with smashed windows on the upper levels. In inclement weather, the project had the appearance of being abandoned, although a number of families still lived there. For shopping, a small grocery store and sandwich shop two blocks away catered to the immediate needs of residents.

The Father Martin Project is a major crack cocaine and heroin dealing area. It is directly off a major highway to the northern suburbs. White buyers who come to purchase crack cocaine seldom turn off their car engines, let alone get out of their cars. Few outsiders, white or black, enter the project buildings. The streets and parking lots of the project, however, provide a safe and accessible area for people who can drive in from the suburbs, buy drugs, and be back on the highway within a minute or two. The project also provides more than a few crack houses for locals.

## The Role of Crack in the Life

For the cocaine smokers on the streets of Philadelphia or Newark, the Life—their lives—is centered almost exclusively on the drug. For the individuals who have committed themselves to cocaine smoking, the daily routine of the Life involves three major components: hustling, or getting the money for drugs; "copping," or buying the drugs; and getting high. This routine has existed for years, although as each new drug enters the ghetto, some changes take place in the content of each component. Smoking cocaine in particular has shaped these three aspects of drug taking because of the intensity and short duration of the crack cocaine high. As a result, the hustles are faster and cheaper. Drug trafficking is more dangerous. Perhaps most important, crack smoking has brought into existence a new social institution in the inner city—the crack house, which differs greatly from the heroin shooting gallery, its predecessor.

### The Hustle

Chronic cocaine smokers, or "pipers" as they are called in both Newark and Philadelphia, usually spend their money on cocaine as soon as they get it. Because of this short-range need, they cannot perform effectively as drug dealers or con artists. Even the "short" confidence games such as the Murphy Game, practiced worldwide by heroin addicts, are beyond the staying power of the chronic cocaine smoker. The Murphy Game involves convincing a prospective trick that if he gives his money to the hustler now, the hustler will leave and bring him back a prostitute. It is also known as whoreless pimping, since the hustler has no woman to bring back. Instead, our men, frequently former or current heroin addicts, resort to lower-status theft and robbery, hustles that are more a continuation of their earlier scams than new inventions driven by crack use, although today their schemes appear to be more erratic.

A few of the men we interviewed had jobs, but many were poorly paid, and the jobs were often "off the books." Joe, a man in his early thirties, owned little but his clothes and the furnishings in his room. His hustle was unloading trucks nine hours a day, for which he was paid sixty dollars per day "under the table."

Other hustles, perhaps less frequent, are outright criminal acts that involve assaults on persons outside the Life who do not use drugs. Unlike heroin addicts who tend to forgo violent hustles, a minority of cocaine users choose armed robbery. Ralph, a 20-year-old crack smoker, surprised us with his definition of extortion during our exploration of his money-making methods:

*Interviewer:* What's your street hustle?
*Ralph:* Extortion.
*Interviewer:* Describe that to me, what's extortion?
*Ralph:* Sticking up people, taking their money, beating em up.
*Interviewer:* Tell me how you do that.
*Ralph:* Somebody I don't know and I want some money, I take my gun, just, you know, pistol whip 'em and take their money.

## Copping

"Copping" is the term used in the drug world for the act of purchasing illicit drugs. The general location of the drug traffic is similarly called a "copping area." Drug dealing in the ghetto takes place on the street, in bars or apartments, from abandoned buildings—from any place where the drug dealer or "cop man" can maintain control over the transaction.

Illegal traffic in crack has introduced qualitative changes in the street drug market. Street-level heroin dealers typically are addicted to the drug they sell. In most situations, they are given the drug on consignment by a higher-level nonaddicted distributor. In turn, street-level heroin dealers are expected to return with their discounted payment before they are given another lot on consignment. For example, a street dealer might be given a "bundle" of ten bags of heroin at the retail price of ten dollars a bag. He must return with sixty dollars to receive another bundle. In this way, the dealer is always "into the man" for the cost of one bundle, but he can get three or four bags for his own use with each turnover. Heroin addicts, or "junkies," are notoriously poor risks as street dealers. Sooner or later, they "blow" the money, frequently injecting more heroin than they can replace with earnings. Nonetheless, they have always been a source of cheap labor for the distributor so their constant indebtedness is tolerated.

Crack distributors work somewhat the same way with their street dealers, but with a major difference, one that reflects the unique attraction of the drug. Crack distributors do not use crack smokers as street-level dealers. They have learned from bitter experience that crack users can seldom be trusted. Unlike the heroin addict, who would slip into unconsciousness, and possibly overdose, before he could use the total bundle for himself, the crack smoker can use fifty caps in a day without risk of a drug overdose. A street dealer who becomes a steady user is usually dropped and replaced with a more reliable worker.

Instead of employing cocaine smokers, many distributors have turned to hiring ambitious streetwise adolescents, who work more cheaply than adults and can be more easily controlled with the threat of violence. The street-level cocaine dealers interviewed for this study ranged in age from 15 to 22 years. Of those interviewed, only one smoked crack. During our study, she became a steady crack smoker, and distributors refused to advance her cocaine. The others, some still in school, earned about fifty dollars on a good day and were part of loose groups of teenaged dealers who bought from the same distributors.

## Buying Crack

In both Newark and Philadelphia cocaine can be bought as a powder (hydrochloride) or as crack. Smokers in both cities prefer to buy powder and base it themselves. In Newark, powder cocaine is most often sold in ten dollar "bottles"—the same containers often used to hold crack elsewhere. The bottles range in size from one-half to three-quarters of an inch in length, and can hold 100 mg or more. Ten bottles, or a "clip," can cost as little as fifty dollars in New York City, where most larger quantities are purchased. Crack has a poor reputation in Newark, and very little is offered for sale, although five-dollar vials can be found.

"Rock" or "crack" has the same poor reputation in Philadelphia that it has in Newark, yet it is more widely available in that city, in five-dollar vials or "caps." Powder cocaine costs ten to twenty dollars and comes most often in bags. Most chronic users in Philadelphia end up buying crack, not only because it is cheaper but because it takes less time and requires no additional preparation; it is the fast food of the drug market.

Procaine, lidocaine, and benzocaine are popular cutting agents since they will "cook up" and convert to the freebase in the same way powder cocaine does. They have all of the qualities of cocaine except the high. These "beats" or "getovers" are called "comeback" in both cities. Several respondents reported that selling "comeback" was a common street hustle.

## The Place: Crack Houses

In Philadelphia, they are called "hit houses." In Newark, the term is "smoke house" or "coke house." Among older users, particularly former or current heroin addicts, the old term "gallery" is employed. In popular parlance— and sometimes on the street—the place is a "crack house." But for everyone who attends them and spends time there, it is a haven: a setting where the users do not feel out of place, a setting that contains people who understand the "basic nature" of crack cocaine smoking and who are familiar with the paraphernalia and procedures that comprise the activity. An overriding theme among our respondents has been their preference for smoking in the setting of a "crack house."

Crack houses have some of the elements of shooting gallery, sex parlor, barroom, and community center. People go to a crack house for many reasons. Some are pragmatic: it is close to the cocaine selling area, thus saving time from purchase to use. The necessary paraphernalia is available so that users do not have to carry incriminating equipment. For the men, sex is virtually unrestricted and at low cost, often only a small amount of cocaine. For the women, drugs are available, often in exchange for quick sex. For many, the crack house is a place to socialize and a safe haven from the fears that come over many smokers when they get high.

Contrary to popular belief, cocaine and other drugs are not sold in most crack houses. Rather, they function as rented space in a safe setting in which either money or cocaine itself provides the basis for a negotiated transaction. Persons who were either currently running crack houses or had once been proprietors explain how this new social institution arose to meet the need for a safe place:

> Most crack houses don't sell crack. I've been at crack houses that sold it and that was shocking. . . . You don't want to buy it off them 'cause they use it. You don't know what they done did to it. They might have put something into it. Most houses don't even try to sell it. Some people do try to make some money. Out of ten houses, eight houses don't sell it. You have to go around the corner and buy it and go back to the crack house just to smoke. A crack house is a place where you smoke it. It's not where you buy it. It's where you do your thing, whatever you do, shoot up or whatever you do. I had a crack house one time. I had my own little apartment. I let certain people come over. Most crack houses, you come and give them a little crack, that's cool, they satisfied. But me, I didn't want no crack. You give me money, I'll buy my own crack. Give me two dollars. It's better.

> This one young lady's house, it is like three or four people sitting around, but it is like a little class, if you consider that a crack house. People sitting

there getting high, using her pipe and paying for it by giving her hits, but they all friends.

Well, when I ran a house, basically they came there to get high. They was people that I knew and there wasn't no cover charge for coming but they would give you something when they come, you know. It was quite a few people, sometime ten people through the course of a day. I seen people come in there spend five hundred dollars. In and out. They might buy twenty dollars and they say to theirself that they not gonna use that much stuff and they leave but they buy more. Then they come right back. When they gone they done spent five hundred dollars running back and forth. . . . A lot of people I didn't let come in cause I lived there. So it wasn't a crack house, just a place that friends of mine or friends of friends were coming by and smoke. It was that particular type of a house.

Certain people wanna come in my house and smoke, then they will come in there and smoke and then they will leave. Now if they wanna come in there just because they know that me and my woman have something to smoke, no. They will not come in. Not to be sitting around thinking I'm gonna get them high for nothing, 'cause you know you can't get nothing in this world without nothing. They have to have they pipe. If not, they use one of ours. I don't charge nothing. All I wanna do is get mine. Give me a nice share or whatever to get off with and that's it. And they can stay there until their coke is gone. Ain't no such thing as laying around. I'm not going to have that. You see once they get too comfortable then they don't wanna leave. And like I said that's me and my wife's place. . . . You wanna get high that's alright.

In practical terms, police raids on crack houses where the drug is not sold are rare. Typically, crack houses are usually small operations in someone's home or apartment rather than large warehouse-type settings. Police concentrate more resources on reducing drug selling and prostitution on the street or in other highly visible areas. In short, small crack houses, frequently hidden away in secret settings, do not have high police priority. Very often, they are set up in impromptu settings such as abandoned public housing apartments by an enterprising entrepreneur. One respondent described such low-cost arrangements: "Most crack houses have no electric, no gas, dirty, like old houses they just put furniture in, maybe sweep em out, no windows. They are abandoned houses, candles for lights."

## Patterns of Utilization

Activities in a crack house are not random events. For the most part, the work hours and pay days of participants determine the incidence of both drug use and sexual activities as they do with drug dealing, gambling, and other entrepreneurial activities in the inner city. Nights are busier than days, although there is a brief flurry of activity at about noon when the "lunchtime trade" comes to the prostitute stroll and possibly for a quick stop in the crack house for a "smoke and blow."

Mornings and Sundays are the slowest times in the crack houses and on the streets. Sunday, we discovered, was a time for family obligations when even confirmed crack users chose to blend in with traditional community activities such as adapting to the influence of community churchgoers. We interviewed Ted on a Sunday morning shortly before noon, a block away from the crack house:

*Interviewer:* What are you going to do after this interview?
*Ted:* I'm gonna get me something to eat and I'm going back in. See on Sundays, I don't get high. Not on Sunday.
*Interviewer:* At all?
*Ted:* Naw. A lot of church people be out here and you be walking around all high and they be looking at you like you crazy. And I got to rest 'cause I got to go to work tomorrow, so I rest up for work tomorrow.

Sundays are also a time for respondents to spend with their families, a practice that belies the common statement that addicts pursue the use of drugs to the exclusion of everything else. Francine, a crack-using prostitute, similarly puts Sundays aside for rest and looking after her two children:

*Francine:* Sundays I get my rest and I eat.
*Interviewer:* Is that because you're religious or . . .
*Francine:* No, no . . . I need that rest one day a week.
*Interviewer:* Then why pick Sunday? Why not pick Thursday?
*Francine:* It might be because it's slow, and then again a lot of times it's because I am tired. You know, after Fridays I'm tired and I can feel that I need food in my system and I need rest. I got to be logical when it comes to this stuff, you know. I got two boys to take care of. Sundays I go by my mother's to be with them.

Fridays and Saturdays tend to be seen as a single day. Many crack smokers binge straight through the two days. Fridays and the first day of the month are by far the busiest days in the crack house.

Other factors affect the frequency of drug use and sexual activities in the crack house. Weather is the most consistent influence. If it is too hot, people tend to stay outdoors. In winter, if the crack house is not heated, it is empty. On the other hand, if it is heated, the crack house provides both shelter and amusement, so much so that the house man—the person in charge—has to limit entrance.

Police activity is another feature that influences the utilization patterns of the crack house. Occasionally police sweeps reduce drug selling and prostitution on the streets. When police activity increases on the street, persons in the Life tend to move indoors where they will not be observed by police and rightfully or wrongfully taken into custody.

When the crack house is in full swing, the tempo of activity increases, and the movement is quick and frenetic. The drug effects of crack cocaine make the movement even more hectic. Lee, a regular at one of the crack houses we visited, described what he called a "classic" crack house. At the time we interviewed Lee, he was very high on cocaine, and he started a frenetic monologue that conveyed the tension of the house. His repetitive use of the word "boom" indicated the speed of the action:

> Knock, knock. "Who's there?" "So and so." "What do you want?" "I got two bottle." She [the person in charge] might not even be answering the door. She'll have a friend who's maybe assisting her cooking up the crack, getting, you know, getting the baking soda and the water at her sign. This person answers the door, questions the person at the door, tells her to come to the door, and she'll have a few words on how much you got. They pay a rock to her and it's like, "Hey, excuse me, sit on the couch." Boom. She sits them down. Boom. She digs out a pipe or stem. Boom. Gives it to them, sets them up, and they get off and shit [smoke]. And she wants some more, you know. Somebody else has rung the bell. They're coming and three more people coming. Boom. They got they bottle. Boom. She's cooking it up. They standing on this side. "Excuse me, could you move over?" Somebody over there waiting for their shit to get cooked up. Boom. She passing them another and the more people, the different kind of pipes. . . . You ever saw liquor bottles. They done drilled a hole in one of those and fixed that up to smoke out of it. You know what I'm saying, or a can of soda or anything you know and it just be going. On a weekend it goes like that 'til she can't even take it. She be like, she be having so much shit [cocaine] stashed after they leave she can smoke for four hours without even spending a dime from the cut she be getting off their drugs. And she can do that around the clock. She does until she just has to have a break just to eat or just something. It gets so crowded where it's dudes just standing in a little nook on the wall smoking and shit, you know laying on the floor and shit. Nobody can't hardly talk. People whispering and like paranoid. Looking at the door, you know. It's frantic. But it's 24-7 [twenty-four hours a day, seven days a week] since I've known her.

## Crack Cocaine Paranoia

"Paranoia" is a psychiatric term that has worked its way into the language of the street. Rather than the construction of a tightly woven plot against an individual, however, the street meaning of "paranoia" refers to any situation where suspicion or apprehension begins to take command. Crack smokers have good reason to be suspicious of anything out of the ordinary. They are, after all, engaging in illegal activity. Living in an environment where exploitation, robbery, and assault are everyday events makes almost everyone wary of actions that are out of the ordinary. And when the nervousness that accompanies the effects of cocaine settles in, it comes as no surprise that crack smokers express their feelings of impending doom as "paranoia."

The expression of paranoia as a theme in the daily life of drug users has been noted elsewhere (Wedlow 1979). As with the marijuana smokers Wedlow discussed, crack smokers share feelings of paranoia that seem unwarranted by the immediate circumstances. One respondent attempted to describe how these feelings of apprehension sometimes dominated his perceptions of his surroundings: "I'm telling you, when you're feeling paranoid, you can step out at night and see a fire hydrant and it looks like someone's stooping down waiting for you. If it's dark at night you would swear to God that motherfucker moved."

The overriding issue that underpins the feelings of paranoia is the combination of the illegality of the drug and the drug effect itself, which creates a nervous tension. One respondent explained indirectly how trafficking in cocaine increased his feelings of paranoia because it increased his chances for arrest: "If they're selling cocaine in a hit house, I don't go in there to get high, 'cause I may take a couple of good hits and get paranoid thinking the police may run in and bust the house."

Crack smokers have devised several methods to manage the disquiet that feeling paranoid produces. Collectively, most crack house operators avoid having cocaine sold on the premises. They understand that drug dealing rather than drug possession has a higher priority with law enforcement agencies. Smokers must leave the crack house to purchase their drug and return there to smoke it or hire someone to buy it for them.

Crack houses themselves put users in company with others who are able to share the "reality" of the paranoia. One respondent noted how the comfort of knowing that other people were available was in itself a counteraction to feelings of paranoia: "I can't smoke without other people being there. Even at home. I can't smoke alone at home. I peek out the windows all day. Lock the door, barricade it. I still worry about someone being out there."

As Wedlow (1979) discussed, drug users can rely on trusted friends to vouch for strangers, make rules for entering and exiting that give a sense of protection, and develop intuitions on assessing dangers. They can exchange selective revelations, which allow them to assuage feelings of paranoia and keep them from intruding into the pleasures of the high (Wedlow 1979).

The quickest and surest way to calm nervousness temporarily is to manage it chemically. Heroin addicts have long noted the balancing effects of opiates in calming the nervousness cocaine often induces. They often combine the drugs—called a "speedball"—under the belief that each drug has counteracting capabilities over the other. In our study, the most common method for calming the jangled effects of crack cocaine was to balance it with alcohol. When questioned why he continued to smoke crack if it left him paranoid, one user explained:

> I just like the high. That's why I always have my wine. Keeps me from feeling paranoid. I always have that wine when I'm getting high. That's a definite. Even if I only have five dollars to buy one cap, I'll sell someone a hit for a dollar just to get a beer.

Most of the crack users in our study were daily drinkers. Rather than spend extra money on heroin, they would buy a bottle of beer or share a bottle of wine to fill in the gaps between cocaine highs and to level off the effects. Cocaine was clearly the drug they would choose over all the others, but alcohol was a strong second choice.

## Social Roles in the Crack House

Although each crack house differs, there are four essential social roles that can be found in the overwhelming majority: the house man or proprietor; the runner or assistant; the "skeezer," a woman who provides sex; and the customer.

**The House Man.** The house man or the proprietor is the person in charge. More than anyone else, he—sometimes she—sets the tone and makes the rules for all activities. He is the director as well as the principal actor. He determines who gets high, and when, who goes first, and who must wait. He decides what sexual activities go on, by whom and with whom. He is the chief executive officer, the boss. Not everyone who has the available space to set up a crack house can achieve the rank of house man. It requires organizational skills. Above all, the person must have the necessary personal characteristics to set limits on behavior, especially the ability to negotiate disputes and to impose authority when necessary. The house man, then, must have earned respect from prior activities either for his physical strength, capability for violent actions, or for logical fairness. One former house man explained:

> When I was running one—well I ran a couple of 'em—we used to charge. We used to charge them a hit and a dollar if they had one cap. And if they had like a ten-cent piece, two dollars and a hit. So the more that you had, the more it's gonna cost the person. Sometimes it cost more 'cause their reactions or their reflexes towards the cocaine. It makes people aggravated, and plus you know it could be like four people that try to take a hit at the same time. And it's gonna be one fight and that's holding me up and holding up my business. So you got to charge 'em more.

When the person in charge is unable to assert authority, the crack house becomes chaotic and is characterized by loud arguments, fights, and sometimes stabbings and shootings. Such actions bring on the attention of the police, and houses where the proprietor loses authority soon go out of business. Crack smokers, as one might expect, prefer houses where the proprietor maintains strict control and where users can feel safe from other users and free of "paranoia." Sweetpea described what he perceived as a "classic" crack house run by a strong-willed woman:

> Say you go and buy like two or three bottles. Soon as you come in the door, she'll crack on you for what you got. And she gets a little piece of what you got. She gets like you know like a rock. She gets a nice little chunk off that rock. I go there cause I'm comfortable there, 'cause she runs the house pretty cool. You know, she don't stand for too much shit like thieving and all that kinda of stuff. She don't even gotta watch her shit like a hawk. I mean you do have to watch your shit, but not no outlandish wild shit going on there. There be from three to maybe twenty people there, weekends.

Most of the house men (and women) we interviewed were somewhat older than their customers and the skeezers that frequented their houses. Coming from the "older" generation, almost all had a history of intravenous heroin use, and se know that at least one is infected with HIV.

**The Runner.** The runner, who is usually a male, assists the house man with menial tasks, such as running errands for customers, buying new pipes, and, especially, quelling a potential argument or fight. In return, the runner receives a quantity of crack cocaine. When the runner provides service for the house man, he is paid by the house man, usually in units of "hits on the pipe." If he runs errands for a customer, it is expected that the customer will pay for the service with a hit on the pipe. The runner does not clean the house or prepare food—if there are kitchen facilities. These household tasks are viewed as "woman's" work and not the proper province of street males.

**Skeezers.** Skeezers, women who regularly trade sex directly for crack, are key figures in the operation of crack houses. With all drugs—from alcohol to heroin—prostitution has been a mainstay in paying for a habit that has gone out of control. There is an old barroom ditty that satirizes alcoholic women: "Get off the table, Mabel, the quarter's for the beer!" In the 1950s and 1960s, female addicts who would exchange sex for a bag of heroin were known as "bag brides."

Prostitutes addicted to heroin have been immortalized in the poetry of the Life in the "toasts" or "jailhouse poems" shared among black players, particularly young men in jails and prisons. One toast, "The Fall," refers to prostitutes "turning half-dollar tricks to make a fix" (Wepman, Newman, and Binderman 1976). Traditionally within the moral code of the street, women who have traded sex for drugs or alcohol have been looked down on, and their worth both as sexual objects or in monetary terms has been devalued, not because of their sexual availability but because they have lost control of their drug use.

In today's world of crack cocaine, females who trade sex for drugs are called "skeezers," the pejorative term for a "low-life whore." In the language of the streets, they "do things for things." Randy, a 22-year-old crack smoker, did not conceal his disrespect for the skeezer:

> A skeezer will do anything. You give her anything, she'll give you some sex. You can give her money. Two dollars. A dollar. Or you can give her a pack of cigarettes. You can give her a little piece of crack. Anything, man. You can get it for anything. They give it up so cheap now.

Compared to prostitutes, skeezers do not hold the respect that a working woman earns when her services are paid for with money rather than drugs. Ali, a former heroin addict and observer of the street scene for many years, noted:

> A real prostitute's doing it for her kids, for rent. They can't get no money now cause the man's goin' to a skeezer down the street and get it for two dollars. They ain't giving a prostitute thirty or forty dollars. Some guys pay it, but not many. Since the crack came in, a lot of things changed.

**The Customer.** Crack house customers run the gamut of local social types. Most frequently, they are local residents and may be unskilled laborers, low-level thieves and robbers, or other crack house operators. In some cases, adventurous men from outside the neighborhood get sponsorship from someone local and visit a crack house. Primarily, they share an interest in smoking crack cocaine. Some customers, however, are more interested in watching the spectacle and, perhaps taking advantage of the available cheap sex. In this sense, they use the crack house as a social and recreational center.

## The Action

The crack house is a complex economic enterprise. The house man gets paid for all the services the house provides. He supplies pipes and matches for customers who bring their own cocaine and will buy cocaine for them if they choose. For male customers, he supplies skeezers and a private room. He can negotiate the fee and has control over which woman the customer sees. This control allows him to collect money or cocaine from both the customer and the woman. After assessing the range of prices per service in several crack houses, we calculated the following scale in both cities:

*Use of pipe*: Two dollars or the equivalent of one "hit" of cocaine calculated to be about two dollars' worth

*Matches*: Twenty-five cents to one dollar a book (or free to good customers)

*Private room*: Five dollars per half-hour.

*Sex with a woman*: Five to ten dollars or an equivalent amount of cocaine paid to the woman and one hit of cocaine to the house man.

One way to capture a picture of the activities in a crack house is to describe in general terms a "good" and a "bad" event.

A good event for the crack house would develop as follows: a working male customer comes into the house with four vials of cocaine he has bought previously. His intention is to rent the house man's pipe and to engage in sex with one of the skeezers. He pays two dollars for the use of the pipe. After smoking one or two caps, he gives the house man a hit and negotiates with him for the services of one of the several women who hang out in the crack house. At this point, he might give the woman a hit on his pipe as an introduction to the sexual encounter. He pays the house man five dollars for the use of a private room and agrees to pay the woman ten dollars. He and the woman then go into the room and smoke the remaining two caps. In the room, they negotiate the kind of sex that will take place. When a half-hour has passed, the house man will knock on the door, tell the customer that his half-hour is up, and assure him that he can stay longer if he chooses. Finally, the house man will ask if the customer would like him to send out his runner to purchase more cocaine.

Now the hustle starts in earnest. The aim of the proprietor is to see that whatever money the customer has brought with him will be spent before he leaves the crack house. Whatever cash is given to the woman will usually be used to buy cocaine, which she might share with the house man. He, in turn, will buy cocaine with the room money and will receive as payment some of the cocaine bought for the customer. In addition, the house man may later also receive extra cocaine from the dealer because of the volume of business he brings.

A bad event for the crack house involves a customer who can hold back on paying the woman until her desire for cocaine forces her to reduce her price. She will eventually give him the sex of his choice—usually fellatio—for as little as a vial, or even a single hit, of cocaine.

## Sex in the Crack House

The most frequently performed sexual activity in the crack house is fellatio. Our subjects sometimes made sharp distinctions in referring to this activity. John, a 31-year-old heroin and cocaine injector who has been smoking cocaine for seven years, at the beginning of an interview mentioned to us in passing that he had traded cocaine for fellatio recently. Later in the interview we asked about his sex life:

> *Interviewer:* When's the last time you had sex?
> *John:* About two years ago.
> *Interviewer:* But you said you've been trading coke for sex.
> *John:* No, only blow jobs. I ain't had sex for two years. The blow jobs take off the tension, and I don't put myself in the way of getting AIDS.

Sex in a crack house is an ancillary activity to smoking cocaine. In concept, it is similar for the woman to what occurs in a strip joint or a massage parlor. There is a pretense of sexual interest on the woman's part but the interest is actually part of the hustle.

The men in our study often like to believe the illusion that the women with whom they have sex actually enjoy it. Most of the men, however, realize the pretense. The following interview with Michael, who enjoyed the "freaky" nature of crack house sex, illustrates the strategy of the crack house hustle:

> *Interviewer:* Are they doing it because they like to do it, or are they doing it because they gonna get the cocaine?
> *Michael:* One girl told me she's doing it because she likes to do it when she gets the cocaine in her. [Long pause] But I believe that's part of her hustle.
> *Interviewer:* Now, put that hustle aside, do you think they enjoy it?
> *Michael:* I don't think so. I think it's wearing on their asses, you know, because most of them have young kids, and they have to run back home. They tell you, "I don't have this much time, hurry up, hurry up."

There are several other distinguishing features of sex in the crack house besides the emphasis on fellatio. First, in the process of getting high, when he is busy concentrating on cocaine, the customer often simply forgets to involve himself with the sex he has paid for. Second, after sustained cocaine smoking, he often finds himself impotent. Many users told us that they have difficulty achieving an erection when they are high, but they attempt fellatio anyway. Finally, they often fail to reach ejaculation. Joe, a particularly honest and direct respondent, stated that finding sexual satisfaction while smoking crack was, ironically enough, a "pipe dream."

> No, that's nothing but a pipe dream. That's all it is. . . . That's what I call it. They always say, "I'm going to get a blow job for nothing off this girl." One hit. Nothing. I've seen people go through their whole bankroll, however much money they got, on a girl because she was gonna give them head for this blast. And she never gave it to him. And after all the coke was gone, she got up and left. So, that's just a dream. Just a pipe dream out of that cocaine pipe. When you be high off of smoking a pipe, you can't have sex because you will not get an erection. I don't care what nobody says. It won't happen. It just won't happen. And people say, you know, "When I smoke mine, I get a hard on." You say that, you's a damn liar. That be the farthest thing from your mind. The only thing be on you mind is where am I gonna get another bottle [of cocaine] from. That's the real deal. I don't care what nobody says. I done seen too many people do it.

Of greater importance than the actual sensation of physical sex was the feeling of power and control many customers experience when they are in sexual contact with skeezers. The issue of control was a theme throughout the sexual interactions between our subjects, although it was seldom directly expressed without our asking. Mack was an exception and provided expression of a power relationship between customer and skeezer other respondents alluded to but could not articulate:

> *Interviewer:* When you're in the crack house and some girl is giving you a blow job, what's the difference between that feeling and any other time that you have sex?
> *Mack:* I feel like I have something on this girl right now, she can't really say anything. I have the ups on her and she's the one down, I'm the one up.
> *Interviewer:* Why is that?
> *Mack:* 'Cause I have what she wants, which is cocaine. If I didn't have the cocaine I probably have to wait on her, I probably couldn't command. She'd be saying, "Look I have to go, could you please hurry up here." I would probably have to wait on her. This way she has to chase me.

Lee is a male homosexual in his early thirties who prostitutes for money and will do sex for coke when he has the chance. He tells us that men seldom want his services in the exposed atmosphere of a coke house and will humiliate him less than they might a woman:

> Women have such a need after that first crack hit that some of these guys want to humiliate them and sort of make them beg, you see. Know what

I'm saying, he might get off on humiliating and having this girl give him a blow job in front of everybody but he might feel a threat to his manhood to have a gay guy do that. That would be done on a more, much more hush-hush sort of thing. And strictly kept between me and him. That's an unsaid, unwritten rule. It could be either for money or drugs.

Because of the study's emphasis on crack use and its potential for transmitting HIV, we were particularly interested in exploring incidents of anal intercourse, the sexual act thought to transmit the virus most efficiently. Our respondents, both male and female, with few exceptions expressed an aversion to anal intercourse, some of them vehemently. The following excerpts from interviews are representative of the general negative view on heterosexual anal intercourse:

> *Interviewer:* Are most of your tricks just blow jobs?
> *Rita:* Yeah, or a little sex.
> *Interviewer:* How about taking it in the butt?
> *Rita:* Oh, no. I don't play that! I do not play that!

> *Interviewer:* Did you ever try it in the butt?
> *Cindy:* I tried it once with my man when we was first together. And I got hemorrhoid problems so bad, it hurt me to go to the bathroom all that month. A trick could not pay me—as bad as I might wanna smoke some cocaine—a trick could not pay me to have no anal sex with him. I can't do that. No way.

As an AIDS risk factor, anal intercourse does not seem to be a practice even skeezers participate in despite their apparent desperate need of either money or drugs.

## Status Degradation

For the women who take on the role of skeezer, the consequence is a severe loss of status and respect in the eyes of all other participants. Skeezers incorporate this reduced image and come to see themselves as permanently tarnished because of their inability to control their yearning for cocaine. It is not that they involve themselves in what they perceive as shameful behavior as much as it is that they are driven to it from an obsessive desire for the drug. "Mom," a 43-year-old former heroin addict who started cocaine injection while on methadone maintenance and then turned to smoking cocaine when she burned out her veins two years ago, regretted losing her reputation as a good street prostitute and saw her use of crack as the cause of her status descent:

> I feel bad because I didn't do the things for heroin that I'm doing for this cocaine. I really below myself as far as taking two dollars. You know, back

then I wouldn't be taking no less than twenty dollars. . . . Right now if I'm desperate enough I'll take two or three dollars. It bothers me, you know, but what can I do. I'm embarrassed inside myself. It hurts me that I be out here giving head jobs for two and three dollars at my age.

Mom's anguish is real, but her need for cocaine dominates her behavior. Her pain and depression are shared by the other women we interviewed. When the skeezer role gets permanently attached to a woman, her relationships with others change according to her acceptance of this low status, which they perceive as unworthy. Francine provided a poignant observation regarding her inability to conceive of sex as an expression of love since becoming a skeezer. In response to the question of whether there was a special man in her life other than her sexual customers, she said:

> You know, every time I get into sex now it's like a job. And that's sorta sad. My feelings aren't into it like it used to be. And now I don't want to have sex unless I'm getting something for it. It's like I'm not human anymore. And that's sad. So that's probably why I haven't had a boyfriend. It's sad. It's not like it used to be. It's not like it used to be with me. I definitely notices a difference.

## Condoms

On the streets of Newark where injection drug users have an HIV antibody seropositivity rate of almost 50 percent,[1] and where noninjecting drug users have a rate higher than 10 percent,[2] HIV/AIDS prevention messages have a ready market of interested people. We found that most street people are AIDS aware and have at least one friend who is either HIV infected or has been diagnosed with AIDS.

We were not surprised when we found that condoms were always available in the neighborhoods we studied. We discovered that many commercial establishments in the study areas, responding to the publicity which the HIV epidemic has produced, have added condoms to their inventories. On Main Street in Philadelphia, there is a twenty-four hour gas station with a small convenience store that sells more than fifty condoms on weeknights and at least a hundred condoms a night on weekends at the low price of fifty cents each. During the business hours of prostitution, they are one of their most popular items. The boxes of condoms are kept under the counter, by the cash register. Only cigarettes are more convenient for the clerk to reach.

The hotel also sells condoms but at the higher price of one dollar apiece. Condoms are also available at the sandwich shop across from the crack house, where they sell for sixty cents. And in Newark, there is a convenience store near one of the prostitute strolls with a condom machine bolted to the outside wall.

We discovered that a "street" market in condoms has developed, created in part by HIV/AIDS publicity. Streetwise individuals have found that a slight profit can be made selling condoms to prostitutes and others in the sex trade. In both study cities, there are always several people on the street who have condoms for sale—condoms that they have commercially purchased or received free from an AIDS prevention project. Mack, a 48-year-old former heroin dealer and pimp who snorted cocaine and heroin for a quarter century before starting to smoke cocaine, has made selling condoms to prostitutes one of his many small hustles. As a known old-timer on the street, he can sell condoms for twenty-five or fifty cents apiece. At night, when most stores are closed, he can demand and receive as much as one dollar per condom.

Perhaps the most consistent supply of condoms comes from the newly developed street-based AIDS prevention programs that target injection drug users, their sexual partners, and prostitutes. Mack, for example, gets condoms free from an "indigenous" AIDS fieldworker, who used to buy her heroin from him and sometimes prostituted for him. The arrangement is beneficial to both of them. The fieldworker, who cannot always be present on the stroll, essentially utilizes Mack as a secondary distributor when she is unavailable. Together they are providing an important health service to the community by ensuring that condoms are available even at night.

Having condoms available, however, is no guarantee that they will be used. We found that most women involved in the sex trades made initial attempts to use condoms, but in the tension between earning money and chancing infection, women frequently opted for the immediate gain of profit and sometimes gambled with infection. As Duriella, an older prostitute claimed:

> *Duriella:* Yeah . . . If they don't have a rubber, I get one.
> *Interviewer:* Even when you give em a blow job?
> *Duriella:* Some of em. [*pause*] You know every dick you suck, you ain't gonna suck with no rubber on it. 'Cause you might want that money. And you ain't got no rubber. So you take that chance. Go home and try to boil your mouth out, you know [laughter].

The pattern of unprotected sex during fellation was common. There was a belief on the street that "blow jobs" were safer than unprotected vaginal sex, a view that is not without some expert support. Because of this, the men in our study sought out oral sex and usually avoided unprotected vaginal sex. Five Star explained how this belief influences his exchanges of crack for sex with skeezers:

> *Interviewer:* Are you getting any sex for coke?
> *Five Star:* Yeah, you can take a half a cap, and you get all the sex you want. And you don't give that coke to 'em; you just let them see it.

Tell them, "This is yours, after you do your job." And they be doing and doing and doing.

*Interviewer:* What do they do? What are they giving you, blow jobs?

*Five Star:* That's all. If you run up into 'em, ain't no telling what you subject to get. I don't use no rain coats [condoms]. I do have a little knowledge to know with oral sex there's not too much in it for you to be getting AIDS. Tell you where I'm at: "I want the jaws. Mail the drawers to Santa Claus."

For individuals who have an intimate and personal knowledge of HIV/AIDS and know or are sexually involved with someone who is infected, there is a compelling necessity to use condoms. Debbie, who along with her husband, a former heroin addict, runs a crack house, always uses condoms:

*Interviewer:* Have you made any changes in your behavior to reduce your risk or make yourself safer from getting AIDS?

*Debbie:* Yes. I've stopped using the needle, and when me and my husband have sex, we use a condom.

*Interviewer:* Why do you use a condom?

*Debbie:* Because he has the virus.

Although the use of condoms may be spotty and subject to the whims of customers who seek odd and cheap sex, the message of the AIDS epidemic has clearly penetrated the networks of all hustlers in the Life. They are acutely aware that HIV/AIDS is transmitted sexually through the exchange of semen and that the use of condoms provides protection. Lee, a male prostitute, explained why oral sex is common and why he insists on condoms:

*Lee:* Mostly it is a blow job. Because it's something quick and it's not exactly like you have a comfortable room and showering facilities to get into fucking, you know.

*Interviewer:* Is it strictly business? Do these guys wear condoms?

*Lee:* Yeah. I'm not gonna give no guy a blow job and let him come in my mouth, and I'm not gonna have no guy fuck me and let him come in my ass. That's out. Both of those are out because of the AIDS epidemic.

## Oral Sex and Disease Transmission

The primary objective of our study was to collect data on the sexual activities of chronic cocaine smokers who exchange sex for crack to obtain an indication of their risk for HIV infection. Since fellatio is the most frequently practiced sexual activity among our subjects, we researched the literature on this activity as a risk factor for HIV.

We found that the subject of oral sex is surrounded by controversy. A decade ago, Shostak (1981) reviewed the sociological literature and concluded there had been a "blank-out" on the subject of oral sex in American society. This has not yet been fully rectified. A search of the *Sociological Abstracts* from 1963 to early 1991 found only five documents indexed on prostitution and fellatio or oral sex.

Even some recent studies, such as Smith and Udry's (1985) study of noncoital sexual behavior of adolescents, do not even mention oral sex. Although oral sex has long been recognized as a standard part of the prostitute's repertoire (Gagnon and Simon 1987; Canfield 1975), some authors fail to note it and, in fact, cast it into doubt. In their classic work, Benjamin and Masters (1964) report that "the American who encounters a prostitute who will not allow coitus, but who is willing to engage in oral intercourse and to masturbate her client, has a good basis for believing that he is dealing not with a bona fide female, but with a female impersonator" (pp. 148–149).

This failure to address the topic extends to the medical literature as well. A search of *Medline* for the last ten years found few reports of sexually transmitted diseases (STD) through oral sex.

The risk for HIV infection through oral sex has not been determined. Only two reports of HIV infection through fellatio have appeared in the literature, although there is reason to expect that this activity puts one at risk. In 1988, Rozenbaum et al. reported on five cases of HIV infection among homosexual males, none of whom had practiced anal intercourse since the last time they had tested negative for HIV antibody. All five had since engaged in inserting fellatio, and three had also engaged in receptive fellatio. Two had no high-risk behavior other than the inserting fellatio (Rozenbaum et al, 1988).

Spitzer and Weiner (1989) report a case of HIV infection in a man whose only apparent exposure was through oral sex (both fellatio and cunnilingus) with an IV drug-using prostitute. They also reported that the man had insulin-dependent diabetes, but they had not considered the possibility that the prostitute might have substituted infected, used hypodermics on occasion for those with which he was taking his insulin during the two-year period they had an affair.

## STD Prevention

Given the evidence that the activities of our subjects put them at high risk for STDs, including HIV, intervention is clearly needed. Recent activities of the Philadelphia Department of Public Health reported by Mellinger and his colleagues (1991) provide direction for future HIV prevention efforts in the population of chronic cocaine users. During the summer of 1990, the department established a screening activity team (SAT) to provide serologic testing in the field at high-risk sites where cocaine was being sold and used. These areas included crack houses, prostitute strolls, brothels, drug-copping areas, and shooting galleries.

The department recognized that infected persons who are users of illegal drugs or prostitutes are often hesitant or unable to identify partners well enough for STD field staff to locate them. In an effort to locate some of these partners, the SAT was accompanied in the field by the infected patient on several occasions; high-risk associates and sex partners were located and tested. This resulted in the detection of fourteen cases of early syphilis.

The SAT then began to provide serological screening at high-risk locations, including crack houses, prostitute strolls, drug sale areas, brothels, and shooting galleries. Of 372 persons screened, 100 tested positive for syphilis, and 44 were successfully treated.

The SAT was eventually accepted at these high-risk locations, although follow-up was a major problem. Of the one hundred reactive cases, thirty-three were lost to follow-up, even though test results were available within one day. Mellinger's report recommends that initial (RPR) serological testing be done in the field at the time of phlebotomy to allow for immediate treatment. The expansion of SAT projects such as this along with the aggressive outreach strategy employed in many cities might provide an effective means for reducing the spread of the HIV/AIDS epidemic.

# Notes

1. Unpublished data from New Jersey Department of Health, Newark Health Behavior Project, 1991.
2. Unpublished data from New Jersey Department of Health, Division of AIDS Prevention and Control, 1991.

# References

Benjamin, H., and R. E. L. Masters. 1964. *Prostitution and Morality*. New York: Julian Press.

Canfield, S. 1975. *Why Men Call Girls*. New York: Dell Publishing.

Feldman, Harvey W. 1973. "Street Status and the Drug User." *Society* 10(4):32–38.

Gagnon, J. H., and W. Simon. 1987. "The Sexual Scripting of Oral Genital Contacts." *Archive of Sexual Behavior* 16(1):1–25.

Mellinger, M. D., M. Goldberg, A. Wade, et al. 1991. "Alternative Case-Finding Methods in a Crack-Related Syphilis Epidemic in Philadelphia." *Morbidity and Mortality Weekly Report* 40(5):77–80.

Rozenbaum, W., S. Gharakhanian, B. Cardon, et al. 1988. "HIV Transmission by Oral Sex" (letter). *Lancet*, June 18, p. 1395.

Shostak, A. B. 1981. "Oral Sex: New Standard of Intimacy and Old Index of Troubled Sexuality." *Deviant Behavior* 2:127–144.

Smith, E. A., and J. R. Udry. 1985. "Coital and Non-Coital Behaviors of White and Black Adolescents." *American Journal of Public Health* 75(10):1200–1203.

Spitzer, P. G., and N. J. Weiner. 1989. "Transmission of HIV Infection from a Woman to a Man by Oral Sex" (letter). *New England Journal of Medicine* 320(4):251.

Wedlow, S. 1979. "Feeling Paranoid: The Organization of an Ideology About Drug Abuse." *Urban Life*, April 8, 72–93.

Wepman, D., R. B. Newman, and M. B. Binderman. 1976. *The Life: The Lore and Folkpoetry of the Black Hustler*. Philadelphia: University of Pennsylvania Press.

# Acknowledgments

I n addition to the chapter authors, many other individuals were instrumental in conceptualizing, planning, conducting, and supporting this study. The National Institute on Drug Abuse (NIDA) of the U.S. Department of Health and Human Services provided primary support for the research on which this book is based through a contract (no. 271-88-8248) to Birch & Davis Associates, Inc. (B&D), a health care research and consulting firm. Gratitude is expressed to NIDA and especially to Dr. Harry Haverkos, this study's first project officer, who saw the need for an ethnographic study of the sex-for-crack phenomenon. Following Dr. Haverkos's promotion to acting director of the Division of Clinical Research and Associate Director for AIDS, NIDA, technical oversight of the project passed to Dr. Sander Genser, an equally persistent and creative supporter of the study. Although NIDA and its staff deserve credit for any positive contribution this work might make to substance abuse research and policy, the opinions expressed in this book are entirely those of the authors and do not necessarily reflect the views or policies of any federal agency.

Staff at B&D effectively provided a full range of support services for the project director and site staff. Willie Davis supplied oversight as the corporate officer in charge. Fred Royster, Jr., Hillard Davis, and Dr. Jack Fiedler were responsible for quantitative data entry and analysis. Production of this book was facilitated by the conscientious word processing efforts of Nancy Smith and Tuwana Slater, by the editing skills of Kerry Treasure, Jennie Heard, and Shirley Kaufman, and by the overall coordination efforts of Cheryl Travis. The transition from manuscript to book was facilitated by the skill and good spirits of the Lexington Books editorial and production staff, especially Margaret Zusky, Carol Mayhew, and Sarah Zobel.

Site ethnographers have asked that the contribution of the following individuals and organizations also be acknowledged:

- *Chicago*: Matthildur Kelley and the staff of the AIDS Outreach Intervention Project, University of Illinois—Chicago, School of Public Health.

- *Denver*: Deborah Puntenney, Tammy Leverenz, Stanley Muniz, John Gooding, and the Counseling and Testing Site, Denver AIDS Prevention, Department of Public Health, City and County of Denver.
- *Los Angeles*: Kimberley Edwards, the Los Angeles Police Department, Transition House, and People in Progress.
- *Philadelphia and Newark*: Atiba Akili-Obika and Adrienne Garrett.
- *San Francisco*: San Francisco Department of Public Health.
- *New York*: Dr. Joyce Wallace and the Foundation for Research on Sexually Transmitted Diseases.
- *Miami*: Rose Anderson, Mary Comerford, Dorothy Lockwood, Dr. Dale Chitwood, Dr. Clyde McCoy, Dr. Virginia McCoy, and the University of Miami School of Medicine.

# Index

# About the Editor

Mitchell S. Ratner is an applied anthropologist specializing in the study of contemporary social problems. In addition to directing the eight-city study of Sex-for-Crack exchanges that led to the writing of *Crack Pipe as Pimp*, Dr. Ratner has conducted major studies of drug-related emergency department admissions, effective low-income breastfeeding promotion strategies, and adolescent socialization in a Romanian village.

# List of Contributors

**M. Douglas Anglin, Ph.D.**  Director, UCLA Drug Abuse Research Center, Los Angeles, California.

**Philippe Bourgois, Ph.D.**  Associate Professor, Department of Anthropology, San Francisco State University, San Francisco, California.

**Kathleen Boyle, Ph.D.**  Research Associate, UCLA Drug Abuse Research Center, Los Angeles, California.

**Sharon Byrd**  Senior Interviewer/Researcher, National Health Study, Bayview Hunter's Point Foundation, San Francisco, California.

**Eloise Dunlap, Ph.D.**  Research Associate, Narcotics and Drug Research, Inc., New York, New York

**Frank Espada**  Documentary Photographer and Educator, San Francisco, California.

**Harvey W. Feldman, Ph.D.**  Medical Sociology Consultant, Oakland, California.

**John French, M.A.**  Sociologist and Director, Data Analysis and Epidemiology, Division of Alcoholism, Drug Abuse, and Addiction Services, New Jersey State Department of Health, Trenton, New Jersey.

**James A. Inciardi, Ph.D.**  Professor and Director, Center for Drug and Alcohol Studies, University of Delaware, Newark, Delaware.

**Antonio D. Jimenez, M.A.**  Ethnographer, AIDS Outreach Intervention Project, University of Illinois-Chicago, School of Public Health, Chicago, Illinois.

**Wendell A. Johnson, M.A.**  Ethnographer, AIDS Outreach Intervention Project, University of Illinois-Chicago, School of Public Health, Chicago, Illinois.

**Stephen Koester, Ph.D.**  Assistant Professor, Department of Psychiatry, University of Colorado School of Medicine, Denver, Colorado

**Lawrence J. Ouellet, Ph.D.**   Ethnographer, AIDS Outreach Intervention Project, University of Illinois-Chicago, School of Public Health, Chicago, Illinois.

**Sharon Penn**   Research Assistant, San Francisco Department of Public Health, San Francisco, California.

**Mitchell Ratner, Ph.D.**   Senior Social Scientist, Birch & Davis Associates, Inc., Silver Spring, Maryland.

**Judith Schwartz, M.A.**   Disease Intervention Specialist, Colorado Department of Health, Denver, Colorado.

**W. Wayne Wiebel, Ph.D.**   Professor and Director, AIDS Outreach Intervention Project, University of Illinois-Chicago, School of Public Health, Chicago, Illinois.